How To Marry Right And Live Happily Ever After!

By
Daniel
Lee
Schinzing

And again, the cover was drawn by a fine man by the name
of Patrick R. Keagan. He's pretty good, huh? I sure hope that
after you have read this book, you think as much of my
writing as you do of his drawing..

ACKNOWLEDGMENTS

I especially want to thank my wife Nancy Lee, and my daughter Dani Lee, for putting up with me during the 14 years I have put into researching this subject of marriage. They have had to endure an almost countless number of mini-sermons about this subject. Dani is only 13 years old, but she can teach this subject of marriage just about as well as I can.

They have also endured having to attend weddings of family and friends without me, after I had come to the uncompromising position that I would not publicly recognize what I considered to be a "married too young" ceremony. This may not seem like a big deal to some, but to my wife, whose one main reason for getting married was so that she would not have to go places alone, this is a pretty big deal. The bottom line is that just being married to me is like being on a mission field.

Also I want to thank the thousands of people whom I have interviewed informally over the years. Please rest assured that I have remembered few of the very personal episodes. You have contributed immensely to my research, and without your responses I may not have been able to observe the patterns that I have. Thank you very much

Some others have given me advice and criticism: Terri Lyons, Mary Lillard, Sandy and Brad Parsons, and my niece, Shannon Schinzing of Sterling Heights, Michigan. And a special thank you to Larry Elwell, though we do not always agree, he is one of the finest men I have ever known.

Again, as I did in my first book, _Eternal Damnation on Trial_, I need to thank my parents, Al and Ruth Schinzing, and Nancy's parents, Jerry and Dolores Dimeis, for giving Nancy Lee and me reasonably stable households in which to grow up. It makes life so much easier to get a good start.

CONTENTS

MAXIMS FOR AFTER THE WEDDING, or HOW TO LIVE HAPPILY EVER AFTER!

DAKE'S ANNOTATED REFERENCE BIBLE

In this book you will find many quotes from the Dake's Annotated Reference Bible. This is a wonderful book that I believe most everyone needs if they are going to do some pretty serious Bible study. For the price, which is not cheap, you will find that your Bible knowledge will increase phenomenally. It is one of the most important purchases I ever made, and I definitely encourage you to purchase one.

You can go to their web site to see their selection, or purchase one at your local Christian Bookstore. I believe that after you have read this book, you will be encouraged to begin or continue more serious Bible study on your own, and I truly believe that there is no better Bible with which to do that. And, no, they are not paying me to say that.

Dake Publishing
P. O. Box 1050
Lawrenceville, GA 30046
1/800/ 241-1239
www.dake.com

PREFACE

The objective of this book is to point out to all who read it that throughout history, mankind, for the most part, has not been following the marriage directive of the God of the Bible, the Creator of this universe. The directive of which I speak is found often throughout the Bible under the most common terms, "What God has joined together, let not man put asunder." This is one of God's Absolutes! There is no plan B! When God has designed for a man and woman to be together as husband and wife, they had better not mess it up.

Just because a man and woman go through some type of religious "wedding ceremony," it is assumed that God has joined them together. Nothing could be more ridiculous nor further from the truth! I hope you will see that early on in this book.

This book is the result of thousands of informal interviews I conducted with people about the divorce situation with which they were familiar, and fortunately most of them lived to tell about it.[Just kidding!] What happened over the years of the surveys is that common trends began to appear that allowed me to actually tell people what had gone wrong in their marriages without them telling me much more than the fact that they had been divorced. Also, through these interviews I was able to come up with certain guidelines single men and women can follow to make their future marriages relatively peaceful.

The main cause of divorce in this country is getting married too young. It will be pointed out how the Married Too Young Syndrome — if you need a name for it — has been the major ruination of countless lives, not only throughout this country, but throughout the history of the world. Hence, the original title, <u>MARRIAGE, WHAT'S</u>

LOVE GOT TO DO WITH IT?, as too many people have let love drive them into marriage. Not a good idea! The survey says that only about 20% of marriages in the past have been truly happy, which in my opinion is a sad commentary on our religious teachings and leadership. If they could get only about 20% of them right, from where I stand, that's not too good, and in baseball, you get fired for such an average.

Toward the beginning of the book I will teach the reader how to marry correctly. It works first time every time. It never fails if you follow the principles. This is probably the first book ever written that will make that claim. What you are going to find amazing is that the method is extremely simple. In fact, maybe too simple for some people to accept, but the fact is, it works! When you have time to think about it for a while I'm sure you will agree with it and maybe we can begin to straighten out the divorce problem that is so prevalent in today's world.

One extremely important point that I've learned in over 16 years inspecting houses is that God never intended for women to live alone, nor to raise children alone. Couple that with the fact that the normal man is happiest when married with a family that looks to him for leadership. We will have many more happy men, better behaved children, and happier women if we solve this "marrying wrong" problem.

My hope for you while you read this book is that you will begin to relate what you read with some of the relationships you have experienced or seen during your adult years, and I sincerely hope that you get a better perspective of marriage and divorce in today's world. The overriding fact that will be established by this book is that marrying right is simple. It is one of the most simple things you will ever do in life! Open this book and let me show you how to marry right, and live happily ever after.

OUR PROBLEMS WITH MARRIAGE TODAY

Chapter One

THE MARRIAGE / DIVORCE SURVEY

This book is the result of an extensive survey I have conducted over a 14-year period. During that time I have talked with close to 10,000 people who have been through divorce themselves or were closely related to someone who had been. The number is certainly approximate, but I truly believe accurate, as my wife and daughter would attest. They would contend that I would talk to a fence post about my survey if I thought there was the slightest possibility that a divorced person may have leaned against it even for a few seconds. What can I say? I was just a man on a mission. For me this survey has been a labor of love, but you need to understand where I came from to get me started talking to people about their personal lives.

Having grown up in a Pentecostal preacher's household, I had some definite ideas about marriage. By the time I left home for college, my ideas on marriage were quite confused because I had read the Bible for myself and saw the inconsistencies from the Old Testament to the New Testament. At that time what bothered me more than anything was that I could not find any Christian teachers who could see the inconsistencies.

I guess my first questioning of the usual marriage teaching was when I was in high school. One evening as our family was eating dinner, a church member came from across the street to ask my father about her friend's situation. Her friend's wife had just walked out and left him with four little girls to raise. [For most men that's a nightmare!] The question she asked my dad was, *"Can [this man] ever remarry?"* My dad's answer was an emphatic, *"Absolutely not, as long as his wife is still alive!"* Something about that answer just did not set right with me, and if I had any inkling at that time of the importance of sex for most males, it really would not have set right.

Divorce and remarriage were always a hotly debated issue in churches as I was growing up. The argument finally got nailed down to the point that most everyone in the Pentecostal/Assembly-of-God movement adhered to the teaching that the sin was not in the divorce, but rather, the sin was in the remarriage. That was until the sexual revolution of the late 1960's & early 1970's. That movement started changing almost everything in the teachings of marriage, divorce, and remarriage for both the churches and the U.S. as a nation.

But, the real shock for my wife [Nancy Lee] and me on this subject came when we moved from ethnically dominated Syracuse, New York in 1981 to Texas. We were astounded by the huge percentage of people we met who were on their 2nd and 3rd marriages, with "hers, his, and our children." This phenomenon was not only among the non-church attender, but was also rampant among the evangelical church attenders.

We had never seen such a phenomenon, both of us having grown up as "Yankees." In my high school of approximately 1000 students there had been only two divorced families that I can remember. Most all of our ex-high school classmates were still married to their original spouses, just as were most of our relatives at the time. But, deep in the heart of Texas, apparently, divorce & remarriage were the rule and not the exception to the rule, as we were raised to believe.

One constant pattern within the Evangelical churches was the large number of honest, "on-fire" Christians who "were believing God" to restore their marriage. This pattern caused me to further question the normal Biblical teaching on marriage. Most of those claiming this belief were, and are, single mothers. They were taught to "stand on the Word," and were clinging to verses such as Matthew 21:22, *"And all things, whatsoever you shall ask in prayer, believing, you shall receive."* I do not remember any of those "prayers" being answered in the way desired.

As I continued observing this pattern, I became convinced there was a problem, but I had no idea as to the solution. I knew that marriage was supposed to be *"till death do us part,"* but reality said, *"If I'm not happy in this marriage, I'm out of here."* I figured that the solution was probably simple, as God *"uses the simple things of the world to confound the wise,"* so at that time in the mid-1980's I must have been pretty wise, because I sure was confounded. It took me about 2-3 years of surveying people about their marriages and subsequent divorces to see how simple God's plan for marriage really is.

To set up my discussion of the survey, let me relate a little bit about my marriage situation. A few months after I turned 25, in 1978, I told someone that I was going to get married in about a year. I just felt like the time was right, even though I had no prospects in mind. Within about a year that prediction came true [some of you may agree that miracles never cease].

To this day, as then, I am convinced that God had His hand in our relationship from the beginning. [Sometimes I think maybe God played an extra special role in my situation, because I could have married earlier, but that woman was not interested in marriage to me. At that time, I did not understand how fortunate I was to be rebuffed.]

It was several years after marriage and also after I had spent extensive time studying the Bible, that I had a strong feeling age 25 was the minimum age to begin thinking about marriage. That impression had no relationship to the fact that Nancy Lee and I had married at age 26, and to prove this I started asking divorcees what they thought to be the minimum age for anyone to be before they even think about getting married. I still remember the first time I asked a divorced single mother that question. I was inspecting a house for her and just started asking questions about her family. When I got to this question and her answer was *"25,"* I knew I was on to something.

Little did I know at that time that I would continue the same survey thousands of times over the next 14 years and receive the same basic response from the overwhelming majority of those respondents.

My survey began with a basic question, *"Are you married?"* If the response was that they had been divorced, I then asked them how old they were when they got married. If the age was less than 26, I would then ask *"Do you think you may have been too young when you married?"* Most answered *"yes"* immediately; others had to think about it for a minute or two.

For others it took, admittedly, a bit of persuasion on my part to get them to admit the obvious. I was really surprised at the high number who had never thought age to be the cause or the root of the problems they had been going through. They had blamed the ex-spouse or themselves, and had never realized that the fault, if it could be put anywhere, could only be put on their parents. Whoa!!

Now, that is a statement that raised a lot of eyebrows over the years with parents whose children married too young. Their most common reply, *"Well, you just can't tell teenagers anything."* I always wanted to shoot back, *"That's the problem! You don't start telling them as teenagers to avoid the danger of young marriage. You start programming them as small children that they are going to grow up, get a proper education, have fun, explore the world, date many people, have fun, develop a career, have fun, then somewhere between 25 and 30 something they will probably find the one that God has chosen for them to marry."* [Did I forget to include the suggestion that young people growing up should have fun? Well, now you have it, if I failed to mention it earlier.]

Most people I talked to knew it was best for children to be disciplined when they were very young, so that as teenagers they already know the boundaries and will be much less of a problem. But it astounded me that these same parents could not see that it was necessary to teach their youngsters about the problems of young marriage. It's like, *"Hello! Can nobody see what the problem is here?"*

But, blaming the parents is certainly not going to solve the problem, because each generation could legitimately blame it on their parents. This blame chain probably goes back to Adam and Eve's children. Why not see if this book will break it?

Chapter Two

THE MARRIED TOO YOUNG SYNDROME

I quickly observed the number one pattern in my survey — the major cause of divorce in this world is getting married too young. It was so simple it didn't take a genius to figure it out, but I think everyone needs to see the results of this huge survey before we move on to drawing some conclusions about marriage and other personal relationships.

I have titled this malady <u>The Married Too Young Syndrome</u>. It is a devastating "disease" of which the world has never heard. Everyone has seen the effects of this disease, but to my knowledge nobody had ever figured it out. The only one I know who ever publicly called for people to get married at about age 30 was Dr. Laura Schlesinger, but I am not sure that she is as consumed as myself with the ramifications of this dreaded plague. I'm not sure this ranks down near the black plague of the middle ages, but it is definitely a plague.

As I mentioned earlier, my informal survey was conducted since about 1985, in which I would converse with people for whom I was doing a home inspection. During the 1-½ to 2 hour inspection I had plenty of time to talk with the buyers of those homes. Just being friendly, at first I would ask them about where they work, their family, maybe their education. Many of them would share with me their history of previous marriages and divorces

It got to the point that I was quite consumed with this survey, and almost any time I could find someone who would listen to me, I would either be surveying them or telling them about the survey's progress.

The overwhelming majority, probably 80-85%, of those with whom I spoke, admitted that they had gotten married too young. Some of these people had lived miserable lives since that wedding and the repercussions from that wedding would stay with them for the rest of their lives. There was a small percentage of people who were able to recover, but unfortunately, not many.

After I had received an admission of a young divorce, my next question was something to this effect, *"What is the minimum age that anyone should be before they even think about getting married?"* At least 80% answered age 25. Some of the interviewees did not think they may have gotten married too young. Mainly, these respondents were females who, according to their maturity, were perhaps not too young for marriage. They just made the mistake of marrying a man who was too young.

During the last 3-4 years, that minimum age has been rising up toward age 30, especially for men. The survey clearly shows that females are much more likely to be more mature than males. Many bitter, abandoned, ex-wives even suggested the age of 35-40 for men.

Keep in mind this survey was unscientific, but from what we see around us, and after you understand the patterns that have developed, I think the results will allow you to recognize what has caused the problems in your life or in those lives around you. Or, possibly they will help keep you from falling into these same difficult patterns.

SURVEY SAYS...

A female marrying young is much more likely to be satisfied with the marriage than the male. I am sure there have been numerous studies about why this may be true, but let me give you the theories that I gathered from the survey. Women appear to have a tremendous nesting instinct which causes so many of them to make serious errors in judgement about men. Their desire to have this security can sometimes cloud their good judgment when it comes to choosing the correct spouse. [This is more of a reflection on the male than on the female.] From this I arrived at a maxim for marriage, *"Never marry anyone until you have investigated your intended's history."* If you find a lie, then that person is not a candidate for marriage. If the intended lied before the wedding, the spouse will lie after the consummation.

For years we have been taught that women have this desire to "fix" men. This instinct, given by God — to think with their hearts instead of their heads — is maybe what causes most women to marry beneath themselves. Typically, they find men who appear to be interested, but have a serious flaw. The females — thinking with their hearts — see only the good and choose to ignore these character defects. Women need to understand that if a man was not raised right, there is no amount of love, except God's love, which can heal those characteristics. Let God change him first. Then you may have a candidate for marriage. Historically speaking, since such a high percentage of men have been jerks, women have to guard their love like their life's savings. You would only trust your life savings with the right person, so why any less your heart?

On the opposite side of the above scenario, one thing that was perfectly clear from my survey was that the female wanted out of the marriage only about 5-8% of the time when the male had given no reason for the marriage to end. In almost all cases, she had married very young, then got a few years older, looked around, and asked, *"What the heck am I doing here?"* She decided she has missed out on a lot of life and the prospects for the future with this guy are not too promising, or she just doesn't love him anymore.

What also appeared as an obvious pattern with these young girls was that they so often had married an older *"control freak." Control freak* being defined by me as a person who not only wants to control his/her own life, but to control other lives as well. This combination of a young, good-looking woman marrying an older man, 5-10 years her senior, is a recipe for heartache bordering on disaster. Almost never did I find that this combination was successful in marriage. Parents should vehemently caution their young daughters from dating or marrying an older man who is a control freak. There is no reason for such a mistake!

Speaking of disasters, how about that Nicole Brown/ O.J. Simpson marriage? Was that a classic case, or what? O.J. had been previously married at an early age, then somewhere around seven to ten years later, O.J. wasn't happy, so he got out of that one by divorcing that wife.. He sees Nicole working in a restaurant. He likes what he sees, even though she is still an 18 year old kid, so he puts the move on her. What woman in Nicole's situation would not have fallen for a man like O.J.? A celebrity, rich, good-looking, personality, what was missing? Yes, she could have and probably should have known better, but what would you do in her situation? If Nicole's family had followed a few relationship principles, this tragedy probably never would have happened.

Then how about that Celine Dione marriage? She's only 26 years younger than her husband, of whom few of us know much. That's a strange age difference wouldn't you say? Then in early 1999 she decides to attempt to have children with this man who will not likely be alive when their child(ren) have children. Children missing out on a relationship with a grandparent must not be any big deal with some people.

I actually found that marriage with a dominant spouse either male or female, almost always resulted in either absolute disaster or a miserable life of repressed resentment by the dominated spouse. To people who have been around this type of behavior, this is not news, but my admonition is for those others who have never seen this type of person. As you already can guess, make sure you shun this type of person like a rodent when you are choosing a spouse. And ladies, this behavior is not always found in a first-born son as is most common, but it can also be found even in a last-born.

If you want to be certain of having a more successful marriage than most people, be sure you choose a spouse who is not dominating. Assertiveness is one thing, but being dominant or controlling is something evil. If you are female and really want to be successful in your marriage— keep in mind the exception— then you'd better find an easy-going man. This especially holds true if you are an assertive woman. Young marriages have a much higher probability of lasting if the male is easy-going and not dominant. I found that about the only young marriages that lasted happily were where the woman was somewhat more assertive than her husband.

Here is a great explanation of what has happened to millions of marriages in the past 30 years. Almost all men who had a "mid-life crisis" had gotten married too young, or had not experienced enough serious relationships before marriage. That's right! It's that simple! How much money and time have been spent on studying and analyzing this subject over the years? Then to learn that it all comes down to simple facts! He either got married too young or he did not have enough previous serious relationships with other women to know whether or not the woman who married him was the best woman that would put up with him. I looked at hundreds of these situations and each one of them could be traced and put into one of these two categories.

Now, for all of you who have been going through, or have already been through therapy, please send me payment for at least one hour's couch fee, since I have, in two minutes, told you what you otherwise would have to spend all kinds of money to understand. Please send that to the address on the back cover. Thanks. [Just kidding!]

Along this same line, an overwhelming majority of males and females who had extramarital affairs also got married too young or did not have enough serious relationships before marriage. Is this a broken record or what? But, you say, *"What about these men who commit adultery more than once?"* My answer is that more than likely he needed several more love interests than a normal male needed before marriage. Or, more likely than that, his daddy didn't raise him right.

If you check statistics on men who have had affairs, you will find that only a small percentage have numerous affairs. For all the adults who have committed adultery, add those adulteries to the marriage, then add that number to the number of pre-marriage love interests and what is your total? I think usually you will find that total will be right at, or around, or even less than the recommended number of pre-marriage love interests. So, where does that leave us? Right in line with how many love interests an adult should have. Some people just get the cart before their horses, or their marriage before the learning relationships. Unfortunately, when that happens, you get difficult lives with scars that will never completely heal.

In regards to women getting married too young, one almost sure way of having a disastrous marriage is by marrying your high school or college sweetheart too soon. Look how many women went off to college to get a MRS. — a Marriage Degree. Many of them got that degree, but flunked the test. Remember that's a "course" of action where the degree comes before the test. Flunk that test and you lose your MRS. degree. But, then again, those degrees are as easy as graduating from a 1999 public school, so hey, just go get another one, right? [With the marriage degree — from your high school or college sweetheart — you'll probably flunk later. With the public school diploma, you've got a very high probability of flunking life.]

Now, there is an exception to the equation. You may marry your high school or college sweetheart, but don't do it until after you're 26 years old. To tell you to absolutely not do it would be trying to put God in a box. All I'm doing is putting marriage in a box, and God is in charge of the box.

One of the patterns which quickly emerged from the survey was that the average male needs to have three to four love interests between high school and marriage. If he doesn't, then you can almost always write that marriage off as a bad investment. This doesn't necessarily hold for a female, but for a male you can almost take it to the bank; that man is most likely going to divorce you if you are number one or two. I hope you won't want to bet against the odds when it comes to marriage. I don't need to expound on this to any great extent, but I cannot overemphasize this issue. It is best for everyone to have at least three to four love interests between high school and marriage!

Probably the most fun and consistent pattern I observed was that marriages of younger couples in the northern United States — east of the Mississippi River, above the Mason-Dixon Line — were much more likely to _not_ divorce than their counterparts in the southern United States. I guess what makes it fun is that it absolutely, totally, unequivocally destroyed the "righteous myth of the Bible Belt!" This aspect of the survey was more confirmation to me that religion (Christianity) in regards to marriage relationships has not been successful.

There has always been this self-righteous attitude by evangelical Christians in the Bible Belt. I observed it the seven years I lived in Springfield, Missouri and the 18 years I have lived in the Dallas-Ft. Worth area. My wife, Nancy Lee, is just as cognizant of this as I , if not more so. There may be larger Evangelical churches in the south, but there appears to be more sinning going on. For instance, in the Syracuse, New York area you would be hard pressed to find

"Gentlemen's Clubs" [topless bars], but in the DFW area you are never very far from one. Now talk to me about the Bible Belt. One instance, you say? True, but it is only representative of the sinning going on in the south, evidenced by failed marriage relationships. My indignation here is not aimed at Southerners, but rather, aimed at the Bible Belt and those who espouse its *"holier-than-thou"* attitude.

But the sinning isn't really the big issue. The big issue that we observed was the hypocrisy involved with the high incidence of sinning. Up north if they want to sin, they just sin and don't spend too much time trying to cover it up. You know where one stands. But down south they will act religious while covering up the sinning. To illustrate this, let me tell you this old joke. *"If you ever decide you want to take a Southern Baptist on a fishing trip with you, don't do it. Take two of them. If you only take one, he will drink up all your beer."* Whether that is true or not I don't know; I don't drink beer, nor do I fish. But, both Nancy Lee and I, and others from the north have indicated they have observed the same pattern.

This issue was brought up to give you a more accurate understanding of the Bible Belt, because the religious teachings of this area have had devastating effects upon the last several generations. You see, it is the Bible Belt which has forced millions upon millions upon millions of young people to get married young, because of conservative Christianity's teaching of absolutely no pre-marital sex. This teaching has forced young couples in love to rush into marriage. Their only motivation was for the sex. I have had thousands of divorcees tell me this, and if I put a percentage to it we are looking at 95+%. Almost to a person, the ones who had been involved in a young marriage admitted it was for the sex.

One couple I spoke with while in front of the candy store at Colonial Williamsburg, Virginia was from Pennsylvania .

I'll talk to anyone who will listen, so I started interviewing them about their marriage. After talking for a while and finding out they had been married 20 something years, I just had to tell them about my survey. When I got to the part about young marriages always being about sex, the husband piped up and said, *"Let me tell you, getting married at age 24 is about sex!"* End of discussion!

[Don't you wish?!] These conservative Christians, obviously, would rather see their grand-children without a mother and father in the home than they would allow their adult children to have pre-marital sex. They would rather have their young adult children have financial problems for many years after the husband deserts the family for another woman than for their young adult child to have pre-marital sex. They would rather be saddled with the obligation of playing a major role in raising their grandchildren, than to let their young adult children to occasionally experience pre-marital sex.

They would rather see their grandchildren as juvenile delinquents, or in prison, caused because they never had their father in the house to discipline them, rather than to allow their young adult children to engage in occasional pre-marital sex. Or, that is the way it seems, anyway. Now, you tell me. Who is more stupid, me or conservative Christianity?

If you have not seen my point yet about the Bible Belt and pre-marital sex, please think about my position for at least the next 10 years as I have, then I'm sure you will agree with me. Conservative Christians, you are going to have to compromise your position on this one. Your interpretation of what the Apostle Paul said is wrong, and because of your wrong interpretation countless lives have been ruined. I call the Bible Belt a "Plague Upon America," because of the untold misery it has spread upon our country.

The next main reason for a higher percentage of northern U.S. young marriages to withstand the test of time is the prevalence of more ethnicity up north, with nationality groups remaining in close proximity. They are more prevalent with the inherent pressures to maintain tradition by marrying within the "clan" and staying married. In the south you do not have many small regions where you have, for example, Italian over here, Irish over there, Jewish on the east side, Polish in Hamtramick, and Scandinavians throughout Wisconsin, Minnesota, the Dakotas.

There are a few ethnic enclaves down South, but other than for Latin Americans, African-Americans, and a few Jewish areas, there just is not the homogeneity as in the north. For instance, one section of Syracuse, New York is considered the Irish section and even the traffic light reflects that local bent, because the green light is on top and red on the bottom. Now, that's ethnicity!

In my survey, the response I often received for why *"married young"* couples are more likely to stay together up north was because of the cold weather. It makes you stay inside more, which either forces couples to grow together or splits them apart. This staying inside includes going often to friends' and relatives' homes to visit, going out to eat, or out on dates. But, the cold up there for 6-8 months causes you to travel exactly to your destination to get into a warm place, so you are less likely to wander out and about as people are prone to do in the South with warmer weather. Warmer weather just simply allows couples to develop separate lives which could cause them to split apart. Thousands have agreed with me on this issue, but you draw your own conclusions.

The next reason is going to sound sexist, but it is so true. The fourth most consistent answer given was the much higher percentage of good-looking women in the South than in the North, east of the Mississippi River. Since men are usually the cause of the marriage dissolution, northern men usually have married the best looking woman who would have them, so it would do no good for them to look around. Southern men, on the other hand, have many more opportunities to find a woman considered better-looking. I have yet to talk to a man from the North, who did not agree with this point. Of course, I don't see all that many men migrating from the north to marry southern women, so it doesn't seem like that big a deal to the overwhelming majority of northern men.

According to the opinions of the hundreds of northern women with whom I spoke, they felt there was a higher percentage of good-looking men in the north than in the south. Now, my personal opinion — if I were to have to make a choice — is that I would rather marry good-looking than be good-looking. In that way I get to look at someone good-looking, and if a good-looking woman is willing to marry me [which she was], then that is to my betterment.

So, northern ladies, please don't despair, because, according to the survey, you get to look at better looking men overall than the women in the South. Enjoy it! Some have suggested that cold weather makes people ugly, but that never happened to my mother-in-law. [I had to throw that in there as I have to do what I can to get up as high as I can in the will, you know.]

The fifth main reason the high frequency of young marriage failure in the South will probably shock some of you. It is the prevalence of country music in the South that contributes to the high rate of divorce. Okay. Let that statement settle in, then read on. It's not the beat or the rhythm of the music, it's the words that can damage relationships. The words will drive you to drinking, cheating, being a redneck, loving the dog more than the wife, and other disgusting things like sleeping with your neighbor's pickup. Think I'm wrong? Go talk to people who work at a business where they play country music all day long, and ask them if they ever go home depressed. You may be surprised at their answers. Does that mean you should stop listening to country music? Until they change the words to the music, be discriminating of the songs to which you listen.

And while I am on the subject of country music, let me give you one more observation I have made, but have no scientific study to back it up. Country music for the past 8-10 years has undoubtedly become much more popular in the northern United States. Along with this popularity I have noticed an apparent upsurge in the divorce rate in these same states. Admittedly, I have not seen any specific studies, but I am just going by what I have been told and seen for myself while visiting in some of these states. According to media reports, northern interest in country music became more popular, and a few years later, I started hearing of many more divorces than I had heard of before. Is there a correlation? You do the study, then prove to me that there is not a correlation.

I have a suspicion that other forms of music— heavy metal, rap, blues, etc. — contribute to situations of infidelity, but I have no survey information to confirm this to be true.

Let me close out this chapter by asking you this question. How many of you have ever contemplated the huge number of problems we have in this world with our many different societies, and correlated those problems with the effect of young marriage? I dare say that there is probably no phenomenon in the entire history of the world that has caused so much personal misery for so many people, as has this Married Too Young Syndrome.

Even the 20th century's greatest evil — socialism/statism — has not had such a devastating effect on so many people as has the Married Too Young Syndrome. It is a killer disease. For some it kills slowly, but for others you know it's killing when you see child abuse, wife abuse, drug abuse, grandparents raising grandchildren, single parent families, undisciplined children, poverty, the Government welfare state, infidelity, psychological and emotional problems of children and adults, etc.. All of these devastating problems can almost always be traced to the Married Too Young Syndrome. Solve that problem, and you have solved almost all of the above symptoms. You see, the above list is not the problem. It is only the result of someone in the family having married too young.

Chapter Three

MARRIAGE AND THE MARRIED LIFE

This chapter is a reprint of a chapter in a book that was published in 1860, titled **MARRIAGE AND THE MARRIED LIFE**, written by J.M.D. Cates. The book was published by Graves, Marks & Co., of Nashville, Tennessee, U.S.A. My brother, Don, brought this book to my attention because he knew that I was on a campaign to stamp out young marriages. He found the book in his collection and lent it to me and I was extremely excited by this man's teachings of more than 135 years ago. At the same time, I was disheartened that so few Christian leaders between him and me had figured out how major this problem of early marriage can be.

I decided to include this entire chapter from his book to let you see what the man had to say about it way back then, so that you could compare it with what I am saying in this book. I hope you enjoy it for its historical perspective. His insight was amazing for his time period.

CHAPTER VII
EARLY MARRIAGES

Among the many errors which are taught and practiced on the subject of matrimony, none, perhaps, exert a wider and a more pernicious influence on the happiness and future destiny of the human family, than misconceptions of duty and obligations in reference to early marriages. [*Where have we heard that before? He just used more high-fallutin' words to say it!*]

The advocates of early marriages, influenced by the love of fashion and popularity, have freely recommended such unions, but without adducing any proof from the Scriptures, or from physiology, to substantiate the correctness of their faith on this subject. The whole doctrine of early marriages is based on the customs of society, and erroneous views of the nature and design of matrimony.

Parents, and especially mothers, are so fully impressed, by false teachings and influences, of the great utility of early marriages, they instill into the minds of their daughters the same erroneous sentiments; and, in order that they may be fully prepared for an *early* marriage, they are hurried through some fashionable school, where they learn a few pretty expressions, and to repeat and sing poetry,---which is calculated to excite the passions more than to improve the intellect,---then they are hurried into fashionable society, without having any time or opportunity to become familiar with domestic business. They are *hurried* through these various degrees of preparation for fear, I suppose, that they will pass out of their teens before they are married, and then their chances to enter the married life will be doubtful.

It is true we find occasionally a kind and wise mother who condemns early marriages, and points out to her children the evil consequences of such marriages. But such parents are very few.

It is contended, by the advocates of early marriages, that as soon as individuals are capable of reproduction they should marry. "Puberty," says a certain writer, "is a declaration of our nature that we should then marry. The Creator himself in that way assures us that it is right." Puberty, it is said, takes place in males about the age of fourteen years, and in females about the age of twelve years.

Common sense would teach us that boys and girls of this age should not marry; and I will show from the Scriptures that God does not design individuals to unite in marriage at the age of twelve or fourteen years. **Reason teaches us that physical maturity, and not puberty, indicates the proper time when we should marry; and that reproduction should never take place previous to this period.** [Bold added.] [*Was this guy good, or what?!*]

When our domestic animals reproduce as soon as they are capable of it, and before they come to full size in body, their growth is generally hindered, and, generally, they remain small and weakly, especially when they continue to reproduce. Under such circumstances, they are of but little advantage to their owners; and according to my own observation and experience, their off-spring is more difficult to raise, and of less benefit, than the offspring of those animals which attained to a proper age before reproduction. So it is with human beings. If the work of nature, in the completion of the physical organization, is interrupted by premature marriage and reproduction, the females, as a general thing, remain of small stature, and become pale and sickly. They do not retain their youthful vigor and animation, but soon their constitution becomes impaired, and premature debility and the appearances of old age are visible before they attain to the time which ought to be the prime of life. We have daily proof of this in the persons of sickly, pale, and feeble women; who, on account of their physical debility, are of but little use or comfort to themselves or to their own families.

Premature marriages and reproduction have the

same influence on the vital energies of men as of women. Premature old age comes on them mentally and physically; and in many instances they live a life of suffering.

It is evident, then, that marriage should not be consummated before each party has attained to years of maturity. But it may be inquired, when does physical maturity take place in males and in females?

In the language of another, "Physical maturity does not arrive, as a general rule, sooner than the twenty-fifth or twenty-sixth year in the male, and the twenty-first or the twenty-second in the female. It requires a long time for the bony frame to become consolidated, and all its parts fully and completely ossified, as they are or should be in perfect physical manhood."

It was the opinion of Dr. Johnson, a celebrated English writer, that for every year a female married under the age of twenty-one, there will be, on an average, three years of premature decay of the corporal fabric. Then, according to this principle, if a female marries at the age of eighteen, instead of twenty-one, there will be nine years of decay, and if she marries at fifteen instead of twenty-one, her physical decline will be hastened *eighteen* years.

Whether this principle is true in every part or not, it is evident that the younger the parties are who unite in marriage, the greater the evil, physically and mentally.

We learn from the sacred Scriptures, that those who united in marriage were *men* and *women,* and not mere *boys* and *girls,* twelve or fourteen years old. "When the Lord first instituted matrimony he brought a *woman* and gave to the *man* for a companion. In this very act, and at this very time, God established a principle by which all succeeding generations should be guided in their matrimonial alliances. But, what is the meaning of the term *man* and the term *woman*?

The term *man* is defined to be, "A male individual of the human race of adult growth, or years."

The term *woman* means, "The female of the human race grown to adult years."

They are individuals grown to *full size* and *strength*.

Christ, referring to the original law of marriage, said, "For this cause shall a *man* leave father and mother and shall cleave to his *wife* (his *woman*).

Paul said, "I will that the young *women* marry."

If early marriages are according to the design and will of God, such marriages would prove beneficial, instead of an evil, to the race of man, both physically and mentally. Strict obedience to the will and design of God is not only productive of happiness, but, also, of health and long life. (Prov. iii: 1,2; iv: 22.)

It can not be true that God ever assured any of his creatures that a certain course of conduct would be right, the performance of which would conflict with any part of his divine law.

Premature marriages have a deteriorating influence on the race of man. They hinder, as has been shown, the physical and mental growth of both men and women, and cause premature decay of their constitutions. The offspring of such persons will be afflicted, more or less, with physical and mental debility; and their offspring, down to remote generations, will feel the evil influences.

From a careful examination of the Word of God, and of history, we learn that the greater number of the renowned of past ages were children of those who had attained to years of physical maturity....

Dr. Johnson said he defied the world to produce a single instance of a man of great intellectual attainments born of a woman under eighteen years of age. [*Interesting challenge!*]...

Individual character should be fixed before marriage. This, as a general thing, is not fully established before physical and mental maturity is attained. Because a man admires and loves the character and person of a girl fifteen or sixteen years old, is no proof that he will love her character or her person when she has attained womanhood. By the time she is twenty-one years old, her character may be entirely different from what it was when she was fifteen years old, and her personal appearance may be greatly changed. The objects of his admiration and love gradually fade and disappear, and the consequence is regret and disappointment, which render the married life unpleasant. [*The end of that chapter.*]

Now, didn't I say that the man had amazing insight for his time period? Was he good, or what? Or, am I the only one impressed with his teachings? If you had spent as many years as I have, attempting to convince people, especially Christians, that early marriage is one of the most ignorant customs ever practiced, you would be impressed with the man.

Chapter Four

DIVORCE BIBLE STYLE

Christians, in their battle against divorce, always point to Matthew 19:6, "...*Therefore what God has joined together, let not man put asunder.*" I agree totally with that statement, but not in the same way as a fundamentalist or evangelical Christian. They have been conned into the false belief that just because a man and woman go through a ceremony where they exchange words, this means that God has sanctioned their union, and He put them together. This belief could not be further from the truth. The truth is, if God really did put two individuals together, then there is no divorce. There is no Plan B. The trouble comes in figuring out if God did put the individuals together.

Since as I stated earlier that I came at my marriage survey from a Biblical standpoint, I want to spend a short time pointing out what we find in the Bible about marriage.

The Old Covenant Law of Divorce is found at Deuteronomy 24:1-4,

> "When a man takes a wife and marries her, and it happens that she finds no favor in his eyes because he has found some uncleanness in her, and he writes her a certificate of divorce, puts it in her hand, and sends her out of his house, when she has departed from his house, and goes and becomes another man's wife, if the latter husband detests her and writes her a certificate of divorce, puts it in her hand, and sends her out of his, or if the latter husband dies who took her to be his wife, then her former husband who divorced her must not take her back to be his wife after she has been defiled; for that is an abomination before the Lord, and you shall not bring sin on the land which the Lord your God is giving you as an inheritance."

I want to quote from "*Dake's Annotated Reference Bible*, page 237, where he analyzes the Old Testament teachings on divorce throughout the Old Covenant. [I welcome you to follow along in your own copy of *Dake's*.]

[Hebrew word] *ervah,* translated uncleanness (v. 1); shame (Isaiah 20:4); and nakedness [many verses]. It comes from *arah,* which means to make bare; empty; destitute; discover; make naked; uncover. The idea here is that of discovering or uncovering something in the wife that was not known before to the husband. Exactly what is included in the word uncleanness in this connection is not known. Judging by the word as translated above, it would be something of the nature of shame, disappointment, and extreme dislike. If the uncleanness refers to moral sin, as in 22: 13-21, the earlier law demanded the death penalty. Perhaps, Moses, seeing that by carrying out the letter of such law, there would be frequent executions because of the extreme laxity of morals among the Israelites and he thus modified the law by permitting a wife, in some cases, to clear herself by a solemn oath. (Numbers 5:11-31), and in other cases, allowing the husband to put his wife away privately without bringing her to trial. (V. 1-4; Matthew 1:19)

The rival schools of Hillel and Shammai in the days of Christ interpreted this uncleanness different ways. Shammai held that it referred only to moral and criminal sins of adultery; but Hillel contended that it referred to anything disliked by the husband, even though it was something trivial...,Christ sanctioned the teaching of Shammai; and if we are to take him as interpreting the uncleanness of this passage as fornication, then that is the nearest explanation of it in Scriptures.

The various translations are as follows: Young, *nakedness of anything;* Rotherham, *some matter of shame;* Pershitta, *some evidence of prostitution in her;* Berkeley, *something improper in her;* Moffatt, *found her immodest in some way;* Septuagint, *found something unseemly in her;* Fenton, *found repulsive qualities in her;* All of this seems to indicate a serious mortal sin.

Whatever the intended thought, it is clear that divorce was not commanded here, but permitted because of the hardness of hearts (Deut. 24:1, Mt. 19:8); that both divorced parties were free to remarry (Deut. 24:2); that the first husband could not take the wife the second time; and the taking the same woman a second time was an abomination to God (Deut. 24:3&4).

Such things must be understood in the light of several things that a wife became the actual property of the husband and he became her lord and master. (Exodus 21:7-11; I.Corinthians 11:3; Ephesians 5:22-23; Colossians 3:18; I Peter 3:5-7); that easy divorces were a common thing in those days among all nations; that Israel had been influenced greatly by such nations and were in the habit of obtaining divorces for the most frivolous excuses; and that Moses simply tolerated certain practices because of the hardness of the hearts of Israel. Hence, this special law of limiting divorce for the one cause of uncleanness was needed.

On page 20 of *Dake's* we find this short commentary about this subject of divorce.

"Rabbis had made void Deut. 24: 1-4. They now permitted divorce on many frivolous grounds, such as careless seasoning of food, causing the husband to eat food which had not been tithed, going into the street with loose or uncombed hair, spinning in the street, loud talk or constant talk in the home, the husband finding one more beautiful than his wife and many other things."

Another good commentary by *Dake* appears at Mark Chapter 10 where he explains the Bill of divorcement, the words of the Bill, and what makes it valid.

"...With the Jews the right to divorce was a right to re-marriage and this was accepted without question by all in Israel.

The question here is not the right to remarry, but only the right to divorce. The Pharisees wanted to know which side of the controversy Jesus was on. It was the prevailing custom to divorce and remarry times without number, hence the strategy was to make Jesus unpopular or even be killed by Herod as was John the Baptist. Jesus agreed with the Shammai that fornication was the only exception (Mt. 5:32; 19: 3-12). He did not change the Jewish universal practice that a right to divorce was a right to re-marriage. He let this be as it was in Deut. 24: 1-4. This is clear from the fact He referred them to what Moses commanded (v. 3). He did not say that Moses was out of the divine will in making a law of divorce, but merely it was because of their hardness of heart that was permitted by God, and that from the beginning this was not the will of God (Mt. 6-9)."

While we are on the subject of Bill of divorcement, *Dake's* gives us the text of an ancient Bill of divorcement and it explains in more detail the custom of Jesus' day.

"An ancient bill of divorcement reads thus: *On the _____ day of the week _ day of the month _ in the year _____ I __ __ who am also called the son of _____ of the city of _____ by the river of _____ do hereby consent with my own will, being under no restraint, and I do here by release, send away, and put aside thee, my wife _____ who is also called the daughter of _ _____ who are this day in the city of _____ by the river of __ __ who has been my wife in time past; and thus I do release thee, and send thee away and put thee aside that thou mayest have permission and control over thyself to go to be married to any man that thou mayest desire; and that no man shall hinder thee from this day forward, and thou art permitted to any man, and this shall be unto thee from me a bill of dismissal, a document of release, and a letter of freedom, according to the law of Moses and Israel.*

_____ *the son of* _____ *witness* _____

The document was valid even if a restriction was put on it as the woman could not marry again, or if it was prepared in a Gentile court. When signed by two witnesses who were acquainted with both husband and wife, the rabbi told the woman to remove her rings and spread out her hands to receive the divorce bill which her husband placed in her hands, saying, 'This is thy bill of divorce, and thou art divorced from me by it, and thou art permitted to any man.' The woman then closed her hands and handed it to the rabbi who read it the second time and pronounced excommunication upon anyone who would attempt to invalidate it."

Now we know what Jesus was referring to when He was speaking about divorce. Knowing some of the historic background on the customs of this time period being referred to helps greatly with the understanding of the Bible passage. [It astounds me how people will read a book [the Bible] in English, a book that possibly was translated from more than one language, and think they know what it all means without having studied any of its original language or customs.]

Let's look at what Jesus said to the Pharisees at Mark 10: 5-9,

> "and Jesus answered and said unto them, 'For the hardness of your heart he wrote this precept. But from the beginning of the creation God made them male and female. For this cause shall a man leave his father and mother, and cleave to his wife; And they twain shall be one flesh; so then they are no more twain, but one flesh. What therefore God has put together, let not man put asunder.'"

Verse 9 is the bottom line on who should never get divorced. That is, those whom God has put together! All others who have gone through a supposed "marriage ceremony," but the two were never intended by God to be together, are just shacking up!

When addressing the Biblical teaching on marriage & divorce it is important, as everyone knows, to check out what the Apostle Paul had written on the subject. It's my opinion that what Paul had to say can be considered more inconsistent than what Jesus had to say. One of the main reasons for this is because the New Covenant was in effect at the time Paul was writing, whereas Jesus was giving an Old Covenant opinion or teaching. The difference in covenants does not make much of a difference in regard to God's original concept of marriage, because God's concept is the same. *"If God puts a man and woman together in marriage, then don't screw it up!"* The fact is, there's a great gulf fixed between the Old Covenant and the New Covenant, but God's principles are the same yesterday, today, and forever. We need to keep our interpretation of the Bible consistent with His principles. Let's now look at how Paul interprets what God says about marriage.

In I Corinthians 7:1-2 Paul begins advice about marriage:

> "Now concerning the things of which you wrote to me: It is good for a man not to touch a woman. Nevertheless, because of sexual immorality, let each man have his own wife, and let each woman have her own husband."

Dake's-"Not that every man or woman is required to be married, but those who choose to be are permitted by Christianity to be married. The gospel does not interpose any hindrance to marriage and normal creative relationship."

V. 3 "Let the husband render to his wife the affection (KJV-benevolence) due her, and likewise also the wife to her husband."

Dake's- "[Benevolence in the above verse comes from the Greek word] eumoia- *good will; kindnesses. It means that the wife and husband must respect each other regarding lawful sexual needs; pay the matrimonial debt and render the conjugal duty to each other, mutually satisfying each other. [Oh, I like that part!] If they do not obey this injunction one may be responsible for the infidelity of the other."*

V. 4-6 "The wife hath not authority over her own body, but the husband does. And likewise the husband does not have authority over his own body, but the wife does. Do not deprive one another except with consent for a time, that you may give yourselves to fasting and prayer; and come together again so that Satan does not tempt you because of your lack of self-control. But I say this as a concession [KJV- permission] , not as a commandment."

Dake's- "The husband and wife belong to each other. Neither of them has any authority to refuse what the other needs or demands in normal temperate, relationship. All acts of perversion or unnatural affection must absolutely be rejected. What you thus owe to each other, do not refuse to pay, unless by mutual consent for a time agreed upon for fasting and prayer. Then regardless of the spiritual blessing either one has received, come together again to defeat Satan."

V. 7-9 "For I wish that all men were even as I myself. But each one has his own gift from God, one in this manner and another in that. But I say to the unmarried and to the widows: It is good for them if they remain even as I am; but if they cannot exercise self-control, let them marry. For it is better to marry than to burn with passion."

Dake's- "It is best to have the gift of continence, but for those who cannot accomplish self-control it is best to marry. It is better to marry than to burn. [In verse 9 the word {KJV-contain} is from the Greek word] engkrateuomai, *have self-control; have command of the passions and appetites. [The Greek word for burn]* puroomai, *to burn; be aflame. Here it means to have difficulty controlling the passions. In such a case, it would be better to marry."*

V. 10-11 "And unto the married I command, yet not I but the Lord: A wife is not to depart from her husband. But even if she does depart, let her remain unmarried or be reconciled to her husband. And a husband is not to divorce his wife."

The commentary by Mr. Dake is the best analysis I have found to put this part of Paul's teaching into its historical setting. For many people who have experienced a devastating divorce and then had to suffer the condemnation of fundamentalist or evangelical preachers, this explanation in *Dake's* should dispel some of that false guilt.

This entire letter to the Corinthians was during a time of terrible persecution of Christians by their enemies. As Dake says. *"They were at the mercy of their enemies with no state protection as we (United States) have today(1963). On this account it would be better for unmarried persons to remain single."* This historical context is extremely important when looking at these next few verses.

V. 27-33 "Are you bound to a wife? Do not seek to be loosed. Are you loosed from a wife? Do not seek a wife. But even if you do marry, you have not sinned. Nevertheless such will have trouble in the flesh, but I would spare you. But this I say, brethren, the time is short, so that from now on even those who have wives should be as though they had none, those who weep as though they did not weep, those who rejoice as though they did not rejoice, those who buy as though they did not possess, and those who use this world as not misusing it. For the form of this world is passing away. But I want you to be without care. He who is unmarried cares for the things that belong to the Lord — how he may please the Lord. But he who is married cares about the things of the world — how he may please his wife."

A large part of the passage above is dealing with the Corinthian people during a time of intense persecution that resulted in much prosecution. Paul was saying some things that could be construed to suggest that celibacy is what God advocates, because their focus could be on God alone, but the above is a flimsy foundation on which to base a theological tenet. It is absolutely true that, if I were not married, I would have more time to think about, and act upon, how I may please the Lord, but that is to assume that God would be asking me to do more than to serve in my immediate environment. God calls few to do more than that, so Paul's inference above is not an edict to not marry. It was simply a suggestion that not being married during Nero's persecution would make life less difficult.

> V. 34-35 "There is a difference between a wife and a virgin. The unmarried woman cares about the things of the Lord, that she may be holy both in body and in spirit. But she who is married cares about the things of the world — how she may please her husband. And this I say for your profit, not that I may put a leash on you,"

Dake put this next subject of virgins in its historical perspective, as this has been misinterpreted by theologians for centuries Here's where we get a great explanation of the virgin's relationship to her father. [v. 36]

> V. 36 "But if any man think that he is behaving improperly toward his virgin..."

Dake's- "In the early times among both Jews and Christians the daughters were wholly in the power of the father, so that he might give them in marriage or bind them in perpetual virginity, and afterwards found that she had her affection centered upon a man, being strongly inclined to marry, he could change his plans regarding her virginity and give her in marriage at any time, even after the flower of her age. He would not be committing sin by changing his plans for her."

> V. 36 (cont'd) "...toward his virgin,..." [Dake's — his virgin daughter, not his sweetheart!] "if she pass the flower of her age, and thus it need be,..."

Dake's-"If she is of full age to marry, wants to marry, and the father decides that it ought to be, let him give her in marriage to her suitor. If she wants to get married instead of being a perpetual virgin. Sometimes the conditions of v. 8-9 enter into the picture."

V. 36 (cont'd) "...let him do what he wishes, he does not sin; let them marry."

Dake's- "Let the father of the virgin do what he will and what he knows is best for his daughter under the circumstances, regardless of how he has already planned her life. He is free from all former plans and vows."

V. 37 "Nevertheless he who stands steadfast in his heart, having no necessity, but has power over his own will, and has so determined in his heart that he will keep his virgin, does well."

Dake's- "If the father finds it unnecessary to change his plans it being unnecessary to betroth his virgin daughter, because of her being inclined not to marry and wanting to consecrate both body and spirit, as in v. 34, then let him keep his daughter from marriage."

V. 38 "So then he who gives her in marriage does well, but he who does not give her in marriage does better."

Dake's-"This explains v. 36-37 and proves that it is a father who gives or does not give his virgin daughter in marriage."

V. 39-40 "The wife is bound by law as long as her husband lives; but if her husband dies, she is at liberty to be married to whom she wishes, only in the Lord. But she is happier if she remains as she is, according to my judgment — and I think I also have the Spirit of God."

Dake's- "Evidently this verse is in answer to a question of the Corinthians about a woman whose husband was dead. Should she remarry? Paul gave the Christian law on this and laid down a restriction that she only remarry a Christian man, not a heathen. He then gave the advice that she would be happier if she remained single in view of the present conditions in the world for Christians. Paul by no means contended for celibacy, but gave sound advice for the present distress."

WELL SAID, MR. DAKE!

By studying the history of the times in which the Apostle Paul wrote we can better understand why he wrote the things he did. Some interpretations of Paul's writings on marriage have helped to ruin countless lives, or have contributed to keeping people in the bondage of wrong relationships— having married the wrong person.

When you take Paul's comment, *"It is better to marry than to burn with passion."* as a universal statement that applies to everyone who is *"in sexual overdrive,"* then it will obviously become problematic for many people, including myself. In fact, I purport that it is this statement, more than any other statement in the Bible, that has gotten us into the terrible divorce mess we have in this world today [2000].

Too many *"hormone driven"* young men found out that they had to get married to satisfy that sex drive. Within a short time they figured out that they should have remained in that situation with *"raging hormones,"* rather than be in a difficult situation with a woman. And you can bet that about the same amount of women, if not more, did the same thing. The reason I said, "if not more," is because most women are disappointed with their first sexual intercourse experience, unless it has been with an experienced man who will take his time to see that the woman is satisfied.

By looking at what Dake had to say about Paul's teaching, we have found that there are interpretations of those writings that could be closer to God's eternal principles. Some past interpretations have run contrary to both Old Covenant and New Covenant teachings of these principles that God was attempting to get across to mankind from the beginning.

I say that, having spent about 30 years studying this issue from the conservative Christian standpoint, and hearing several times from people who had experienced being in some of these churches after being divorced. They told me that Christians would forgive anything but divorce, that they could have found it easier to be forgiven of murder or robbery than divorce. I have never experienced divorce. Up until about 1990 these people were right. But by that time, so many members had been divorced and remarried that these same churches would lose too many members [money] if they came down too hard on divorce.

We have to keep in sight God's principles which can be seen throughout the Old Testament and into the Gospels. God put people together and He meant for them to stay together, but never, so far as I can determine, did He advocate staying in a marriage that never should have been. He allowed divorce when a mistake was made. Why can't we do the same?

Did we see anything throughout this entire section which did not line up with God's absolute of sundering? No. Also, it appears that if a husband and wife both desire to split up, there is no law or condemnation against it. To do so, was certainly not an almost unpardonable sin, as has been taught for so many years in modern Christianity.

It seems to me that many Christian teachers over the years have missed it two ways when teaching this subject of marriage and divorce. First off, they never correctly taught how to marry. Then they never taught people that they could get out of a wrong marriage without condemnation. I don't like divorce, but I dislike a man and woman in the wrong relationship more than I dislike divorce. The key is to not get into the wrong relationship. Stay tuned.

HOW TO MARRY RIGHT

Chapter Five

INSTRUCTIONS ON HOW TO MARRY RIGHT

WORKS FIRST TIME, EVERY TIME AND IT NEVER FAILS

Marrying the right spouse is actually rather simple when you look back on it, but when you are in the process it can seem to be extremely complicated. After you see the principles you will then recognize that it is not a complicated process, just a long one.

This part of the process is quite simple, as you are looking for someone to balance out your life. As a teenager, but mainly as a young adult, you are learning about yourself, about your weak points and your strong points. You are learning what things you like to do and which things you don't like to do, what activities you are good at and the activities at which you are not good. That's pretty simple isn't it? All it takes is time to learn these characteristics, which is one of the main reasons why young adults need to do a lot of dating, to focus their interests, to expand horizons, to simply experience many different aspects of life.

What I was looking for was a woman who had characteristics opposite of me. Where I was lacking, I wanted a woman who was not lacking. [And you thought you had problems?] How could I find a woman with so many positive qualities, to whom I would be attracted and who would actually want to spend the rest of her life with me? Talk about a tough order! God probably thought it would be easier to create another planet or two, than to find a woman who would fit with me. But, miracles never cease.

First off, I had to know for sure what deficiencies I had before I could get serious about looking for a woman who added balance to my life. I know I keep talking about my life and not Nancy Lee's, but at the time I was single, I was thinking about me, not her. I figured God could get her prepared.

All the time you are finding out about yourself, you have to be working on the other major piece of the puzzle. How do I describe it? For me it was difficult, but now for others it will be extremely easy. At the time I really was not sure exactly for what I was looking.

If you want to find the one spouse God has chosen for you — the best person in all the world to balance our your life — you have to know what characteristics that person possesses, which could only apply to that one. I know, now you're thinking I'm crazy, if you had not thought that already.

I can best explain this by, again, telling you about myself. I was looking for a woman with a perfect nose. Now, you know I'm crazy! Yes, I was looking for a woman with a perfect nose, only at that time I had no idea how important a point that was. [No pun intended.] Also, what I didn't know was that attached to that nose was going to be the best woman who would ever put up with me.

Since my high school days I had this thing about noses. One of my girlfriends from high school, who was good looking, never did know why I broke up with her. It was the nose. I never could tell her the truth, and she will not find out from this book because she died in 1996 as a result of an auto accident. There was nothing wrong with her except the nose, but I couldn't tell her. Despite that, we became very good friends after that. A normal guy would have not had a problem with the nose, only me.

This thing about noses has since that time been a constant with me. I held out for the only woman I have ever found who has a perfect nose, so perfect in fact, that it is the nose by which all other female noses will be judged. [Just kidding!] I just wish I knew without a doubt when I was in my early twenties that the perfect nose was what I was looking for. If I had known that, I would have dated a lot more different women just for the fun and experience. [I know my last statement is a whole lot presumptive, like there would have been other women who would have actually gone out with me? I know, I'm probably dreaming.]

But, all that aside, what I have been able to put together is that God knows who you need to marry, so He is going to reveal to you as you grow up the specific characteristic or characteristics which would only apply to the person who would best balance out your life. He can do some of the strangest things to get people together. Let me relate our experience, or actually my experience as Nancy Lee just stayed in Solvay, New York, USA, while I moved around. I am telling this story as an example of the "crazy" things God might do.

My oldest brother, Dwayne, graduated from high school in June of 1963, at Petersburg, West Virginia, and as many graduates of West Virginia schools did at that time, he went to Washington, D.C., only about 155 miles to the east, to find work. He found work alright. Within a few months he joined the Air Force and got shipped for basic training at Lackland A.F.B., in San Antonio, Texas, USA. After the required weeks there he was sent to Syracuse University in upstate

New York, USA to study a foreign language since he would later be shipped to a foreign country.

During the time he was at the university he attended a local Pentecostal church. The strange thing about this particular church was that the sermon was preached in Italian and then repeated in English. As a descriptive term, you could call it an Italian-Assembly of God church, as that will give you a better idea of the teachings of the church.

There were other Assembly of God churches in that area, so I don't know why he chose that one, but, within a short time one of the families invited him home for Sunday macaroni dinner. Since this family had at least one good looking single daughter, and the food was great, it seemed that he got hooked on the food and the daughter. Within a short time they were engaged and we were traveling from West Virginia to Syracuse for a weekend visit to meet his intended in-laws.

While my brother was overseas, the rest of the family moved to Michigan, just 30 miles northeast of Detroit. From the hills of West Virginia to the suburbs of a huge city was quite a change for a hillbilly like me. This was June of 1966 and the wedding was scheduled for September, just after school began.

At this all-day Italian wedding I saw things that a country boy had never seen before, like mounds of delicious Italian food and a strange custom of the bride throwing the bouquet, the groom throwing the garter and whoever it was that caught the garter had to put it on the leg of the one who caught the bouquet. Well, guess which two teenagers ended up with those two items. That's right! Nancy Lee caught the bouquet and I caught the garter, and never in anyone's wildest dreams could you imagine that 13 years later we would marry. Sounds crazy, doesn't it?

It would be crazy if we lived in close proximity, but I lived in Michigan, and would later go to Missouri for college.

While in high school we would see each other when our family was in Syracuse to visit my brother, and she was just a part of the clan, kind of a cousin or a distant sister type. Certainly not someone you would ever think about marrying, and I'm sure her feelings toward me were similar. We just knew each other.

The last time I spent any time at all with Nancy Lee was September of 1971 when she took me to the New York State Fair and we just hung out together that Labor Day weekend. Even at that age, I was not interested at all. I can't remember ever thinking about her again until Thanksgiving 1978, when my sister-in-law suggested I "come up to see Nancy." [Why is it that New Yorkers always refer to themselves as being up? Does that mean they think everyone else is beneath them? Just wondering.]

During the six years I had spent in Missouri I really believed I would be there the rest of my life, and being so busy as a sports official I did not have time to travel to New York to visit a brother. It wasn't until I was suspended from refereeing for a year that I got an opportunity to go visit in New York.

This year of suspension was in my opinion the only way that God was going to get me to New York. I spent the first six months driving a truck around the country. I had to get away from the love of my life, refereeing, so driving a truck was a great way to do it. I had been driving a Pepsi delivery truck for the 1 ½ years after graduating from college and I had driven a truck before college, so I had experienced that "keep on trucking" thing before. I even wonder if God had prepared me for this period of truck driving by having my brother Doug buy a moving company for which I worked after high school. [Nah! I must be reading too much into this.]

The six months of driving was mainly throughout the western states, so I was surprised when my dispatcher told me my request for a load to New York was exactly where he wanted me to go. I want the reader to understand that it was very rare for this dispatcher to send one of his trucks to New York, as he had stated to me that all bridges over the Mississippi River should be burned. A true westerner, obviously.

It was amazing how quickly my life changed, but God was in control all the time. I certainly did question Him many nights when things weren't going well on the road, as I'm sure any over-the-road truck driver will attest. [If there ever was a profession in which Murphy's Law rules, it is over-the-road truck driving.]

I don't mean to belabor the point of what I had to go through to find that one woman with that one characteristic [perfect nose] which God had shown me was the woman who would best fit me, but I want you to stay with me on this one. Once you are convinced that God has shown you that you are to marry, and He has shown you the specific characteristic(s) for which you are looking, then you hold out without compromise.

This follows God's principle of prayer in which he prefers you pray specifically. The principle I believe is clear, that we need to let God give us the specific characteristic of our future spouse and we need to hold off getting married until we find it present on a person who balances us out. There are three mandatory points: *1) Opposite sex; 2) Must be the balance you need.* And once you have found the first two points then: *3) Does that person have the characteristic(s) that God has shown you as the way you will know you have the right one?*

You may find the characteristic(s) in a person of the opposite sex, but if they are not strong where you are weak, and/or weak where you are strong, then you are barking up the wrong tree. A marriage to that person is headed for disaster. And these 3 principles hold true with second and third marriages, for those of you who have not successfully chosen the right one the first time. Remember, it's like a BIC pen. It works first time, every time.

The main reason that these 3 principles are not listed as a maxim is that it may or may not hold true for females. My wife, for instance, wasn't looking for any specific characteristic in a man, fortunately for me. From what I have ascertained the female might be looking for one, or maybe two general features.

One of our friends from the jungles of Mexico told me that since her dad and brothers had been such rough — bordering on mean — men, she would only consider a gentle man. That's what she got. An 84 year-old female friend, "Jimmie" Haines, was looking for a man who did not drink any alcohol. She found a Seventh-Day Adventist, and she stuck with him over 50 years. I talked with other women and got similar answers, and I am sure you can see how general the characteristics are. Some other women gave more than one characteristic, but none of them were specific.

My theory for this is that I do not think women should be out looking for a husband. It appears to me that God wants to bring the man to the woman. Remember how the Bible says, *"a man shall leave his father and mother and cleave to his wife."* [Genesis 2:24; Matthew 19:5; Mark 10:7; I Corinthians 6:16; Ephesians 5:31]

You may be suggesting that I am reaching on that one, but I'm not so sure that I am. After all, there is a very high probability that I am right when it comes to relationships. I had never even thought about this until I met an African-American woman in Dallas while inspecting a house for her. I was relating to her my survey and when I got to this part about looking for specifics, she suggested that her interpretation of the Bible was as I just mentioned — the woman can have some general characteristic(s) she must see before they marry, but that God has not required that they be more specific. Why that is, I'm not sure. He hasn't told me everything. Hey! If He ever tells me that one, then I can sell you another book. [Just kidding!]

Here's my theory as to why God does not want women out on the prowl looking for a husband. The average female is programmed to think with her heart and not her head. There is nothing wrong with this statement as long as everyone understands that it does not hold true in all cases

With that explanation out of the way, can you now see why it is not a good idea for the female to be on the hunt? If she is hunting, then she will be more susceptible to falling for the wrong man.

Here's how you check-up on your choice for marriage, to prove to yourself that you have the right one. When you think you have found that Numero Uno/Una, it's time to pray about it. I didn't mean to get so preachy in this book, but I want to give you all I've learned about choosing the right spouse and this last part is your insurance policy against making a mistake.

If you pray about the choice, God will give you the answer some day when you wake up, either in the morning or it may even happen after a nap as it did for me. At that moment you'll have either a good feeling about it, or you'll have a negative feeling about it. It's kind of hard to explain, but you'll know it when you feel it, because if it is negative you may have cold sweats, too. If it's a good choice then you will feel great about it inside, a really happy feeling.

While Nancy Lee and I were "negotiating" our possible togetherness, we had several major disagreements, arguments, "can zones" as the Italians say. A couple of these were so serious that it looked like there was no way a wedding would follow, much less a marriage. But, after each of these, I awoke with a very positive feeling that everything was going to work out, as it has. It is a supernatural feeling and you'll know it when you feel it.

The opposite is also true. Cold sweats and bad feelings usually accompany wrong decisions. This principle holds true whether it is a decision on whom to marry, what automobile to purchase, what college to attend, or whatever. A while back I experienced just such a situation when I decided on a business deal the ended up costing me a bunch of money and, more importantly, a lot of embarrassment when it didn't pan out. I awakened one morning knowing I shouldn't be doing it, but I did it anyway. STUPID!!!

In contrast to the above expensive and embarrassing lesson, a few weeks after this episode, I began in earnest the typing of this book very late almost every night. Most mornings during this process I awoke with very positive feelings about this endeavor. Not once did I awaken with any negative thoughts or feelings during four months of concentration on this marriage book. Some nights/mornings my awakening was accompanied by words going through my mind, if not my spirit; words that did not appear to be from my own head. [I will discuss this issue in another book titled, _Christianity Is Simple. It's Religion That's Hard._]

It's simple. When you are doing things God's way they will be successful, but if you are bucking Him, things are not going to go so well. In fact, it will usually be disastrous! And that may be putting it mildly.

The positive feelings are what I was getting when I decided that Nancy Lee was a marked woman, marked for me, that is. Everything about it was positive, even when I left her in New York and I moved to Texas. Within minutes of leaving, I had this positive, peaceful feeling that everything about our marriage was going to work out okay, though it looked like hell on earth. It's somewhat difficult to explain to someone who has not experienced this peacefulness.

And that's what you need to feel about your marriage. If you don't have that "peaceful, easy feeling" about your pending marriage, then you are headed for disaster! You can take that to the bank! And you'd better hope you have something in that bank, because you are going to need it for your divorce! It's that simple!

Just ask God the question, *"God, am I doing the right thing marrying this person?"* Wait for the answer. That answer will usually come at a time just after sleeping for a while. If you wake up thinking about the wedding, your fiancé, your marriage, etc., and you have negative feelings along with those thoughts, then you only have one option. That option is to immediately call off the wedding. It's probably a good idea to pray this simple little prayer before you have spent much money on the invitations, party supplies, and other assorted items that females think they need for a funeral/wedding. Believe me, it can save a lot of money.

In review, if you wake up thinking about your marriage to this person, and you have negative feeling accompanying these thoughts, then it's all over. Make the phone call, and go your separate ways as friends, remembering that God just saved your butt from misery. Hopefully, your intended prayed a similar prayer and has gotten the same message.

Take my word for it, please. Don't attempt to buck the odds that you are going to be successful at going against God's intentions. Ain't gonna happen! You may be good, but you ain't that good! Take the hint and move on. Embarrassment is much cheaper than a divorce, child support, and the other miseries that accompany such. You'll be glad you did.

Now, get out there and choose well.

Chapter Six

RELATIONSHIP MAXIMS

In the past, religions have had varied numbers of absolutes or principles. This is a sin, that is a sin. Do this. Don't do that. Each violation thereof was a major offense which could result in any punishment including eternal damnation. From what I can see, few of the past absolutes had anything to do with true Bible teaching or reality. So, over the next several chapters I would like to look at some of these principles to see if they really are consistent with what the Bible says.

Look at a couple of the absolutes from Catholicism. No pre-marital sex was an absolute. Divorce used to be an absolute no-no, and it still is in some areas of the world. However, American Catholics are getting around this issue by annulment, if they have the right amount of money or their name is Kennedy.

Evangelicals and Charismatics, have had similar situations on their hands with rampant teenage pregnancy and divorce. It is my understanding that annulment has also become quite a popular exit from marriage among this group. Furthermore, abortion, which you would think would never enter the minds of this group of people, can be kept quiet with the right amount of money, whereas teenage pregnancy can be seen by all.

The sexual revolution of the 1960's-70's seemed to be instrumental in changing these previously mentioned absolutes. Most religions have been left with theories and totally wrecked theologies. Even today [2000], Evangelicals are conducting a campaign where they get teenagers to sign pledge cards. In essence these young people are pledging to not have sexual intercourse before marriage. This is possibly a commendable objective, but when reality sets in when these "pledges" reach age 22-23, that pledge is going out the window, or a disastrous marriage is about to commence. The sex drive in the early 20's is tremendous, but of course, for the most part, the people passing out the pledge cards are married and probably getting all the sex they want, or they are older and the drive has died a bit. Perspective makes a big difference.

This revolution was not totally bad for all of us. Instead of Christians being silent on sex, or talking about how evil it was, as was done for centuries, the Church began to teach about its benefits for both men and women. In my opinion, it's sad how the previous generations' failure or refusal to understand sex resulted in extremely frustrated men and women. This led to major marital problems which were seldom addressed.

We don't need to dwell upon the pluses or minuses of that time period because we who lived through it are well aware of the results, both personally and as a group of people. The ruinous results of the sexual revolution probably would not have been so terrible for most, if we had observed a few reasonable principles which could pass Biblical muster. Now that we have gone through such upheaval in our traditions, where teachings were challenged, it seems to me that it is time to re-establish some Biblically based principles upon which we can rebuild our belief system.

Those of you who do not think our belief system needs to be rebuilt may want to stop and take a look around at how many problems we have in this world with the lives that have been so messed up. I am convinced that the number of dysfunctional lives will decrease if we only adhere to the maxims or principles that God wants for us to understand, live by, and teach to our children. The following sections are a few of these principles which I am convinced that God has shown me about family relationships.

Chapter Seven

DON'T MARRY TOO YOUNG

DON'T EVEN THINK ABOUT MARRIAGE BEFORE AGE 25

Bottom line! Don't even think about getting married before age 25! There are no ifs, ands, or buts about it! This maxim/principle holds true no matter which historical time period, or where in the world a person lives.

Now, here's how we prove this one. You the reader, give me a reason right now in the next 60 seconds why a person should think about getting married before age 25. Go ahead, time it. I'm waiting......Anything yet?......You must have a good one by now!......No?......Time's almost up......Okay, time's up. What did you come up with?

Oh, that's the same one everyone came up with. *"Because they are in love."* Remember what the original title was of this book? Are we ever going to do this marriage thing God's way, or are we going to continue to screw-up millions of lives every year just in this country alone? Which way is it going to be? Love's got nothing to do with marriage, if we would only let God do it His way! I am convinced that there is almost nothing more dear to Him at this point in history, than to solve this marriage thing.

The answer is simple. Only marry the one that God has chosen for you to marry. If He can make a universe, He shouldn't have any trouble with a spouse, if you are supposed to be married, that is.

Why should anybody be in such a hurry to get married? That answer is simple. Sex! Almost all of the interviewees in my survey admitted that they got married for the sex. The few who did not readily admit to sex being the objective were females. That is not unusual seeing as females are wired differently than males. Still, approximately 80% of the females admitted that it was for the sex. People who got married at an older age seldom did so for the sex, as that had already been taken care of by most. I only met a few who got married after age 25 who had not engaged in sex, and almost all of those married because of religious beliefs.

For those who want to disagree with me on this issue all you have to do is turn on your TV and wait for pictures of poor people, whether in this country or out of it, in so called third world countries. Look at the parents of the children. How old are they? Pay close attention to the pictures from the Appalachian Mountain area of eastern USA. that are used by some charitable organizations that use children as the "tear jerker."

I strongly feel that problems should be solved at the root cause, and in the above mentioned charitable situation— feeding the children—is like having a doctor give you a tissue to wipe off the blood after you have cut off your finger, or pain medicine after you broke your leg. Obviously, in those situations tissues and pain pills would certainly help, but they wouldn't solve the problem. Use those tissues to dab the blood without closing the wound and you will dab that thing for a long time. Don't reset the broken bone, and you may wish you had pain pills for many years, for possibly as long as you live.

Even these examples do not come close to illustrating the seriousness of the Married Too Young Syndrome, because that self-imposed malady seems to continue on from one generation to the next like an inherited disease. In the above examples of a cut-off finger or broken leg, the problem would stop with the person injured. In the same way, when we expose the Married Too Young Syndrome as the evil it is, it should stop with the present generation.

One of the main reasons for not getting married before age 26 is because almost everyone does a lot of changing right around age 25. I know this was true in my own life, and in the interviews I conducted, thousands of others said it happened to them and/or their ex-spouse also. There have been scientific studies done about the lifestyle, emotional, and physical changes which take place in people between high school and age 25. From what my survey says, these changes don't take place for some people, mainly men, until even later than the age of 25. *"He had not grown up yet,"* *"He refused to grow up," "He will never grow up,"* or some other variation on that theme were very common descriptions given by a lot of women complaining about their "exes."

The fact is, as was reinforced by the survey, a female is much more likely to be more mature at 25 than a male at 25. Men are much more likely to still be self-absorbed at that age than women. Most men, it appears, are also still not done playing by that time. Perhaps this is due to the competitive juices which are much more common in the male than the female. Most of this is probably not news to anyone above age 25, but if you are younger, you need to be aware that changes are inevitable for each person between high school and age 25-28.

One of the most obvious changes which will occur in almost everyone before age 26 is in physical appearance. A lot of people refuse to believe this has anything to do with divorce, but the survey says otherwise. To be honest, I do not have statistics to back up my statement because the interview surroundings were not conducive to this type of personal question — I found that few people wanted to talk about it.

But those who did, said it certainly does play a significant role in aiding all the other perceived negatives about the spouse to boil to the top. Everyone knows that men are more attracted by appearance or repulsed by appearance than women, so it was not a surprise to find that many men who responded said that it really bothered them that their wife's appearance had changed so much from the time of the wedding to her mid-20's. She wasn't the young babe that he had married. You know my answer. He should have thought of that before he decided she was the one.

In my situation, when I was checking out Nancy Lee to see if she might be the one for me, I spent a lot of time observing her mother. I will readily admit that my wife's future looks were as important as her appearance at the time I asked her to consider marrying me. I was a believer in a lifetime marriage and I wanted to be relatively sure that I would like her looks when she was 60 as well as I did when she was 25. What can I say? I'm a male.

Now, 20 years later, what amazes me is that I still love to look at her face. I mean. I really love to look at her face! I know this may sound surprising to some of you but I was concerned, years before I got married, that at sometime I would get tired of looking at my wife, whoever that would be. I was that way when I was a teenager; I got tired of looking at the same female, so I would change. But I have never come close to thinking that about Nancy Lee. The fact is, she is much better looking now than she was as a teenager, or even when we got married. She keeps me excited! This in my opinion is just another one of the ways that God can work out perceived problems when you choose the right spouse.

From what I gathered from the women in my survey, the female's perception of the looks of a man is way down at about number 5-6 on the list of important qualifications needed in a husband. Being a man, I had trouble understanding this, so it's about here that I would like to make some wise crack like, *"But, how smart are women? They marry men don't they?"* but my niece, Shannon, would not appreciate such a statement.

Financial considerations are another extremely important reason to wait until after age 26 to marry. I am well aware that many divorce surveys blame financial problems for the cause of most divorces, but this could not be further from the truth. Financial problems are usually a result of being married too young, but they seldom can be considered to be the cause of the problem.

How many 20 year olds have secure, well paying jobs or careers that would give them a good base upon which to begin a family? Now, wouldn't a 26 year old be more likely to have a more optimistic financial future to accomplish that? A 26 year old is more likely to have finished 4-7 years of post-high school education, more likely to have begun a permanent career, or even at a lower rung, more likely to be making more per hour at age 26 than at 20. That's not to mention that at age 26 each one has already setup housekeeping, owns a personal automobile, and has come to some understanding of the principles of budgeting, prioritizing bill paying, and juggling family pressures from mom and dad and siblings. Also a 26 year old is more likely than a 20 year old to have developed specific hobbies, entertainment interests, and set more long term goals.

I'm probably forgetting several hundred other reasons why a 26 year old is much more apt to have a successful marriage, and if I have not convinced you by now, then I am a poor communicator, or maybe you are young, with raging hormones and refuse to look at your life long-term. If it's me, then please ask for a refund. If it's you, then I'll dedicate the next paragraph to all the reasons I can think of that support advocating a 20 year old's marriage.

Please be honest with me and yourself. Are there really any overwhelming reasons to advocate marriage for someone younger than 26? There really are none, are there? So now that we have been unable to establish one good exception to the maxim that says under no circumstances should anyone even think about getting married before age 25, let's get busy programming our children with this reality.

Chapter Eight

NEVER MARRY FOR LOVE

NEVER, EVER MARRY BECAUSE YOU ARE IN LOVE

Not ever in the history of the world should anyone have married because they were in love. Whoever it was that got that idea started should be hung in effigy daily for having been so stupid. I know I have mentioned it before, but something so important cannot be overemphasized to any degree. This incorrect thinking has caused countless wrecked lives throughout history.

"So, Daniel, if we are not supposed to marry because we are in love, then what are we looking for when seeking a mate?" That one is simple. You're looking for balance!! The proof for this one is all around you. Everything in the whole universe is balanced, except for the marriages in this world.

You are looking for someone to balance out your life. In areas where you are weak you need someone to be strong. Where you are strong you need someone who is weak, so that your overflow will flow to them rather than be wasted. For instance, my wife is an organization nut! She would organize God if He would ever let her. As she was growing up, whenever the preacher talked about saving the lost or unsaved ones, she always thought he was talking about the disorganized. So, since then, it has been her mission in life, her "Macedonian call" so to speak, to see that the entire world gets organized. What a noble calling. If you are one of the disorganized ones you may want to glance over your shoulder occasionally, she may be after you. I am fortunate that this strong gift is hers, because it is one gift that I lack.

This is another of the main reasons for never getting married before age 26. Before that age few people are aware enough of their weak points or their strong points. Seldom, in my opinion, unless you have lived out on your own for a few years, will you know your assets and deficiencies when you are young. If you go right from mom and dad to a spouse, then you have not had time enough to learn those things about yourself. While you've lived at home, mom and dad have been your balance. I know, you can learn some things about yourself while with mom and dad, but not enough.

I love this letter from Dear Abby that I found in our local Cleburne Times-Review in December of 1997. It talks about this exact subject:

*"**Dear Abby**: What percentage of people find their soul mates? You once advised a young man who had doubts about his relationship to keep searching. How long does one search? I am married to a man who is decent and has similar values to mine, but he is definitely not my soul mate. If I had kept searching for my soul mate, would I have found him? What if he lived in another state? How would I ever find him? Would I have been too old to have children by the time I found him?*

I have pondered these questions all my life. In my experience, love is not equal. I once found a man I thought was my soul mate, but he didn't really love me; and some men in whom I had no interest pursued me. This confuses me. Isn't it supposed to be that two people find each other and fall madly in love?

My husband and I have children, and they are the joy of my life. I suppose I love him, but it is more like loving a brother — there is no passion. I thought he would open up eventually, but he never did.

I have seen people who have happier marriages, but I think it is basically dumb luck that they found the right person and that person loves them back with equal fervor.

Abby, I don't expect you to have all the answers, but I needed to ask someone. Thanks for listening. --
EXAMINING LIFE IN OHIO

ABBY'S REPLY

Dear Examining: *I'm happy to listen, and wish I could answer all your questions. Just as no two people are alike, no two marriages are alike. Some couples are content with "brotherly" companionship, which can include a deep and meaningful love. Others enjoy a fiery passion. Some have both. However, it is important that there is a vast difference between real life and fantasy. If these pluses in your marriage outweigh the minuses, you are better off than many."*

Doesn't this book answer this woman's question? You have to admit that she had a great question, and it took a courageous person to ask it. I'm certainly glad she did, because her timing was excellent as it fit right in with this chapter.

Balance is the most important ingredient for a happy marriage with your "soul mate." When you are looking for balance in a person, one of the best characteristics to look for is the birth order. I would highly recommend reading a book about the subject of birth order. There are several out on the market. One that I read was written by a Dr. Leman from the Phoenix, Arizona area. His most recent book is titled, <u>The New Birth Order Book: Why You Are the Way You Are</u>. If there is anything that will make it easier for you to find someone to balance out your life, it would be to understand the characteristics which commonly accompany the birth order of the person you are considering. I have found these birth order characteristics to be patterned throughout the

Bible. It is obvious that the pattern of birth order characteristics does not hold true in all cases, as it is a generalization, however, from my extensive study and interviews with thousands of people, it is quite obvious that the pattern holds true consistently, whether male or female. It also cuts across racial and cultural lines as few other characteristics do. It makes hunting and being hunted much easier.

Another important lesson to learn while growing up and when you are getting more serious about dating, is to educate yourself about the opposite sex. If you are hunting something, you need to educate yourself about what you are hunting. If you don't know the characteristics of what you are hunting, how are you going to know if you found it? Reading books, watching videos, etc. about the huntee or the hunter, will benefit you greatly. Learn as much as you can about that huntee and you will be more likely to succeed in the hunt.

Also, a very important consideration when looking for balance in a prospective mate is what I call "level of mentality." This subject gets me into trouble more than most other subjects I discuss, mainly because most people think it is rude and prejudicial to speak in generalities when discussing people. But, what most of these same people have not comprehended is that mentality level is something we are all born with and it is allowed to develop by parents or guardians. It is what you naturally think about.

To alleviate a lot of arguments between males and females both must recognize the difference of mentality levels of different people. Almost everyone has heard the old line about small minds [Level 1], medium minds [Level 2], and great minds [Level 3]. Whatever level you put on it, the situation exists that some people think mainly about other people, some people think mainly about things, and some people think mainly about concepts and ideas. Almost everyone, and I would venture to say everyone, fits into one of these categories.

It amazes me that people get defensive when you ask them what category they think they would fit into. Yet when you quiz them about their thought patterns during their normal day, you find that they definitely fit into one category or another. Whether the patterns are desirable or not, one cannot deny their existence.

The people that tend to be easily frustrated with these generalizations are the ones who primarily spend their mental activity dealing with things. They spend almost all of their time with their minds on day to day affairs of life, seldom spending mental time on ideas and concepts, yet they become offended by a suggestion that they do not have a grasp on a subject that they have not spent 10 seconds of time analyzing. You can determine whether people are on Level 2 if you question them about their command of certain subject matter outside their realm of thought life.

When I was younger, I spent a lot of time arguing points with Level 2 people, and seldom found that I would get anywhere with them. After a while I began to recognize a pattern and figured out it was a waste of time to argue with them.

To understand the differences between the different levels of mentality is a major part of growing up. It is my opinion that there is not enough emphasis on this subject. The education mainly needs to be for people to recognize their own level and the teaching of this subject probably needs to be done in the late teens. By that time most males and females can recognize their own level of mentality.

It is extremely important to recognize these different levels when it comes to male/female relationships. This is due to the fact that God made males and females different. The basic generalization is that God made women to think about things and men to think along the lines of ideas and concepts. And from my research, it is one of the most accurate generalizations I have come across. But despite the accuracy of this generalization, it makes neither species better than the other, it just makes them different.

As I said, it amazes me that people get defensive when discussing the probability that the overwhelming majority of females are going to have a Level 2 mentality. This by no means indicates that these are less intelligent humans, as nothing could be further from the truth. From what I've seen, the level of thought life has nothing to do with how mentality sharp, alert, or aware a person really is.

Nancy Lee is an example of this. She is a classic Level 2 person, whereas I am a classic Level 3 person. The conclusion I came to many years ago was that she is smarter than I am. She has a quicker mind than I do, and I came to that realization after spending several years with her. What really hit me was how often she would figure out a movie ending before I would on a regular basis. This would happen in other areas of our life also. When I came to this admission of her superior intellect, it really brought freedom to my life, because I no longer felt I had to be the one to figure everything out. And it wasn't that I had always felt it necessary to be the smarter one, it was just that I always thought myself to be pretty smart. I'm glad she's smart, because it makes me look good. I was smart enough to marry her, and how smart is a woman who would marry a guy like me?

Smart as she is, Nancy Lee spends almost her entire thought time dealing with things. Almost never does she concern herself with ideas and concepts. She does not sit around thinking about how she/we can solve the crime problems in this country, or what affect the Russia/China relationship will have upon the economies of North America. She just naturally does not care about those and similar issues. Does that make her less intelligent than someone like me who spends almost all his time thinking about similar issues? Absolutely not! It just makes her different.

Even if a female is able to intellectually discuss concepts and ideas with a Level 3 person, there is only a small percentage of those who can maintain that discussion for extended periods of time. Most shut off the conversation because their minds just don't want to take it any more.

A huge percentage of men do the same thing only in reverse. I'm a prime example. Get me into an extended conversation with a Level 2 person or persons, and after a short period of time I do my best to shut off my mind, mainly because I find it boring. The same applies when I am forced into a shopping situation. Women shop. Men buy.

While listening to Rush Limbaugh's talk show during the Clinton scandal period in the summer of 1998, I heard a female caller explain to Rush and the audience the entire list of Clinton scandals with personal analysis. It was the best synopsis I ever heard from anyone, male or female, about the intricacies of all the different scandals in which that man had been involved. Her analysis was brilliant! Much better than I could have done! But, the fact is, she is rare. The average female does not operate on that level.

I honestly feel that when almost all females spend extended time on Level 3 subjects, it causes a strain on their brains because of the electrical energy circuits in the brain. I also have a theory, which I have never seen studied, that a lot of females who suffer from headaches are spending too much time thinking outside their Level. I have not observed this type of phenomenon in males because a normal male will just be rude and get out of the Level 2 conversation or activity. If you want to prove this one, tell your husband that he has to quit his job and become "Mr. Mom." I say that there are very few men in the entire history of the world who would look upon that as a good idea, and that is because God never made the normal male to think about "things" as they would have to do in a home setting.

A Level 3 discussion rejuvenates me, but I feel dragged down by Level 2 conversations or activities. Nancy Lee, on the other hand, feels rejuvenated by those things. You want to get her juices going, just take her discount shopping all day, getting home about 10 p.m., and she is going to be too "pumped" to go to sleep quickly. I sometimes think the phrase, *"You Go Girl!"* was a description of Nancy Lee shopping. Is she better than me, or am I better than her? Neither.. We are just different, and that helps create balance in our marriage.

My choice in clothing is pathetic because I don't spend more than 10 seconds of my week thinking about clothing unless Nancy Lee tells me I need to, or I have some event to dress for. I spend even less thought time on my wife's or daughter's clothes. I just could not care less, unless I should deem their attire as totally inappropriate for where we are going [but with Nancy Lee that has never happened]. This is just a simple illustration of the differences in the thought Levels and the resulting actions of each of us that makes for good balance.

Level 3 people should be looking for someone on Level 2 or else your home will probably be a mess, your clothes will not be stylish, and there is a very high probability that you will be out of touch with the real world. Could you imagine two college professors married to each other, with children? Now, I bet that could be a mess. Who's going to remember to wash the clothes, buy the groceries, pay the bills, mow the lawn, fix the roof, paint the house, clean the house, etc? These are just some of the things that Level 2 people think about. I know that if I had been raising my daughter Dani by myself, she would have been a mess up until she was at least 8-9 years old, when she was better able to care for herself. I just do not do the mental preparation for such activities. It's just not me.

It is the same with writing this book. Why did Nancy Lee

not write this book? It is certainly not that she does not care, because she does. She just does not spend her thought time on these issues when that is all I do. The only conclusion I can come up with is that Nancy Lee was born the way she is, and I was born the way I am. [That's my story and I'm sticking to it. I have been pleading my case with my mother-in-law for 20 years. I say I was born this way, she still insists I was possessed at an early age.]

Incidentally, for all you ambitious people who are not too good at details, I would recommend looking for a detail oriented person, because they can really be a great support for your activities. Plus you can be serving them by allowing them to use their talent for detail.

The Female Mental Circuit Breaker

While I'm on the subject of thought Levels, I want to warn men of the fact that God built into females a "mental circuit breaker." This is a phenomenon which I have never heard discussed in polite company, nor in any publication, so I named it the "female mental circuit breaker."

This "circuit breaker" can be an asset and a protection for a male if that woman is a mother, or sister, or wife. No matter what trouble you get into with females of the above three categories, there is a very good probability that this "circuit breaker" will trip and they won't be too mad at you. Once that "breaker" has tripped, there is nothing you or anyone can do or say to make you look any worse in their eyes. They are going to love you anyway.

This "mental circuit breaker" can also cause problems, especially when a man is attempting to discuss an idea or concept with a woman, or is attempting to tell her something negative about one of her loved ones. Men, you will get to a point in the conversation when she just turns off her mind. What has happened is that the "mental circuit breaker" tripped and you may as well shut-up because there is absolutely nothing you can do except wait a few days to let the "breaker" reset.

This can be a great thing for guys like me who do things somewhat out of the ordinary. People who do not know me can lambast me to my wife, but she trips that "breaker" and she does not let those things said about me bother her opinion of me. The average man does not have that capacity. Sometimes it's a blessing and sometimes it's a curse. It depends on which side of the argument a man is on.

This may sound sexist or maybe chauvinistic, but it is not. It is just one of the facts of life. As you read this book you will see I have come down quite hard on males, but these facts about the normal female speak for themselves. I can only explain this phenomenon as I have observed it.

Before I leave this subject of thought Levels let me touch on Level 1 humans. This is a level reserved for the least intelligent human beings, where they invest their thought time in other people. The Bible calls them "silly women:"

"For of this sort are they which creep into houses, and lead captive silly women laden with sins, led away with divers lusts."
II Timothy 3:6

Personally I have found the overwhelming majority of this category is female. The males I have found in this category are those total sports nuts who conform their lives around sports. Level 1 males are just as bad as Level 1 females. They sit around talking about, reading about, and watching personalities. Often times, Level 1 people are too shallow to get through life alone successfully.

Please keep in mind that these opinions are usually generalizations given to help people sort out things they will find while establishing relationships, whether short or long-term. They do not hold true in all cases, and should be read and applied with that in mind. They hold true a high percentage of the time, but not necessarily in specific situations. [End of disclaimer.]

Chapter Nine

ADULTS AND CHILDREN DON'T MIX

ADULTS NEVER DATE OR MARRY CHILDREN

There is a great gulf fixed; a wall; an impenetrable obstruction between adults and children in regard to boyfriends and girlfriends, or significant others, and never the twain shall meet. This subject is one of the most important that will be touched on in this book. As I have said, this is a subject which the Church has neglected to address for too many years. The only reason I can think of for this neglect is because they obviously have not figured out there is a problem.

How do we arrive at the dividing line between adults and children at ages 19 and 20? The answer to that is rather simple, because if you ever spell out the word twenty you will notice that the word "teen" is not at the end of it. For the most part I am kidding, but really, God clarified it very well thousands of years ago:

> "Take a census of all the congregation of the children of Israel, by their families, by their father's houses, according to the number of names, every male individually, from twenty years old and above — who are able to go to war in Israel. You and Aaron shall number them by their armies." Numbers 1:2-3

If age 20 was good enough for God, it is certainly good enough for me.

There are probably numerous reasons to never allow love interests between adults and children, but I will only touch on a couple. If someone cannot see that a wall of separation should exist between the two groups, they have never seriously looked at the situation, or possibly they may be as dumb as dirt.

For starters, children can often be easily swayed and influenced by adults, rendering them less able to make mature decisions. Come to think of it, why should children be forced to make mature decisions anyway? They're children! We adults have enough trouble making mature decisions, so how can we expect children to make the right decisions about adult situations?

One of the obvious examples of this type of relationship by well-known people would be Elvis and Priscilla Presley. She was 14 when Elvis started making a move on her. How long did that marriage last? How about Don Johnson and Melanie Griffin? What was he, about 30 when she was less than 18? How did that one turn out? Melanie, at the end of 1999, was off with Antonio Bandaras and Don Johnson was doing a TV show somewhere. I don't think that would qualify as *"til death do us part,"* do you? And I almost forgot Sonny and Cher Bono. How could I have forgotten that experiment?

Another great marriage which I love to point out is Princess Di and Prince Charles. Everyone in the world knows these two, and many people were up early enough in the morning to watch their wedding. He was 30 something and she was, what? Eighteen? We all know what happened to that marriage. She grew up and got smart, and got out, just as Nicole Brown Simpson, Melanie Griffith Johnson, Priscilla Presley, and untold billions did before them. These are only some of the countless million, and possibly billions of problem marriages throughout the world today and throughout history which were due to adults becoming involved with children.

In 1993 I interviewed a distant relative whose parents allowed her to marry at age 15 to a 30+ year old man. Needless to say, 50+ years later she is an extremely nice lady who has had a pretty miserable life, and will bitterly talk about it.

The ones who dislike this maxim, besides the male control freaks who can only find young girls to put up with them, are the ones who are presently around this age. Some of those with whom I have spoken cannot understand what difference one or two years makes. That is why when addressing this subject it is necessary to look at the big picture of history and the entire world. Well, forget the world, just look at the history of the southern United States, as this custom is rampant in the Bible Belt. [And why was it always an older man marrying a young girl, and seldom an older woman marrying a young boy? Just think of the names a woman like that would have been called. But, it was okay for a man to do it. Yeah! Right.]

Children need to remain children for their entire 20 years and should not be rushed into adulthood. Adulthood comes soon enough, so why rush it? My attitude that I attempt to communicate to my daughter, her friends, and anyone who is willing to listen, is to milk childhood for all its worth. Do not grow up until you have to. It will happen soon enough. What is wrong with that type of attitude?

> "When I was a child, I spoke as a child, I understood as a child, I thought as a child; but when I became a man, I put away childish things." I Corinthians 13:11.

> *Dake's-"The Greek for 'put away' is* katargeo, *and means the things that cease are to be superseded by a more complete life along the same lines, in the same way that adulthood is so far advanced beyond childhood as to be on another plane entirely."*

When I read this comment of Dake's, I had written the above section only two minutes before. His statement fits exactly along the lines that I was writing, *"to be on a different plane entirely."* I love it! It is accurate because as anyone who has ever had a high school geometry class knows, a point or a line from one plane cannot get out of that plane into a non-intersecting plane without breaking all the universal rules. And that is exactly what I am attempting to get across. The mixing of children with adults is breaking all the rules.

The only people affected by this principle are those passing through or close to this barrier. Quite often this barrier will necessitate changing relationship status right around this age. This is good, but uncomfortable. Humans, especially females, love to get into a comfort zone, and woe be unto the man [namely me] who attempts to shake up that comfort zone. But that is the way it is. A maxim/principle/absolute with exceptions is not one. Now, you may totally disagree with me on the need for this barrier, but we have to draw the line some place, and I am convinced that God drew that line thousands of years ago.

If you are in a relationship when reaching that barrier, all that needs to be done is to dissolve the love relationship but remain friends. Why is that so terrible? You are not going to marry anyway until after you each have had several other serious relationships. Shoot! By that time, you are going to be totally sold on each other or extremely thankful you found someone that suited you better. Anyone who gets bent out of shape on this one is strictly looking at the issue through a telescopic lens which makes it look humongous. They need to take out the wide-angle lens and see the big picture from a distance; then it will appear as it really is, an extremely small issue, except when an adult attempts to cross that line. That should be a crime.

Chapter Ten

SHORT-TERM RELATIONSHIPS BEFORE MARRIAGE

ALL LOVE RELATIONSHIPS BEFORE MARRIAGE NEED TO BE SHORT-TERM

Now, that's a strange one for the books. I know what you are saying. *"Here Schinzing is telling us that 'one-night stands' are sexual immorality, and that marriage is forever, and now he is telling us that love relationships before marriage are to be short-term. What's it going to be, long-term or short-term?"* As I said, short-term before marriage and long-term [until death] after marriage.

One of the most predictable relationships you could ever find which will almost certainly end in divorce is one in which the man and woman dated for many years before marriage. I would be very surprised if more than one in ten of these relationships made a successful marriage. I admit that I have found a few of these relationships which worked at least up until the couple was in their 40's, but you will only find a small number of gray-haired couples who have been together since their early teens. One such exception would be baseball great Nolan Ryan and his wife, who are now gray, and who, as I understand it, have been together since high school.

One of the most common statements which divorced women agreed with, when talking about their ex-husbands, is that *"They did not have enough different relationships before marriage."* If this is such a common problem with so many men, then the solution would seem to be to encourage more short-term relationships, at least among males.

The rule that men must have 3-4 serious relationships between high school and marriage requires that these relationships be short-term. If a man graduates at 18 years old, marriage is 8-10-12 years later, and taking into consideration several periods of being unattached, that does not leave much time with each relationship.

Did I say, *"periods of being unattached?"* Absolutely! You have to grow up on your own to find out about yourself before you can come into a permanent relationship when it is time to marry. Do you remember hearing about men and women who had been married for several years, who ran off to find themselves? Back in the olden days [the 1960's-1970's] this happened quite a lot. This "finding yourself" phenomenon has simply progressed into the "mid-life crisis" which many adults experience around the age of 40. Almost always, as I have stated, this "finding yourself" or "mid-life crisis" phenomenon was preceded by a young marriage. Almost always, these crises can be eliminated by "finding yourself" before marriage.

Short-term relationships begin during the teenage years, when there is no reason to "date" the same person past the last day of the school year. That way you can be free to have fun all summer. Being that young, you need to be free to meet and share experiences with lots of members of the opposite sex.. You are not going to have sexual intercourse, nor are you going to marry, so have fun.

Then, once you reach age 20 it is time to change again. Remember that great gulf fixed between adulthood and childhood? Unless both have their birthdays on the same day, when one of the two of you turns 20 then you have to break up, as there are no exceptions to this rule at all. [Not one!] Again, keep in mind, it doesn't matter because you are not going to marry anyway.

It is after the onset of adulthood that the relationships may get a bit longer and the between periods may become a bit longer also. It is all a growing up period, but you are attempting to experience those 3-4 required serious relationships. Adult relationships should never be longer than two years at the most, with a lot of dating different people between those relationships.

Staying in long-term relationships is comfortable, but it is not necessarily productive, from the standpoint of growing up. Long-term relationship breakups can also be personally quite devastating for one or the other, and can negatively affect that person for years. Usually females are the most devastated, as they are much more likely to get comfortable in the relationship, and it is extremely tough for them to recover from the breakup. The solution? Keep it light! If you are younger than age 25, and you know the relationship is going to be short-term, then you are not going to put everything into that relationship like you would a long-term or marriage relationship.

Probably the saddest example of a long-term relationship gone bad which I came across was the case of an 89 year old woman I met at a local tire repair shop. After just driving in on a low tire, she sat down beside me in the waiting area, so I figured she was fair game to be surveyed. [Hey, if you don't want me to ask you questions, then don't come close to me. If you sit next to me when I have time on my hands, I may just get you to open up and tell the world some of the hidden secrets in your life. Just as this lady did.]

She couldn't hear a lick, but she talked just right. All I did was ask her if she had ever been married. She went on for about 10 minutes after that, with me shouting an occasional question.. She had been divorced, but she did not get married young, probably age 25 or 26, she couldn't remember. My first thought was that maybe she would be an exception to the rule of the Married Too Young Syndrome. Then she admitted that they had dated for 10 years before getting married.

After that bit of knowledge her divorce was easy to figure out. Her husband did not have enough serious relationships before marriage to know that his wife was the best woman who would put up with him. Within a few years after marriage he began drinking heavily and wife beating to the point that she was injured several times, needing medical attention. She never remarried and she still loved him. Only a woman and God would do that.

This lady's situation is rather typical of long-term relationships from what I have seen in my surveys. In her situation during the depression of the 1930's, divorce was a no-no, and the husband wanted out. He just reached out the only way he knew how because society wouldn't let him just say, *"Hey, this isn't working out, I want a divorce."* Both wife and children had to suffer because one man dated one woman too long.

Speaking of dating a woman too long, or at least being with the same woman too long, take a look at the history of the NFL quarterback, Warren Moon. He married his high school sweetheart and then 20 some years later he had legal problems for something along the lines of spouse abuse. I predicted that one. I had read a short biography about Warren as being one of the greatest quarterbacks of all time and how he had married his high school sweetheart. That situation usually leads to problems later. Spouse abuse is definitely a strong possibility with a long-term dating situation. Maybe it is true that familiarity breeds contempt?

How do you end a short-term relationship? Since you knew going into it that it was not going to be long-term, there is no reason to end it on negative terms. Be friendly about it and thankful for the time and experiences together and move on.

Chapter Eleven

STAY WITHIN YOUR AGE GROUP

DATE AND MARRY WITHIN YOUR AGE GROUP

*"**Dear Abby:** I am 34 and divorced for three years. I met a very nice man I'll call Jim at my boss's Christmas party. We hit it off very well (at least I thought we did). He is about 20 years older than I and in the process of getting a divorce. Also, he is a friend of my boss. They play racquetball every week.*

At the party, he told me I was "too young." I felt I met a nice person to be friends with, and the age difference doesn't bother me. I have been through a six-year relationship, live on my own and pay my own bills.

It's been two weeks, and I would like to know how I can see him without jeopardizing my job or a friendship. He didn't ask for my phone number, but he knows where I work. Should I sit back and wait, or should I call him? I don't want to embarrass him or myself, but I don't see why a younger woman can't date an older man. I will abide by your advice. -- INTERESTED IN ILLINOIS"

One of the dumbest phenomenon in which earthlings have ever engaged is in developing love relationships outside of a specific age group. I have noticed for many years that people really don't approve of these relationships, but they tolerate them. A particularly disgusting part of this phenomenon is the "May/December" marriage. [This type of marriage is one in which one spouse is much older than the other.]

Probably the most offensive violation of this rule that has been clarified in another section of this book, is adults dating and marrying children. As we learned earlier, this activity is strictly forbidden, with absolutely no exceptions to this rule. There is therefore, no need to discuss this activity any further.

It has amazed me how often people develop love relationships with someone who is many years their junior or senior. Almost everyone accepts this as okay, none of anyone else's business. So often those relationships develop because one or the other of the couple have a problem with which they refuse to deal, so they attempt to placate or suppress the need to deal with it by having a relationship which allows them to not deal with it. For example, male control freaks love to marry a woman at least several years younger than themselves. Almost always this is because they cannot find anyone their age who will put up with their evil ways. Usually only a younger woman would be naive enough to tolerate their garbage.

[While I am on the subject, if females are usually considered to be more mature than males, why do so many of them marry such jerks who should never be married? With maturity is supposed to come intelligence or wisdom, but it obviously does not hold true for a large percentage of females. Why do they marry these jerks?]

One other occasional relationship that I see becoming more prevalent is one in which the female is quite a bit older than the male. I think it is pretty simple to pinpoint why males marry younger, but I have not been able to determine a pattern of why women marry younger men. I believe that one reason is because they want to train them right, which might indicate control freak tendencies on the part of the female. It may be an ego trip for the female knowing that she is still attractive to a younger man. And don't get me wrong on this issue, as I don't think it is wrong for an older woman to marry a younger man, just so long as their age difference is reasonable.

So, what is a reasonable age group? It depends upon the age, and the age gap widens as the age increases. In the teen years that should never be more than one year. When you have more than one year age difference you have too much pressure from the older one [usually the male] and the younger one may not be mature enough to resist. When you come to that age barrier, I'd recommend a break up, since you are not going to marry anyway.

When you pass that adult barrier at age 20 [You remember that "great gulf fixed", don't you?] the age group can be expanded two years. I know I sound like a control freak, but is it okay for a 26 year old male to find the new 20 year old "babe" and start dating? She just became an adult and he is probably starting to look for a spouse, so why should a 26 year old hit on a 20 year old? Maybe he is a control freak and looking for a relationship that he doesn't realize will be a disaster.

So, if it's not a good idea for a 26 year old and a 20 year old to date, then wouldn't the same principle hold true for a 25 year old, as that is too close to marrying age? And then if we look at age 24 we find that age is just one year away from 25, the minimum marriage consideration age, so don't you think that age is still too far away from age 20? Now, we are down to three years aren't we? So why can't we just draw a line at two years? Why is there anything unreasonable about that? You are probably saying that is quite arbitrary, but I truly do not think so. Why can't we just have some basic guidelines for dating and love relationships, instead of what we have today, where anything goes and many problems result?

If you think I'm a nut then you need to be thinking about the male species of the human race. If you find a man who is still a virgin past his 24th birthday you have a very rare person. I remember speaking with one fine Christian young man who plainly stated that he was not going to wait much longer, when he was talking about his marriage at age 23. But, I being a man knew he was not referring to his marriage, but rather he was speaking of his lack of sex. He was not going to go without much longer than age 23. And this is typical for the man.

It is for that reason that I want to warn females about men in their early 20's. They are on the prowl for sex, and they will promise a female almost anything to get clean regular sex. [A term borrowed from *Fixing The Broken Boomers* by Maryjane Brady] Don't mean to be crude, but that's the way men are made. Now, does my warning about the age barrier in the early 20's sound so unreasonable? A man at age 25 should appear even predatory to a 20 year old. The two are not in the same league. Keep it that way.

We have a little problem at age 25 because that is the pivot age for those who plan, or at least, hope to get married. If you date too far above, the one above is likely to be looking for something permanent and the one at 25 is just beginning to think about something permanent. This age, I think is where you have to be very careful which direction you date, whether younger or older it's your call. Just please choose carefully.

At age 26 I see no problem with a three year difference and at age 30 a five year difference is not unreasonable. as long as that five years is going up and not down. In other words a 30 year old going down for a 25 year old is the wrong way to go, but a 30 year old going up for a 35 year old is not a problem. The main reason for this is because above 30, from what I have observed, things have leveled out quite a bit across age lines up until about age 40.

At age 40 that age barrier can be stretched upward about 5-7 years, but going down the barrier still remains at five. You have to be careful at 40 also, because you are over the top of the child-bearing years and anyone younger is still there in that child-bearing age. The younger one may still have a desire for children, which the older one does not, which causes concerns about the male and female coming together as "one flesh" [common interests, goals, objectives, etc.].

This also holds true up to age 45, where caution must be exercised going downward below 40 where child bearing is still possibly desired. At 45 it's time to expand upward to 7-8 years. At 50 going up, 10 years seems reasonable, and there appears to be no reason to ever expand that age barrier. I know there have been a large number of couples who have led happy lives after hooking up outside of their age groups, but how large a percentage have had happy marriages? I say it is a small percentage when you consider all relationships from teenager to the grave. The bottom line is that I feel pretty safe in saying that there have been many more lives ruined because of marriage outside these barriers than have been happy ones.

In dealing with this issue, you have to keep in mind the future, not just the present day generation. Also, you must take into consideration different parts of the world where there might be few moral absolutes. There are certain actions which should be considered immoral and this, in my opinion, is one of them. If you cannot stick to your age group, then I think you are not following God's directive for your life.

Chapter Twelve

DON'T GO FROM PARENT TO SPOUSE

Live Alone For a While

Everyone needs to live alone before getting into a marriage relationship so as to continue the growth process. It is a detriment to a marriage relationship to go from your parents' house, where they have almost all responsibility, and not have been on your own with all the responsibility. This fosters a dependent person who never had to take the ultimate responsibility when things happen around the house or apartment. It may not follow that dependent people will have trouble making it in a married situation, but they will be more likely to have problems for which they will have to rely upon someone else to solve.

Life is basically dealing with challenges, but while living at home, those challenges are few. One of the main life lessons to learn is budgeting and paying bills. This is where so many young couples mess up, in the financial end of their relationship, and this is where most of the divorce surveys hone into as the cause of divorce. Financial problems are only a symptom of not being prepared for marriage — they are certainly not the cause of the divorce.

When a man or woman are self dependent for several years before they get married, they are much better prepared to bring more into the marriage, and better able to do everything on their own, such as the household chores, finances, job, education requirements, and other family arrangements.

If you have experienced these challenges on your own, as a single adult, they can come easier as a couple. That is, unless you are too set in your ways and refuse to compromise a few things when you come into that marriage relationship. In that case, you are in for problems and a lot of "head-butting" with your spouse. If you married correctly, where balance was the key, then there should not be a whole lot of "head-butting" after mutually laying down the ground rules. But when you go from mommy and daddy to a spouse, you are much less prepared for marriage.

In my situation I was on my own for about seven years before marriage and I certainly faced a lot of challenges that came up. I had even compounded the situation by living a long way from family that could be relied upon for occasional assistance. Nancy Lee, on the other hand, had spent her 26 years in the same house. Even as screwy as I can be, I would still say that I was better prepared for marriage away from family than was she. She even admitted several years after marriage that if she had it to do all over again, she would have lived on her own, away from her parents before marriage.

Probably the main reason for not going from your parents' house straight to your spouse's house, is that it teaches you how miserable and un-godly loneliness really is. I have never heard anyone talk about this subject and its correlation with being a self-dependent adult before marriage, but I can see a direct connection. If you know what living alone is all about, where you do not have anyone over, even to visit, for weeks or even months at a time, most people will decide they don't want to do that anymore and will work harder on their marriage relationship when it comes about.

Loneliness can be like a slow death. It was never God's intention for men and women to be alone for long periods of their lives. Young people need to be taught to plan for their financial future and just as importantly, to plan for their relationship future in the battle against loneliness.

Chapter Thirteen

WAIT BEFORE MARRYING YOUR SCHOOL SWEETHEART

DO NOT MARRY YOUR SCHOOL SWEETHEART UNTIL AFTER EXPERIENCING OTHER RELATIONSHIPS

Marrying a school sweetheart is a recurring cause of divorce throughout the country. The wedding pages of newspapers are full of engagement announcements by couples who were obviously high school, or more often, college sweethearts. It saddens me that their parents made a major error by not informing them that they should never marry school sweethearts until after they have had other relationships since their sweetheart days.

From what I have seen during my survey these sweetheart relationships seldom ever last *"til death do us part."* From the maxims/principles mentioned earlier in this book, we know that no high school sweethearts are old enough to marry, and coupled with the requirement for short-term relationships, that certainly outlaws the possibility of high school sweethearts marrying right after high school.

College sweethearts also cause me great concern. At the age that most young adults graduate from college they have spent a few years as an adult, those feelings of invincibility start setting in and clean regular sex is the quest. Historically, college sweetheart marriages have been the thing to do with the more educated population, especially females; go to college, get a college degree, but more importantly, get an M.R.S. degree.

This attitude is very, very prevalent in prestigious college towns. I did most of my surveying in the Ft. Worth/Dallas,

Texas area, where this phenomenon was very prevalent around the Texas Christian University [TCU] of Ft. Worth and the Southern Methodist University [SMU] of Dallas. And from what I have gathered, it is prevalent throughout the country around college campuses, except those which would be considered commuter schools.

It seems that the thing to do is go to college to find a mate. Unfortunately, this does not appear to be the best way to find a mate, or to begin a marriage. These young men and women are to be commended for seeking a mate who would be considered upstanding, probably a goal setter, motivated, and an achiever, but right after college is not the time to marry that college sweetheart.

Everything will be great for a few years, probably, but there is the possibility of that seven year itch. Then when the man is around 40 years old, there is a high probability that he will be confronted with the "mid-life crisis" syndrome. As I stated earlier, most all young marriages, if they last until he is 40, will face these problems.

In the classic case of marrying a college sweetheart, couples get married within a year after graduation, set up housekeeping in a small house or apartment, get jobs or start careers, and possibly, one spouse goes to graduate school. A few years later two or three children come in sequence, and if they get out of their early 30's without divorcing, they move into that dream house with the large mortgage. At around 40 years old, watch out! If you can get through that time and hold the family together, then there is the post children period which you have to survive. There seems to be several obstacles along the way for a college sweetheart marriage. It simply happens too young.

One very interesting situation I came across was a couple who had dated for a while during college at Baylor. They broke up or drifted apart for some reason. Both graduated, moved on to jobs in Dallas, quite a distance away from their college town, to begin the rest of their adult lives. They met up with each other a few years later, found that they were right for each other, have married and hopefully are living happily ever after.

I found this scenario to be very <u>uncommon</u>. The classic case described above is much more typical of what will happen if college sweethearts ever marry. The bottom line is that it's not worth the risk. Both the possibility and the probability for divorce is extremely high. Why try to beat those odds?

The best way to deal with either a college or a high school sweetheart situation is to break up friendly with each other around graduation. Let the other develop a new life apart from you. You may end up marrying some day. You never know!

Chapter Fourteen

AVOID THE MISTAKES YOUR PARENTS MADE

This is one principle which everyone thinks about when they are young and growing up under their parent's care, but somewhere along the line something like hormones, money, fun, etc., clouds our memories of what we said when we were young. Each one of us made some statement such as, *"When I grow up and have kids, I am not going to _____."* Or, *"When I grow up I'm going to _____ with my kids."*

We've all done it, and almost all of us have not held up to what we said. Some of us were peeved at our parents for little minor things such as the way we were spanked, we thought we had too many chores, we didn't get enough allowance, had to go to work too soon. There are thousands of different things which children wish their parents did not do, behavior which at the time, the parent could not see as a problem. That is why we as parents need to always be re-evaluating ourselves to make sure we are serving the child.

Probably the worst parental offender, who makes the highest percentage of discontent with children, is the perfectionist. To be very blunt, these parents can be, and usually are, a Pain in the Butt! Too many of these perfectionist parents refuse to compromise, even when it comes to children. How stupid can you be?! How can any adults be so stubborn as to force their perfectionist ways onto a child and expect a child to measure up to their standard of perfection? Millions of these types of parents have infested the earth for centuries, and the Church has not put them in their place. Many children have been adversely affected by these types, always trying to come up to mommy or daddy's standard. A child should not have to live up to any parent's standard. Parents who have acted in this way should be exposed as the idiots they have been.

Another parental characteristic which has caused all kinds of problems for children is the parental control freak. In a later chapter I lambast ferociously the evils of these people. Control freak parents can be just as bad as the perfectionists, and sometimes these traits are in the same parent. Any children who can endure this type of parent and come out normal have accomplished an amazing feat, and maybe should earn a big gold star for their tombstones. Control freaks can either stifle a child's creativity or attempt to mold what creativity the child had in the wrong direction. What a detriment that can be for a child. Remember, children are to be served, not controlled.

Another parental deficiency is a lack of personal discipline; which can be prevalent in males or females. In this malady, the parent has poor personal habits which carry over to the children. Some of these can be related to health, cleanliness, neatness, or with some, particularly men, safety. If parents do not show care in these areas, then the child grows up with bad habits which can cause them problems when they are on their own and when they marry. I don't have to get specific with these, do I? You know what I'm talking about.

Most of these and other detrimental parental characteristics can be balanced out if the ones who have these problems recognize their deficiencies and marry someone who can balance out their problem areas. Nancy Lee, for example, has control freak tendencies, so fortunately for Dani, I am the opposite of a control freak. I think we strike a balance.

One major problem I see with parents is that as children they were never programmed to be introspective and honest enough to admit their deficiencies. This is especially true of perfectionists and control freaks, who refuse to be introspective and honest more often than normal people. They are to be exposed for the problems they cause for their children.

Some of the other mistakes parents make, which I have learned from my survey, and which lots of children fail to correct when they grow up are these: marrying too young, teenage or out of wedlock pregnancy, divorce, parents arguing too much, parent working too much, one parent having an affair, alcoholism, physical abuse, sexual abuse, poor spending habits, poor saving habits, laziness, poor housekeeping habits, uncooperative with mate, lack of attention for children; and the list could go on and on.

The above complaints are ones I have heard about, but quite often the complaining children end up doing the same things they did not like their parents doing. Why do we do that? I know one of the problems I had when we got married was that I thought I had to be the boss. I was the man and my dad had been the boss, so that meant I should be the boss. Now, how stupid was that? Stupid enough to cause us more problems than we needed. Things got a lot happier around here when I decided that it didn't matter who was boss.

I sure wish I knew then what I know now. I never liked that my dad had to be the boss so, why didn't I decide I was going to change that in my marriage? My parents argued a lot, but I determined I was not going to live that way, and we've done pretty well with that one. [Don't tell Nancy Lee this, but usually when I aggressively discuss something with her it is just to see her get riled up.]

I really think the best way to overcome the mistakes your parents made is to write down the things they did that you did not like. Just before marriage, take your list out and study it so you can recognize when you start doing the same things they did. And to keep it honest, give a copy to your spouse for accountability.

Chapter Fifteen

GET OVER IT!!

So you think you have had a rough childhood? You got cheated out of many years of fun and most of the other activities that a normal child experiences? Well, you can keep blaming your parents or blaming the whole world for that matter, but the best thing I can tell you is to *Get Over It!*

Almost everyone in the world has had the screws put to them at one time or another, but we all cannot have the luxury of standing around, or better yet, lounging around, and putting the blame on someone else. We have to *Get Over It!*

If you really feel that your parent(s), guardian(s), or overseer has done you wrong in your formative years [I heard that term on a TV commercial when I was a kid and I always wanted to use it, so I did.], which affected your growth, whether physically, mentally, emotionally, or spiritually, then the best thing for you to do is to seek the path of least resistance.

The Path of Least Resistance

1. Analyze what they did wrong and the effect that wrongness had upon you and others. The best thing to do is to write it all down on paper or on the word processor. Do not forget anything that bothered you; anything that you could bring up later as an excuse for why you are the way you are or why you do the things you do.

2. Now, delete it. That's right, delete the file. Burn that piece of paper or delete the file if it is in on your word processor.

3. Do your best to forget it and never bring it up again. In other words, work on forgiveness, as hard as that is to do sometimes. That is why I say, *"work on forgiveness,"* as it can be extremely difficult to do in some cases. Do not make excuses; that work begins immediately. The actual "state of forgiveness" may not show up for a while, depending upon how deep the wounds are.

That "state of forgiveness" is a condition, a state of being, like happiness, sadness, being wealthy, being intelligent, being tall, being short, whatever. True forgiveness is a state of being. That's the way it has to be to *Get Over It!* We have to get to the point that we are no longer bothered by the person who did damage to us, or the things they did. That is being in a "state of forgiveness." When you have arrived into that "state" you go about your life as if it never happened. You will know when you have arrived, when it or they do not bother you anymore.

The 1990's have been characterized in many ways by victims. The humanist teaching says that almost everyone is a victim and the welfare state socialists reinforce this malarkey. The media of course does its best to also reinforce this teaching so that our society has a condition that some people call *"victimitis."* This condition causes people to always look for excuses for why one does what he/she does. The problem with this type of condition is that excuse makers do not get very far in life. In other words, they usually do not get any higher than their excuses.

Okay, we all need a little bit of whine time, which I think is good for us. We need to get it off our chest about how bad we had it compared to everyone else while we were growing up. That is what the Path of Least Resistance file [above] is all about. It is our "whine list." We are going to whine for a little bit, then we are going to *Get Over It!*

How long is a little bit? That probably depends upon what was done to us and how good we are at this forgiveness thing. It can sometimes be tough when we do not want to release whatever it is that we are holding on to. It also can depend upon what age we were when we were put through the ordeal or perceived ordeal, and how long that ordeal lasted.

Get Over It!!

On the same night I am writing this, I am sort of watching a TV show while Dani and I throw a ball across the room between sentences. [Nancy Lee seems to duck much better since her laser eye surgery.] On this show a male doctor is in a funk, demonstrated by his playing golf through a hospital. His dad was one of those scum of the earth, you know, a first-born control freak. This doctor is hitting age 40 at least, and he still refuses to get over the way his father treated him, so his being a victim, controlled his whole life. He could not have a good relationship with a woman, he had a gambling problem at one time, and just has an overall problem adjusting to others. All because he refused to *Get Over It*.

Now, you're probably saying, *"Daniel, keep in mind. It's only a movie. It's only a movie."* Yes and no. I have met a lot of people during my survey who lived a similar existence, though they probably never played golf through a hospital, but they did other things that were just as stupid. All because they refused to *Get Over It*.

Are you asking why I say that this character in the TV show and the folks I interviewed "refused" to *Get Over It*? Logical question I would say, and a very simple one also. They made a conscious effort to not *Get Over It*. When they didn't *Get Over It* by the time they grew up, they made a decided effort to hold onto the hurt, the pain, the scars, the whatever. They had plenty of time to figure out what it was that caused them to be the way they are or to do the things they do, but they decided to dwell more on the problem than on the solution to the problem. Is that counterproductive, or what?

Come on. Do your best to let it go.

Chapter Sixteen

NO SHACKING UP!!

As touched on in other sections of this book, I am totally convinced that shacking up is not God's design for male and female relationships. Shacking up is defined as a man and woman [or if under age 20, a boy and a girl] living in a conjugal relationship without having taken the marriage covenant vows. When did God ever allow this type activity under the New Covenant? The answer is, He didn't 2000 years ago, and it should not be encouraged today.

This lifestyle is one of convenience. Sex is convenient and abundant. Expenses are shared to a certain extent similar to pre-1980 days when same-sex roommates were the norm. [I wonder if part of the move to shack up is to discourage other people from thinking that same-sex roommates may be in a homosexual relationship? That one I can understand somewhat, but since when did Jesus advocate being worried about what someone thought or spoke about you?]

God is a God of commitment, and shacking up is not commitment. The door is always open for one or the other to leave the relationship. Yes, you're right. Other young adult relationships can be ended at any time also, but the understanding is that they are short-term relationships. A living together arrangement is a more permanent and easy style. It is much too easy to fall into this type of relationship, and it restricts growth of other relationships, both same-sex and opposite sex friends and acquaintances.

The main reasons I have seen for shacking up vary with each couple, but they usually revolve around sex and finances. Most often, with the younger ones it's for sex; with older couples it is usually for financial reasons. It is mainly the easy or convenient sex which makes this shacking up arrangement wrong. Adults not in a covenant marriage should not be having sex on a more than occasional basis. If you are having sex more often than once a month, you are running too great a risk of pregnancy. I cannot stress enough that it is sexually immoral and should be criminal to create a baby outside of marriage.

It is wrong for you to create a baby without being prepared to give that child a loving family home life. Even if you do create a baby, place it for adoption, and the child grows up in a loving family atmosphere, that child has the lifelong stigma of adoption. Some children get over it, but many do not. So, when you are allowing your hormones to get out of control at a young age you need to keep in mind the baby you may be creating and how that creation will pay through a lifetime for your moment of pleasure.

When you are in a shacking up relationship, the risk of yielding to the temptation is too great, and you should never put yourself into that situation. *"Resist the devil and he will flee from you."* We have to resist extremely tempting situations.

Another aspect of shacking up which many young people fail to take into consideration is the splitting up and what your financial outlook is like at that time. One 30-year old man I met said he had been in two of these relationships during which time he bought his partners two cars each and fixed up two houses. Now, at 30, he has almost nothing to his name. He would have had much more if he had lived by himself and she by herself, and that is exactly what he recommends for everyone to do. She have hers. He have his. And continue growing up separately, while learning how to treat the opposite sex from a distance.

In the above situation the man took the brunt of the poverty at the time of the break-ups, but most surveys say that it is usually the female that gets the screws put to her. This is especially true if she has children, or is an African-American,

Hispanic, or Native American.

Spain, Caphne and Suzanne M. Bianchi concluded in their section of <u>Wives and Single Mothers</u>,

> *"This section concerns itself with the growing disparity of earning power between working wives and working single mothers. It is claimed that the later is disadvantaged in the labor market, which leads to a higher degree of poverty among single women and their children. In 1992, adult women's poverty rates were higher than men's at every age. Gender disparities are a result of women's experience in the labor force (less participation, lower wages) and their greater responsibility for children outside of marriage. Female-headed households have access to ½ the resources of two-parent or male-headed households. In 1990, more than 1/3 of white and Asian female-headed households and over ½ black, Hispanic and Native American lived in poverty."*

Looks to me as if these authors did a scientific survey and came up with the same message as my informal survey. Shacking up is probably not a good idea, especially if you are of the female persuasion.

To give equal time to the "shacking up advocates", at *Cncurrency.com,* you will find some answers to financial questions about cohabitation. One question caught my interest: *"Does it pay to get married?"* According to their "answer man/woman," *"...working couples with similar incomes usually pay more because of the way the tax brackets work. Two singles, each with $45,000 in adjusted gross income, would owe the IRS about $1,400 more once married."* But this only applies to federal employees as they are the only ones to whom the income tax applies in 2000.

If you thought I was going to leave even a possibility that shacking up is okay, let me share with you one of the latest articles on the subject that I found in *USA Today* on February 3, 1999. This daily newspaper's headline reported that, ***Live-in couples may miss out on wedded bliss***, definitely a headline which caught the attention of a lot of people. In fact, I heard about the article on *The Regis and Kathie Lee Show,* so lots of people knew about it. I sure hope everyone got the message that writer Karen S. Peterson attempted to convey. She had quoted at least three researchers, David Popenoe of Rutgers University, Linda Waite of the University of Chicago, and Alan Boothe of Pennsylvania State University.

Ms. Peterson quoted Mr. Popenoe saying that *"living together is not a good way to prepare for marriage or to avoid divorce."* She then indicates that Mr. Popenoe *"finds overall that living together is not 'marriage friendly.'"* Unfortunately he also thinks that *"Fresh studies are needed."* according to Ms. Peterson. Personally, I do not see the need for that, as too many of us have done plenty of asking questions of people who have experienced shacking up and for the most part it does not work very well for the majority of participants.

One other important point of Ms. Peterson's article was her interest and mention of the fact that *"The study finds that living together increases risks of domestic violence."* [This was an area on which I did not get any information as I was not looking for it in my survey.] Mr. Popenoe is reported as finding that *"Living together increases the risk of domestic violence for women and the risk of physical and sexual abuse for kids."* Researcher Linda Waite reportedly found the same situation, as she is quoted as saying, *"the violence rate for live-ins is almost double that of marrieds."* Two experts on shacking up saying the same thing about the violence would seem to me to be yet another good reason not to shack up!

One of the best books that covered the subject of cohabitation and its accompanying problems is the book *Marriage Savers*, The Revised Edition, written by Michael J.

McManus. In this book Mr. McManus quotes different surveys as saying the same thing I learned in my marriage survey. Comparing the studies at which he looked with Ms. Peterson's article in *USA Today*, they seem to say the same basic things, yet Mr. McManus' studies were at least several years older. It seems to me that Ms. Peterson is already reporting about "fresh studies." Wouldn't that make any others totally unnecessary?

Look at what the *National Council on Family Relations* reported when they studied 309 newlyweds in 1983. Mr. McManus quotes that study *"found that those who co-habitated first were less happy in marriage. Women complained about the quality of communication after the wedding."* This seems to compare exactly with what Ms. Peterson reported in her 1999 article. In the third column she wrote, *"Unmarried couples have lower levels of happiness."* Here Ms. Peterson is writing at least 15 years later than 1983, yet the "happiness factor" does not seem to have improved in that time. Could you tell me again why we need "fresh studies" on this subject?

Getting back to *Marriage Savers*, Mr. McManus is a marriage counselor at his church which allows him to talk to those engaged to be married. In one of these classes he said,

> *"I don't know if any of you are co-habitating with your fiancé(e), but I want to report the results of the* **National Survey on Families and Households**. *After Interviewing 14,000 people--ten times the number interviewed by Gallup in a presidential poll--it concluded* 'Marriages that are preceded by living together have 50% higher disruption rates than marriages without premarital cohabitation.' *With those odds, I would urge any of you who may be cohabiting, to separate and increase your odds of a life-long marriage."* — *Marriage Savers*, The Revised

No Shacking Up!!

Edition [Zondervan Publishing, Grand Rapids, Michigan, USA, (49530),1993,1995.]

Mr. McManus goes on to quote another minister who conducts similar counseling sessions, who says that his "students" who take that advice report back that *"The quality of our relationship has never been better. Our love continues to grow and amaze us."* Why was it again that we need "fresh studies" on this subject? I seem to have forgotten.

God designated that man and woman come together in a covenant marriage and become one flesh, which means common interests, common goals and objectives, two bodies acting and moving in the same exact direction. This cannot be done by shacking up.

If you do not believe me, then take a closer look at the studies mentioned above and those that have been done by other college professors and other researchers, or better yet, do your own survey with those who have shacked up and then married. I remember hearing one professor from a large mid-western university, not mentioned above, on a radio talk show several years ago. His research came out just like the others, that living together before marriage did not lead to a happy marriage; in fact, the opposite was more likely to be the case.

My survey was certainly not scientific — I purport that it may have been a bit more honest than some surveys — but the results I received from men and women who had co-habitated before marriage said they were dissatisfied with the results of their experiment. The answers were fairly consistent. Living together before marriage did not very often contribute to a happy marriage.

One thing that I have found interesting is that young people still consider it a good idea to be co-habitating, as one recent Internet survey reported. An overwhelming majority of the respondents voted that shacking up was a good idea. Other survey results I also saw on the Internet indicated that agreeing or disagreeing with living together without intending to get married was approximately 50/50. [From what I see as a plague of shacking up going on today, that one didn't surprise me. I guess I'll someday be interviewing these men and women after they have been there, done that, and have the divorce decree to prove it!]

Another survey asking if it would be recommended for a woman to live together with a partner before marriage got a majority of respondents to say that it was a better idea to "marry without living together first." I found this survey on the Internet by doing a search for "cohabitation" under the heading of GSSDIRS. The researchers asked several questions along these lines and got fairly consistent responses. It appears that a majority does not think it a good idea to shack up before marriage, but the gap was not as significant as it was 30 years ago.

And to quote a study by *Spain, Caphne and Suzanne M. Bianchi,*

> *"Cohabitation is a sky-rocketing phenomenon with over half of all marriages beginning this way. This phenomenon also accounts partly for the delay in marriage."*

This is the same result that Mr. Popenoe [mentioned above in the <u>USA Today</u> article] got in his research. My research and casual observation agree with the term "sky-rocketing." I wonder if there are too many men out there thinking with the wrong head? And too many women looking for security? Do you think I'm onto something here? Maybe?

Chapter Seventeen

SAVE YOUR BEST SEX FOR MARRIAGE

Have you ever seen a chapter heading/title that looked like this one? This time, you can believe what you read. This is a problem for sexually active people who decide to shack up before marriage. They have 2 to 3 years of great sex, then after that, *"The Thrill Is Gone, Baby."* They then sit around looking at each other, thinking, *"Is That All There Is, My Friend?"*

And the words for these songs are not far off. I was rather surprised at the large number of men, and women even, who opened up to me about this subject. For people who have married since the sexual revolution of the 1970's this is a rather common situation, as premarital sex is less likely to be frowned upon by both genders. However, few people have ever contemplated the importance of saving their best sex for the marriage.

As I have stated in another part of this book, premarital sex should <u>never</u> be done as children, and only <u>rarely</u> as adults. But today there are too many young people, male and female, having steady boy/girl friends as teenagers or young adults, and engaging in sex way too frequently. I have interviewed enough young people to know that there are some of them having sex almost every day. This behavior is being carried on by teenagers on a massive scale compared to what it was like in the 1960's & 1970's. Back then, premarital sex was rare.

One young man with whom I worked closely at one time was shacking up with his present wife at the time we met. She was 22 years old, he was 25, and they had been in this living

arrangement for about a year. When I asked him how often
they had sex he admitted that 3 to 4 times each week was
normal. For some unknown reason she got pregnant. [I
wonder if they were running a risk having sex that
frequently? Without a doubt!]

This episode turned out okay so far — they later married,
have a beautiful daughter, and work together in a couple
successful businesses. At this time they are extremely happy.

Another young man I met in jail was 20 years old and
related that he and his girlfriend had sex every day. Since we
all know you can only believe not more than half of what
almost all inmates say, the above statement would lead us to
believe that this couple, like the last, not married, is having
sex 3 to 4 times each week. Obviously, they are running an
extreme risk of creating a child who will quite possibly grow
up without a mother and father in the house, unless, of course,
the baby is put up for adoption.

One big reason that young people engage in sex so
frequently is that our society has not heaped enough shame
upon the adults who create a baby outside of marriage.
Society, in the past, looked down upon the child of such a
relationship more than they looked down upon the parent.
Now, in 2000, for the most part, neither one is shamed. That's
fine for the child, as no fault lies there, only sympathy.
However, great shame should be heaped upon both adults,
especially the male, when they act in such an irresponsible
manner.

A society that does not publicly expose participants of
such an extremely irresponsible act will pay a terrible price
for that irresponsibility. It will be reflected in crime and
delinquency rates, family violence, the break down of the
family, a bankrupt welfare system, etc.. It may not be readily
apparent, but all the factors add up to cause a more chaotic
society. If taking or damaging the life of another person is
considered as irresponsible behavior in a civilized society,

why is it not considered equally as irresponsible to create a baby, who for as long as he or she lives [maybe 80 years] will have attached the stigma of the parents' irresponsibility. That is terrible to force upon a human being. Label these parents as negligent. You do so in the negative, in the damage of something, why not do so in the positive, in the creation of something? Negligence is negligence, whether positive or negative.

My 14-year survey revealed a pattern of high frequency sex at young ages, especially with couples shacking up. This is very similar to those couples who go the marriage route. Sexual activity is much more frequent during the first few years of marriage because of the newness of it, the love you have for the spouse, and now that you are married you can do it anytime you want.

But, if you have already experienced this newness, and the doing it anytime you want, and you thought you were in love at that young age while shacking up with someone, then you have already experienced the excitement of things I believe God intended for spouses to experience. These experiences get a marriage off to a good start.

If one or the other spouse has experienced unlimited sexual activity, what happens to the other spouse at marriage? The one who experienced the great stuff in another relationship before marriage is possibly not going to be as receptive to the unlimited sex after marriage, especially if that one is the female. If the female has already had the great sex, but the male has not, I'll bet there's going to be trouble, due to the sex drive of the normal male. If the situation is reversed, there may not be trouble, again, due to the male sex drive.

Don't you want the greatest sex memories of your life to be with the one you have chosen to spend the rest of your life with? I strongly feel that if those greatest sex memories are not with your spouse, then it will have a tendency to draw the two of you apart during the marriage. Great memories certainly help hold a couple together, just as bad memories can help break up a relationship. That is pretty obvious. And it should be just as obvious that people should not have their greatest sex before marriage. Why has our society, and especially Christianity been so stupid as to have not addressed this issue? Oh, yeah. Christianity has been too preoccupied with demanding that young people get married to solve their "horniness" problem. Go ahead, argue that one with me! Forcing children or young adults to marry in order to have sex has proven to be disastrous for everyone, not just Christians. It is a ridiculous theology because it contributes to the high divorce rate.

There is another angle of this issue that needs to be addressed. I had finished this chapter, then met a man who put into simple words what I think needs to be read by everyone who has not come close to marriage. After he had already told me of his failed marriage, he related that it was in large part because of the lack of sex. When he said that, I already knew that he and his wife had violated the maxim of this chapter. I have seen it too often. If the man ain't getting much after the wedding, then you can bet the farm that he probably had more than he should have before the wedding. Either that, or he's just a lousy lover

The quotable line he gave me to describe his situation, I just have to use. ***"I wanted to get married so that we could have sex more often. She wanted to get married so that we would not have to have sex so often."*** The simple point is that if you have been doing it a lot before the wedding, a normal female is probably going to be thinking the same way that this wife did. *"After the wedding, I will have him so I won't have to put out so much."* Let me assure you females out there, if that is your attitude, from what I have gathered in my survey, you better start putting money away for your divorce, because it will be yours sooner that you may think.

If that man is the right one, you make him wait until after the wedding for the good stuff! Do it in that order, and it is less likely that you will need to start saving for your divorce.

Now, that you have read the logic behind the title of this chapter, do you see my point? Admittedly, I did not interview everyone who had ever shacked up before marriage, but I am satisfied with my position on this issue. I hope it has allowed some of you to look back on your past sex life and see where you may have been a little too active before marriage. I found very few people who were finally in a happy marriage but had shacked up with someone previous to the present marriage, who were not at least somewhat sorry for their extensive sexcapades at a younger age. Perhaps this experience will make a positive difference in the way they train their children for marriage.

Chapter Eighteen

SEX IS NOT FOR CHILDREN

SEX IS FOR ADULTS IN A COMMITTED RELATIONSHIP

Throughout my extensive survey, one point which kept coming up, and which remained very consistent among the thousands of interviewees, was the fact that children should not be involved in sexual intercourse. In fact, I was quite surprised at the wide response to such a moral standard. After all, few of these thousands of interviewees could be considered Christian or religious, but the overwhelming standard was the same: *"Sex is for adults, not for children."*

However, we need to interject one more standard into this equation, lest rampant sexual activity occupy the lives of too many adults. And this is not interjected because I am a control freak, but rather, as an attempt to establish morality. That new absolute is *"Sex is for adults in a committed relationship, not for children."* This type of restriction forces young adults to practice relationship skills, rather than what has been since the sexual revolution which gave credence to a free love concept of "anytime, anywhere, with anybody." That is absolutely not God's way of doing things!

One of the main reasons that sex is for adults and not children is because of a previous maxim, which clarified the great gulf between adulthood and childhood. As we have seen, adulthood begins at age 20 and not earlier. [That is a mental age of 20, not a physical age of 20.] The Church has been negligent in the past by not establishing a minimum age for adulthood even though governments for years have established age limits for different adult activities, such as voting, military service, drinking alcohol, etc.. Amazing, isn't it, how a secular, supposedly religious neutral entity could make an attempt at morality, while the Church has not taken a stand on such a critical issue?

Governments have even established a minimum age for marriage, such as in Texas, where it is age 14. One other state I read about has age 16 for males and 14 for females as the minimum for marriage. But, our great "spiritual leaders" to this day have not arrived at a minimum age for marriage or sex. As long as you were married, even at age 14 or 15, or whatever, you could have sex. But, if you were 30 and not married, you still could not have sex. How stupid is that?

This point really hit me when my younger sister got married at age 19, about a month before her 20th birthday. From that day forward she could have all the sex she wanted, but I, being over 21, could not engage in sexual intercourse. From that time on, I knew there was a problem that needed an answer. Of course, Church leadership at the time talked about pre-marital sex being the sin of fornication, and woe be unto all those who engaged. Also, they had no answer to the question, *"What if this couple is just getting married for the sex?"* That was one they did not want to address. After all, *"What God has joined together let not man put asunder"* was the standard answer for all these types of questions. For that one they never heard me respond, *"Good answer!"* Even then I knew God had to have better answers than were being given by Evangelicals, and Conservative Christians.

It was during the mid-1970's, while attending college, that I saw the problems beginning with this type of teaching. At that time, and I think it is the same today, there were several church related colleges with campuses in Springfield, Missouri. The three which I had the personal opportunity to observe were B.B.C. [Bible Baptist College — a fundamentalist Bible college], C.B.C. [Central Bible College — basically an Assemblies of God minister training campus], and Evangel College [an Assemblies of God liberal arts college].

I participated in an incident which illustrates the type of mentality that was so prevalent, if not dominant, on those campuses. There was a new freshman co-ed at Evangel whom I had met through some friends. She had caught my eye some weeks earlier, but at that time she had a steady boyfriend. I was the next guy she decided to date, and so she said yes when I asked her to attend a football game at our school one Saturday afternoon. Keep in mind, we had only spoken a few times while among friends, so we really did not know anything about each other.

At the game we happened to sit in front of a bunch of guys from my dormitory hall, so I have witnesses to this episode. All during the game this girl was almost climbing all over me, not touching in a sexual way, but more of a hanging all over me, which is something — my friends knew — I absolutely hate! The more I moved away from her, the closer she moved. At the end of the game she and I were about 5 yards away from my buds.

The guys got such a good laugh out of my discomfort that most of them would remember it, even today. It may have been hilarious for my friends, one of whom is now my brother-in-law, but it was absolute misery for me. I could not wait to get her back on her campus, as her clinging continued in the automobile on the return ride.

After I got rid of that girl that day, I had to put up with the normal ribbing from the guys, who kept singing the phrase, *"Cling to me, clinging vine."* I don't ever remember seeing her again, but within weeks I learned that she was engaged, and then within six weeks or so, she was married.

Unfortunately, on these church campuses this type of behavior was not uncommon. In fact, a not so funny nickname was given to Central Bible College. Known by millions of people as "Central Bridal College", it was where girls went to get their "Mrs degree." Even at that time I was not impressed with a church body which would allow such a reputation to continue to grow, particularly in the secular world. Some testimony, huh?

There were several other similar colleges within a 60-70 mile radius of Springfield from which had come to me very similar stories. I knew they were from first-hand knowledge, because during my teenage years, I had attended Assembly of God churches and youth camps, so I knew some of the students at the two A of G schools from years before.

In the ensuing years I have heard the same basic stories about church related schools from all sectors of the U.S.A.. Only the names were changed, but that was not to protect the innocent. It was because those church groups were guilty of being stupid.

The only innocent ones I can think of in those schools were the ones who escaped without their marriage degree, and those in the administration who may have been discouraging marriage among the students. And from what my niece, Stephanie Schinzing, of Syracuse, New York, indicated in 1995, this type of behavior is still not uncommon on the A of G campuses.

Of course, the Mrs. Degree recipients always credited God with finding their mate for them. I wonder now, 20+ years later, if they are crediting God or blaming God? From my standpoint, I always put the blame exactly where it belongs, on their hormones! And to give my opinion more credence, I heard about a survey conducted by an Evangel College alumni group. The survey found that only about 27% of those students who had gotten married while in school were still married years later. Interesting!

Young adults are unprepared enough as it is for a sexual relationship, and for children the complications can be enormous. How many teens or young adults who, when they first become sexually active, actually totally understand their own sexual characteristics, nuances, and idiosyncracies? Then they have to know what makes this other, totally different being function in the way they do. This type of test can only be prepared for after many years of serious study and interaction from a distance. It is my opinion that, of all of life's tests, our ability to understand the opposite sex and tend to their needs, are the tests that have been failed by more people than any other tests.

Childhood is a time of learning about yourself and the world around you. When it comes to learning about sexual proclivities and feelings, even as a 20 year old, it is somewhat early in the ball game, as this age is only a few years away from puberty and adolescence, with all of the mixture of feelings accompanying that period of life.

Childhood is the time to be learning responsibility, not fully demonstrating responsibility. The age of 20 is the age to which parents should aim in the training of their children. By that age, children, if trained correctly, should be able to be on their own as contributing, effective, responsible adults. That is not a commandment that they have to be on their own, it is only important that they be able to do so if the need arises, or they have the desire to be. Of course, this may not hold true if children have a physical or mental challenge which would not safely allow them to be on their own.

If children are not allowed to have sexual intercourse, then how are they to relieve their sexual tensions? How have they been doing it for centuries? Self relief, masturbation, whatever you call it. I know this has been a taboo subject in Church circles for hundreds of years. That, in my opinion, is because the Church has never totally rid itself of false Roman Catholic teachings — Masturbation is taboo! — which should have been debunked centuries ago. If this type of instruction had been taught by the Church from the beginning, just think of the millions of lives that would not have been ruined as the result of a sexual urge that was not controlled.

Now, there is a term that religion loves to harp on —
control. Of course, the word is usually put with the word
"self," to form the term "self-control." They love to preach on
this issue, and just because the subject is the urge of sex, then
everyone should just have self-control. They order no relief
for the urge when it comes to sex, but when it comes to the
urge to eat, sleep, drink, work, acquire, own, control, or
whatever, it has been okay to give into these urges without
condemnation or sin. But, woe be unto him or her who should
touch themselves in a sexual manner! That's a major, almost
unpardonable sin! How did something that is healthy for you
become taboo? [I would call them, "theological idiots," but
my niece Shannon would jump my case.]

Using Christianity's logic, a man or woman should not
ever eat or drink a bite or ounce more than they absolutely
need to sustain their existence. Nor should they sleep a
minute more, work a minute more, make a dollar more, own
a possession more, buy an item more than they absolutely
need to sustain their existence. Why has it been that when it
comes to anything relative to sexual activity, Christianity's
ability to think is nonexistent?

The Church does have a responsibility to teach, and even
demand, that adherents abstain from sexual immorality, but
the historical concept of sexual immorality should never
have included a total ban on masturbation. Believers would
have been better served by the teaching that sexual activity of
this type by children is to be a private matter.

I am by no means stating that all children should use self-
relief in order to deal with the sexual drive while they are
young. If a child chooses to deal with it by will power, then
God bless them. But, for those who choose self-relief, God
bless them also. Neither is right and neither is wrong. The one
who is right is the one who successfully deals with the
problem of sexual immorality.

As I hope I have pointed out to you, the problem of sin to overcome is not the release of sexual hormones, but to overcome the problem of sexual immorality. If you have reached your first committed adult relationship without having publicly displayed, lewdly discussed, touched another or allowed yourself to be touched in what would be considered a sexual manner, nor participated in any other activity which God considers immoral, then you will be considered to have successfully overcome the desire to commit sexually immoral sins.

There is a principle which applies to this discussion of sexual self-relief — *"You must control this activity, and not let this activity control you."* As a youngster the urge will come often, but does not have to be relieved each time, each day, each week, or each month. It is different with each person, and that is who must decide. When you are older you may not have the urge as often as you need to relieve yourself in order to help fight certain adult diseases such as prostate cancer in men and some cervical problems with women.

One point of information of which you need to be aware, is that there appears to be some type of demonic activity associated with excessive masturbation. I was made aware of this possibility in 1982 while I was doing telephone counseling in Bible College. A man called in wanting deliverance from a demon of masturbation; he said it was sitting on the TV at that very moment, laughing at him and us on the TV program. Whether he was mentally ill or under the influence of a demon, I to this day do not know, but this information should be an incentive to control this activity.

Now, there may be several of the narrow-minded persuasion who, because of this last mentioned possibility, would adamantly oppose my instruction on this matter of masturbation. But, if you are going to take that position, then I expect you to be just as adamantly opposed to eating, sleeping, dieting, working, owning your own business, alcoholic beverages, raffles, and sex with your spouse, as each one of these can easily be dominated by demonic activity and lead to excesses and ruination. Get real!

Having pretty thoroughly covered the issue of sexual activity as it pertains to children and adults not in a committed relationship, we must address the issue of what would entail sexual immorality for an unmarried adult in a committed relationship. The list is rather short, since we do not have to include those listed in the Bible; they obviously apply universally.

I will define a committed relationship as a steady monogamous relationship for a minimum of 4-6 months. During these months as the relationship deepens, possibly leading to sexual intimacy, it is imperative that people find out about the partner's past sexual activity, and have all the necessary medical tests taken, prior to becoming sexually active with that person. Anyone not willing to expose all personal medical details is certainly not a candidate for sexual intimacy. In this day [2000] of sexually transmitted diseases, any intimate sexual activity without intimate medical knowledge of the prospective partner is certainly sexual immorality.

Sexual intercourse in this type of relationship without taking the safe necessary steps to prevent pregnancy is sexual immorality. The same also with painful, unhealthy, and unsanitary sexual activity. There are absolutely no reasons to participate in the above mentioned types of sexual activity, as it only leads to problems.

The sex hormones of a non-married committed couple must still be held in check to a much greater extent than in a God ordained marriage. In a Godly marriage, my commandment is, *"Do it long, and do it often!"*

"Often" of course depends upon the spouses involved. In a non-married adult situation the commandment is, *"If you are going to have sex, do it very seldom."* Yes, it is not immoral to engage in sexual activity while in a committed adult relationship, but to do so irresponsibly, as I stated above, ranks right down there with having sex outside the relationship, a.k.a. adultery.

If you want to have sex outside the relationship all you have to do is end the relationship, then begin again with a new relationship. If you are ending the first one because you want sex with someone else, then you have a problem that sex won't cure. Sounds like the problem is you, not them.

These types of relationships should end amicably, because unless you are 25 years or older, then you should not be getting married at this time anyway. You may marry this person later, but absolutely not now, so there is no reason to get bent out of shape about the end. It should be a congenial time as it is the possible beginning of a new committed relationship, but hopefully, not right away. Also, you are just that much closer to the one for whom you are looking.

Between each committed time there should be a lot of dating. For years I have been amazed how much a female could shop around for every item they ever buy, but when it comes to choosing a male for a serious relationship, they take on the male shopping characteristic. Why would they want to do that, considering how stupid men can be when it comes to shopping? We habitually choose the first one that looks right and we have a high probability of being wrong. Don't believe me? Ask my wife, or any other wife for that matter. Ladies, stop being as stupid as we men are! Take your shopping skills into the dating arena and never select a rotten one. History tells us that when it comes to men there are a lot of rotten ones! Why am I preaching to the choir?

Virginity

In case you missed it, I am not a believer in being a "virgin" when you get married. I'm not necessarily against it, but I'm not for it, as it doesn't matter when you marry the one

God has chosen for you. That's the key. A few years after we had been married I decided that it didn't matter what or if Nancy Lee did before we were married. She was the one God chose, so anything else was unimportant. She herself today thinks the same way about it. It just doesn't matter. This, of course, doesn't give license for promiscuity because you have to remember that certain activities can come back to haunt you. Bed down with the wrong person, and your reputation may suffer significantly.

One of the most ridiculous stories I ever heard for not having pre-marital sex was played out by a young couple, or should I say, played out by the wife. Come to find out that the wife was a lesbian and she only got married to experience sex with a man. Seems she was not impressed with heterosexual sex, told him she was a lesbian, and said her goodbys. I never did hear if he had remarried, or if he found a good lawyer or both. Personally, I hope he kicked her legal butt for breach of contract, alienation of affection, and fraud, among other things.

Hopefully, this is a one of a kind story, as I would not want any other man to experience such a tragedy, and I am not using this situation as justification for my virginity teaching. I just honestly think that too much has been made of keeping your virginity until marriage, like it is something special for your husband or wife. What God intended to be special for your spouse is that the relationship is for life! You can't get any more special than that! For me, it is a whole lot greater to know that Nancy Lee is with me for life, than to know that she saved her virginity for me. In the overall scheme of life, the latter is insignificant.

Chapter Nineteen

WHEN CHILDREN HAVE SEX

Having sex without being married is risky! It is risky enough for adults in a committed relationship to have occasional sex, taking into consideration that adults should have more maturity and be more prone to keep their hormones in check until the appropriate time. But to allow children the option of sex will in some way have disastrous consequences.

I am about the last one in the world who would be in favor of prohibition for adults, but when it comes to children, adults have been designated by God as their protectors, so that we have the responsibility to forbid certain things from them. I am of the opinion that if children are taught the proper way to behave from the time they are small, then when they get old, they will not depart from it.

Programming children is not that difficult, and the subject of sex should be similar to the instruction for other potentially dangerous activities such as driving an automobile or boat, handling a gun, caring for pets, working at certain types of jobs, learning how to take care of things around the house [pilot lights, small electrical appliances, the roof, etc.] baby sitting, and the like. All these activities should not be engaged in without training. How extensive the instruction should depend upon the child, of course.

I know some of you are questioning my equating sex with handling a hunting rifle or automobile, but for children, those are probably about the closest potentially dangerous activities in which they may ever engage. Don't you find it interesting that we cannot think of any other activity even close to childhood sex, yet for centuries the Church has refused to address the issue of sexual instruction for children? Which one is more important?

To quickly deal with the issue of sexual instruction, it is my opinion that the most extensive education should be in the home, and be as extensive as the particular child requires. The only instruction in a public setting should be in the study of biology or the like in school. Specific classes on the subject are absolutely unnecessary and, more than likely counter productive, as evidenced by rampant teenager pregnancy rate of the 1990's. When sex education first began to be taught in the socialist [public] schools in the USA in the 1960's, the incidence of teen pregnancy was minimal. But, some intellectuals decided that a solution was needed for a problem which did not exist. What was the result of that sex education? A MAJOR PROBLEM! [Of course, that's what happens when you follow ungodly leadership, as they will lead people astray.]

Sexual instruction in a home does not begin at puberty when the sexual urges begin in earnest. Proper instruction begins as babies and toddlers by not making a big deal about nudity around the house. This obviously cuts out the curiosity factor later. The children have seen private parts for many years so to see another one is actually pretty boring. You are doing your children a disservice by keeping nudity a dark secret. This is only to be taken to the point of being voluntary, not mandatory, and of course, must cease with any possible arousal. Nudity in the house is not to be sexual except with husband and wife.

While I was growing up my parents were extremely modest, never allowing the children to see them in fewer clothes than a T-shirt and boxers for dad, and nothing less than a slip for mom. One of my brothers reminded me of an incident where our dad would take the 5 boys into a public rest room, let us go, then have us go stand off to the side with his back toward us while he went. This type of behavior can only lead to curiosity, which can lead to premature sexual activity, which of course can damage lives big time.

In-home nudity is just the beginning of sexual education. It progresses through answering the child's questions with age appropriate answers. It is actually relatively easy if openness is there from the beginning. The child already knows what the parts look like, so the next step is where the parts go for making babies. Years later the sexual arousal information can be taught by answering questions, reading books, instructional video products, and such. It is obvious with modern technology/animation that personal demonstration is not necessary to educate about sexual arousal, its causes, effects, results, and possible consequences. This type of instruction should be open, structured, with the objective of having all questions answered at the appropriate time, with emphasis on appropriate time, as each child is different. I know for a fact that it is best to have all questions answered, plus, as stated in an earlier chapter, teaching the child the method of self relief. I don't care if you don't want to address this subject, it needs to be addressed.

I also think there needs to be some discussion of basic ground rules for childhood relationships, dating and such activities. These by no means are absolute, but may be pretty close. If we have basic rules to which everyone can refer, I think it makes life easier for all. Again, these rules are not etched in stone as is the edict that *"Sex is for adults, not for children."*

The first thing that people need to realize about what they are about to read is the fact that by following our maxims/principles the marrying age has been moved back several years. It logically follows that the dating age must also be shifted back by several years. With the new marrying age there is no reason for teenagers to be looking for a mate. This releases a lot of pressure off the normal teenager so that all they have to do during this period of their life is to have fun and grow up. Few people have ever given this subject much thought, so it may take a bit of pondering to really see the simplicity.

Prior to age 16 children should only date in groups of at least 6-8, with appropriate chaperoning. There is no reason for pre-16's or even pre-18's to be single dating! They still need to be spending time finding out about themselves and their teenage relationships with others of their own gender. That can be enough of a challenge so why compound it with single dating? When your children display the maturity of their age, alone and among others of their gender, it is then that they should be allowed to move to the next level in relationships with the opposite sex, but the age barrier should be close to those listed above.

That next level, to be determined more by age than by anything else, should still involve others, along the lines of double dating, for a short period. Maturity may have something to do with it, but that type of thinking is what has gotten us into this mess in the first place. Controversy arises when you have to debate about the maturity of a child. One child will fuss about how one sibling was allowed to date at an age that he/she was not allowed to date, or vice versa. Why not just set a reasonable age where single dating should begin? What is unreasonable with the age of 18 for single dating?

I know a bunch of you or your children are going to come unglued about this, but you need to keep in mind that under our system of principles, marriage is 10-12 years away from 16 so there is plenty of time for single dating. In the old days when people were stupidly getting marred at 19-20-21, age 16-18 was pretty close, so you needed to be running scouting trips. However, these scouting trips are no longer needed at such a young age. Youth should be spent having fun, learning about the world, having fun, observing the opposite sex from a distance to figure out what kind of animal that is over there, with emphasis on the "over there" at that age.

Of course, the goal of teenage dating is to learn about yourself, about the opposite sex, how to relate to the opposite sex, and especially how to publicly treat the opposite sex. There is no rush to participate in sexual activity at that period of your life, as that should be several years off into the future.

Physical touching of the opposite sex before adulthood should also be limited. I know it sounds as if I am a control freak, but I really am not. I just think we need some guidelines. Don't you think we need to ask a question here? Why do dating teenagers have to touch? It's natural, right? So is sex, but remember you are years away from that action so why hurry the touching? You have probably seen some of these young teenagers hang all over each other like a coat? What did you think when you saw it? Pretty disgusting, right?

It is a fact that much touching leads to permanent consequences, so limits need to be put upon this aspect of teenage life. When children are young, begin teaching them that all relationships, except family, are temporary, and after a reasonably short period of friendship, relationships will get stale. Teach them to move on to others until they find one with which they will begin a family. Non-"significant other" relationships are the same way. Almost always they are temporary when you take into consideration the length of a lifetime. They will have many different friends during their lives — tell them to enjoy each one for the time period.

The temporariness of teenage love interests basically goes along the line of the popular song from the 1960's-70's, *"Love the One You're With."* I know that is going to raise the ire of some of you, but I want to use that line to help demonstrate the temporariness of the relationship. It does not exactly fit, but it is pretty close. At that age if one wants to move on, then let them move on with blessings, because that is just one less relationship you must experience before you find that one that is permanent.

Before age 16 there is no reason for teenagers to be touching in a loving way. Hanging around each other, being at events together, sitting with each other is okay before this age. At 16 you can add hand holding at certain limited times. Even an occasional congratulatory hug, as friends are prone to do is not unreasonable. But the more serious lengthy hugs and short kisses should be reserved for age 18, always keeping in mind the temporariness of the relationship. Teach your children to not do stupid things!

The single dating age should be cautiously approached due in large part to dating methods of the early 21st century in the more modern countries of the world. Things can be potentially dangerous out there, so parents have to be very careful with whom and where. It is toward ages 19-20 that more serious single dating should commence. Oh? You think that is terribly unreasonable? Why? Remember, marriage is still 6-8+ years off, so why the hurry?

One important point with which we must deal is the issue of touching private parts of the body in a sexual manner during the teenage years. This type of activity is forbidden and should be considered sexual immorality. When children are faced with this type of temptation they must fight it off with self control or self relief. They must be programmed early in life about the principle of "right to privacy." A person's body is one's alone until adulthood when he/she can make a decision about with whom, if anyone, to share.

This "right to privacy" needs to be programmed into children at an early age, not just in sexual matters, but leading all the way to political governmental affairs. The "right to privacy" is one of God's most important gifts to mankind and children should be taught to always cherish it and guard it against intrusion. As children grow older it is necessary that they be allowed more privacy. It's really kind of a natural progression that should not cause any upheaval in the family when the child starts exercising more privacy. If you have done the job right from the beginning, you will have no problems.

If you are having problems, then the parents did something wrong. Remembering that age old principle, *"If there is something wrong with an organization, look to the leadership as the problem. Solve the leadership problem and you will have solved what is wrong with the organization."* With raising children it is the same story. Raise them right and you will not have any problems with them. Raise them wrong, and you will.

Personal privacy of certain parts of the body cannot be emphasized enough at the right age with children. There are certain parts that are off limits at almost all times to other people [except, of course, parents and doctors and such]. For example, in my situation as father of a 13 year old daughter, the last time I touched her private areas was many years ago, the last time she took a shower with me. I still pat her on the butt, and I will probably never stop the occasional butt patting until she marries some guy bigger than me. The one thing I had to stop recently was the touching of her chest when we are goofing around. Once breast development begins, the chest is off limits, because this is just the natural progression of the relationship between fathers/men and girls.

Now, if someone else is patting my daughter's butt, they may have a problem. In situations such as this, children must be taught to report such improper conduct to parents, guardians, or law enforcement authorities. This principle holds true even as an adult. Your "right to privacy" of your body can only be relinquished by you, and not by force. Any forceful submission needs to be exposed to the limit of the law and punishment dealt to the offender. The main reasons that children need to expose these kinds of wrongful acts is for the action/abuse to stop, as well as for the protection of others who could also become victims if the perpetrator is not exposed.

Exposing a perpetrator is following the Biblical principle laid down by Jesus when He said, *"A new commandment I give to you, that you love one another as I have loved you, that you also love one another."*[John 13:34] You are not loving [serving] perpetrators if you let them by with such an offense. They have a problem and need a solution. Also, you are not loving [serving] others if these persons should possibly do this action against another child.

We began this chapter with the discussion of children having sex so we need to address the issue of punishment of the offenders. When a child should violate any of the above, a court should determine the severity of the offense and determine punishment of the child, or the father of the child. Yes, that is what I said. The father of the child should be punished in severe cases due to the fact that God holds the father of the child responsible for that child's behavior. The only time that the birth father cannot be held responsible is when paternity cannot be determined, the birth father is not alive, or a final adoption has taken place, in which case the adopted father is held responsible. The mother should suffer punishment only if she has refused to disclose the name of the father.

Punishment for the child can be by restitution or jail time. That is right, jail time for those children over 10 years old. Give children jail time, locked up in a room nights, or weekends, and/or vacations, and there will not be too many problems with delinquency. I know ladies, that sounds cruel, but when it comes to discipline God never put it into females to be the disciplinarians, therefore hold the fathers responsible.

If pregnancy should ever result from teenage sexual activity, again, the father of the boy should be held responsible to the tune of $15-20,000 [2000 value] plus all medical expenses. The baby must be put up for adoption to a family with a good home environment, meaning husband and wife. The only circumstance under which the child should remain with these children or their families would be if they have exhausted all possibilities for adoption. And do not even think about the two of them getting married. That is about the stupidest thought you could ever have, because if God did not put them togther, then it will be put asunder.

If we just observe a few simple rules of respect for the opposite sex, we can turn our society in the right direction. Notice I never said *"Turn it around."* We can't do that because we have never been going in the right direction. I, for one, would love to see that change.

Chapter Twenty

PLACING CHILDREN FOR ADOPTION

ANY BABY CONCEIVED OUT OF WEDLOCK SHALL BE PLACED FOR ADOPTION

"Dear Abby: Of all the phrases and terms we use, the one that offends me the most is "illegitimate child." I guess I'll go to my grave wondering what a new born child does to become illegitimate. What horrendous crime did he or she commit? How did he or she sin beyond all redemption to become forever illegitimate?

If there's a stigma to be attached to a child born out of wedlock, let's put it where it belongs — on the parents. Put the word out, Abby, there is no such thing as an illegitimate child. There are only illegitimate parents. — Gene in Olympia, Wash." [Dear Abby, Cleburne Times-Review, January 28,1999]

YOU GO, GENE! Simple, yet profound.

God designed that babies are to come into the world as a wanted and loved child of a mother and father in a God ordained marriage relationship. This is the best atmosphere in which to raise well-adjusted children. There should be no exceptions to this rule. Every possible effort should be made to prevent pregnancy at all times when pregnancy is not desired. If you don't desire pregnancy, then prevent it. What's so difficult about that?

How many young men have I spoken with, having just learned he had caused a pregnancy, made the statement, *"I'm going to do the right thing and take responsibility for the baby."*? Who was it that came up with this definition of the "right thing" to do for a man in this situation? So, you mean that the right thing to do for the child you created is to grow up without a father in the house? Yeah, right. How is that the right thing to do? The right thing to do is to allow that child the best opportunity to grow up in a stable two parent household. The best opportunity for that is to place the child with a fine established family.

Dear Abby on January, 22, 1999 had a great letter that I think also fits this chapter.

*"**Dear Abby:** I am writing to encourage "Scared in Vista Calif.," who was uneasy about meeting the daughter she had placed for adoption 18 years ago.*

I am 27, and it suddenly became very important to me that I know my heritage, medical history, and the reason I was placed for adoption. I have never felt abandoned or unloved because of my birth mother's decision to allow someone else to raise me. To me, such a decision is the most unselfish act a woman can ever make.

Abby, I recently located and met my birth mother. My adoptive mother, who is my mom, also recently met my birth mom. It was by far, the most amazing event in my life to date. It has been several months since my first call to her and I have visited with her and her entire family four times now. We frequently telephone one another.

There were many reasons I wanted to meet her but first and foremost, I wanted to thank her. Mom expressed the same sentiment when we met my birth mother.

Please tell "Scared" that there is no reason to be

afraid. She will experience many emotions on this journey and will need to allow time for everyone to adjust, but I guarantee that her daughter has been looking for her, and she is probably just as nervous as the mother. However, the meeting should not be feared. They should not back off now. The rewards are just around the bend. — NO LONGER GUESSING IN NEW JERSEY"

Mothers who place their children for adoption with a stable two parent family should never feel guilty for that action. In fact, they should feel proud since this was the ultimate act of service that they could possibly do for the child who was the result of a major mistake. The only guilt they should feel is for being so careless to have allowed the pregnancy. That regret should be felt for a long time.

If the mother abandons a baby in a negligent manner, the guilt should be tremendous as there is no reason to ever abandon a baby, especially when there are families willing to adopt babies. Placing a child for adoption is not abandonment, as abandonment is leaving the child in an unsafe environment when a safe environment is available.

Once a pregnant woman has placed her child for adoption, that decision is final when the contract is signed with the adoption agency or the adopting family. There is no reason to allow for a mind change, as the opportunity for that is before the contract is signed. To not abide by the contract would be to compound the major error of the pregnancy, which only compounds the guilt.

Immorality should be accompanied with guilt. Having a baby outside of a Godly marriage is immoral and should be looked upon by others as such, just as abandonment is immoral behavior and has been looked upon as immoral behavior. It is in this vein that I feel called to inform the reader that it is also immoral behavior to not place a child for adoption that has been born under circumstances outside of marriage. There is no legitimate reason for this behavior, unless there are absolutely no families in the entire world with whom to place the child.

While we are dealing with guilt and blame, did any of you happen to notice that I have not mentioned the truly guilty party, the male? Of either party that should walk around with a scarlet letter, it would be the male.

As everyone knows, the male caused the pregnancy, so he is responsible. Okay. Go ahead and say it. *"It takes two to tango."* I'll assume that is true, as I do not know anything about different dances, but that does not fit this situation. It takes only one to naturally cause a pregnancy. The fact is, God put a greater responsibility for serving on the male than He put on the female. He gave to the male the responsibility to create new reproductive spirit beings with his sperm.

Spirit Beings

God put His spirit into the first man and put into that man the ability to pass along the original spirit by the electrical energy within the sperm. This energy is passed into the child when the sperm joins with the egg to energize the egg of the female. It is at that moment that a new spirit being is created to begin forming a new human being. Things do not always go exactly as God originally planned, but that is the basic operation.

In simple terms, our spirit is made up by electrical energy. The sperm has electrical energy as part of its makeup, which when attached and joined with the slightly different type of electrical energy of the egg, will result in a baby with a human spirit, if everything goes according to God's plan.

The egg is obviously energized by the sperm, as has been observed by medical researchers. This energizing is, in my opinion, the spirit energy contained within the sperm. Obviously this electrical energy grows as the fetus grows, which would explain how people who have been privileged enough to have visited heaven, have seen children there. I haven't been there, haven't done that, but I have heard others say this is a fact.

It seems that I have strayed a bit from the original subject, but I wanted you to understand what I have perceived is God's plan for conception and upon whom He has placed the greater responsibility for preventing pregnancy. This responsibility is on the male, not just because of biological reasons, but also because God made the average male physically stronger than the average female. Since he has the greater responsibility, how could he be serving the female by causing a pregnancy without her permission? And, to keep and attempt to raise a child under such circumstances would certainly not be serving the child.

Now, we all know that the humanist religion would tell us that we have the option of abortion. However, if my biological description is for the most part correct, then it logically follows that, since the spirit of the fetus [baby] is put into the child, and actually is what gives the child its life from conception, then how is abortion an option? It really isn't, is it? That is, unless you do not believe in spirit beings. But only dishonest people don't believe in spirit beings.

There is a very simple way to determine that abortion is wrong, and that is to turn around and make an absolute judgement on the definition of death. If we determine what causes, or is accepted as the determination of death, then the rules of logic will determine the cause of life. Several years ago I sat around thinking on this subject and it came to me in simple terms.

If you find a corpse lying outside in the road, can you be charged with murder if you go outside and shoot it several times? Most people would answer that they could not be charged with murder. Why not? The answer to that is always *"The corpse was already dead."* The next question is, *"How did you arrive at the fact that the corpse was dead?"* Their final answer is that since there were no heart beats or brain waves, death was established.

So, if the absence of heart beats and brain waves is the absence of life, then the presence of heart beats and the presence of brain waves means the presence of life. When are these two conditions present in a fetus? There's the question that needs to be answered.

From my research, they may be detectable at about 14 days after conception at a minimum, and some information I have read says that the heart beat is present in the 7th week. If it is wrong to stop heart beats and brain waves at one time, then why wouldn't it be wrong to stop heart beats and brain waves at another time? Why should it matter how or when the stoppage occurs? What is so difficult about this?

While we are on this subject, what do you think it is that gets heart beats and brain waves started? How about that spirit, which is that electrical energy, that is in the sperm of the male? Do you think that could be it? I certainly do! It is the system that God set up with Adam and Eve to put His blood [spirit] into mankind. If the presence of the spirit gets the heart beating and the electrical brain waves going, then wouldn't it also follow that the absence of the spirit would cause the death of the human? So, the reports of people who have had an out of body experience, then returned to the body and regained their health would not be far-fetched, or a dream. It would also follow that the involuntary muscles of the heart and breathing parts maybe are not so involuntary after all. Maybe the humanists who originated the idea of involuntary muscles should have asked God what caused this phenomenon of these muscles just working on their own without any help from any other muscles. How did these humanists think that happened? Magic?

Our discussion of a maxim/principle against abortion is also along this vein. Conservative Christianity, for the most part, is anti-abortion in all cases. But, I cannot hold to that position. The reason for that mainly has to do with the health of the mother. If the mother's life is in danger, and the only solution is to take, or abort the baby, then abortion is viable. These situations are so rare, especially with modern technology, that it certainly is not worth spending much time on it. The mother's life is much more important due to the fact that she is breathing and functioning on her own in contra-position to the baby still dependent on the mother. A human breathing on her own takes precedence over one not breathing on its own.

Abortion in situations such as rape or incest is not an option if the definition of abortion refers only to the removing of a fetus [baby] after conception. But, if abortion refers to the removal of the male ejaculate from the female within 10-14 days after the act of rape or incest, then abortion is okay. I think this type of procedure is called, in gynecological terms, a " D & C." From my information this entails the scraping of the interior walls of the uterus to prevent pregnancy. This is a reasonably simple procedure which can be done in a doctor's office.

This or similar types of procedures should absolutely be done within 7-10 days after the act, which is prior to any proof that a pregnancy exists. The only sin in this type of situation — rape or incest — is in not cleaning out the uterus area to prevent pregnancy. This is not an unreasonable or un-Godly teaching. To force someone to give birth to a baby as a result of an activity outside of the control of the female is totally unreasonable and ridiculous! For the Church to have been opposed to this simple solution in the past speaks of a lack of spiritual understanding.

The same holds true for possible pregnancy not by force. There is still that 10-14 day period where a cleaning procedure is allowed, as there is no evidence that the egg has been fertilized. Until proof of fertilization, there is no proof of pregnancy. Even though I don't recommend this type of birth control, it's none of my nor anyone else's business, as there is no proof of pregnancy. After proof of pregnancy exists however, you have to do everything within your ability to protect the unborn child.

When it comes to dealing with pregnancy outside of marriage in regard to the child, it is best to follow this sequence in doing what is best for the child.

Plan A – Place the baby for adoption. After exhausting all possibilities then see **Plan B**.

Plan B – See **Plan A**.

Plan C – See **Plan B**.

Plan D – Place the baby with family or friends.

Plan E – Either father or mother raise child.

Plan F – Shoot the guy who even suggests a shotgun wedding? [Just kidding!]

Abortion is never the solution to an unwanted pregnancy, but adoption is. Everyone wins in an adoption situation, where a major screw-up is turned into a blessing all the way around.

When you adopt children, that adoption makes them equal to any other children you may have. It is damaging to adopted children to treat them any less than equal; many never get over being treated less than equal. I am totally convinced that God has established that adoption brings equality, exactly like it is when you give your life to Jesus: you come into the family of God by adoption which gives you all rights and privileges. Look at what *Dake's* says about it.

> *"Adoption - the act of God whereby a repentant sinner is made a member of the family of God, as if he had been born in the family; the placement as a son with all the rights and privileges of a son."*

Then Dake lists several blessings of adoption into the family of god, which could, of course, for the most part, apply to the human family.

1. Love	John 17:23; I John 4:7
2. Care	Luke 12:27-33; Hebrews 12:4-12
3. Name	Ephesians 3:14-15; I John 3:1
4. Likeness	II Corinthians 3:18; Philemon 3:20
5. Spirit	Romans 8:14-16; Galatians 5:16-26
6. Service	John 14: 12-15; 15:16
7. Gifts and grace	Romans 12; I Corinthians 12; Galatians 5a;22-23
8. Inheritance	Romans 8:17; I Peter1:1-9
9. Supply	Matthew 6: 33; Philemon 4:18
10. Health	Matthew 8:17; John 10:10; Romans 8: 11; I Peter 2:24; II John 2; Psalms 91
11. Home	John 14:1 3; Revelation 21
12. Fulness	John 1: 16; 7: 37-39; 5:32; Ephesians 1:3

Dake's is great for categorizing Bible verses; it gives you a quick reference guide to verses which fit together. I recommend that you research these verses for yourself.

When we take into consideration this subject of creating a child outside of marriage I am of the opinion that the father and mother need to be punished. A society that does not hold this as one of the most important aspects of its norms is pretty pathetic. Obviously, in our society today, the emphasis is on sex, and since there is no longer any stigma associated with conception outside of marriage, it is not going to get any better. I say that a stigma needs to be connected with this type situation, never on the child but always on the parents, and especially on the father as he has a greater responsibility for keeping it in his pants.

I know that a bunch of you are, or will, come unglued when you read my form of punishment for the mother and father as too many people in this world today get squeamish when talking about any type of punishment. There is too much acceptance abounding in our society, and that spoken by this author of the statement, *"The essence of Christianity is not in the "not sinning", but rather in the forgiving."* But the fact is, there is a time for forgiving and a time for punishment, and in this issue of the importance of parenthood, punishment is more important than forgiveness.

The punishment of the mother has already been discussed at the beginning of this chapter. Probably you female readers caught it immediately, but the men probably missed it. Requiring the mother to place her child for adoption is punishment enough for the mother's lack of discretion. Show me a woman who can easily give up her child, and I will show you a disgusting human being.

Speaking of disgusting human beings, let me lay into the fathers of such children. This group of people have skated for centuries. No, make that for millennia. I see nothing wrong with sentencing such a man to two years behind bars so that he can reflect upon his major disregard for the rights of another spirit being, the child he created. And, if the child is born into a negligent atmosphere— poverty, drug/alcohol abuse, violent parent, etc. — as determined by a competent court of justice— something unheard of in the year 2000 in the U.S.— then give him four years. That's four years in a very small room from which he never sees the light of day. In other words, NO MERCY!! The reason I say this is because I believe God intended for an infant to have a right to be born into a loving family with mother and father having made public marriage covenant vows. Do I sound unreasonable?

How many teenage or unmarried pregnancies do you think there would be if boys and men knew they would be held responsible with a prison term for doing what men have historically done without consequences. Therein lies the major problem. Where there are no consequences, there is less likely to be responsibility taken. I say let there be consequences, or punishment, and your problem just may disappear.

Chapter Twenty-One

HOMOSEXUAL BEHAVIOR IS WRONG

HUMAN SEXUAL RELATIONSHIPS ARE RESERVED FOR
Adult Males with *Adult Females*

God has never allowed for any variance on this issue. Anything else is wrong and should be considered to be deviate sexual behavior.

As covered in my first book, *ETERNAL DAMNATION ON TRIAL*, God created the original man from His own blood, or spirit; the Bible teaches that the spirit is in the blood. Since Adam was created in God's own image, he was created with both male and female characteristics, just as God has both male and female characteristics. [The Hebrews have believed this from the beginning, but most of Christianity missed this one.] All God had to do to create Eve was to strip off the female characteristics from Adam and clone these into another body. When the two come together as husband and wife they become one as God is one. Of course, this is the simplified version of The Garden Of Eden story in Genesis, but it will do for now.

I truly believe that if the Bible had been translated a bit more clearly in this section of Genesis, there would not have been such a controversy. What God really did when He "cloned" Adam was to make a co-equal partner for him [study this in the Hebrew language]. [I wonder when it was that woman had that co-equal status wrested from her?] Once we understand the beginning we are more inclined to get it right later on. The only way that two can become one, as God is one, is by the merging of the two sets of characteristics. Anything else was never God's intention. We have to stick with God's intent on the issue.

There are many different beliefs on sexual lifestyles in the world today, and there probably always have been a small percentage of people who have adhered to different lifestyles. I happen to believe that one man with one woman is right, not only for the above reason, but also because that is the way the overwhelming majority of people throughout history have done it. Therefore, I think we can conclude that one man with one woman is the natural way. This remains basically true no matter what political or economic system people live under. It was that way under Hitler's Democratic Socialism, Mao's Chinese Communism, Hong Kong's quasi-Free Market system, the majority of Native American Tribes, Hindu India, the Muslim world, and even some of the tribes in New Guinea. Wherever in the world, or whenever in history, for the most part, men and women have naturally paired off and started a family.

I honestly don't see how this natural progression can be challenged, but it has been and is at this present time, not only by a politically active homosexual segment of the world's population, but by other groups such as "Polyamorists." The latter name describes their beliefs; *"many loves."* I came across the name for this belief system when I was researching on the Internet under the subject of co-habitation. Let me show you a little of what they have on their web site; then you decide if heterosexual monogamy or polyamory is closest to what God had in mind:

"Most Polyamorists have a 'live and let live' attitude. They are happy for those people who have found happiness in monogamous relationships. However, most polyamorists are impressed by the fact that the divorce and adultery statistics indicate that monogamy fails a great deal more than it succeeds.

Polyamorists tend to see the modern American nuclear family as an aberration in the course of human history and believe that larger, more complex extended families or tribes have been the natural human family structure. Children are seen as better off when they have a broad range of adult role models to relate to, instead of a single, monogamously married couple. [Think that's where Hillary Clinton got her idea for Bill's sexual freedom and her book title, It Takes a Village? — Just kidding!]

Polyamorists believe in freedom of choice and consider Polyamory as a viable alternative to monogamy. They acknowledge that real love and a committed relationship is in no way free. Intimate love relationships, whether monogamous or Polyamorous are complex and challenging and their success requires maturity and hard work. Polyamorists, being outside the mainstream of our society, are taking on the extra challenge of trying to do something which is unpopular among their monogamous peers. Polyamorists do tend to object to our culture's idealization of monogamy and suppression of alternative lifestyles.

"Polyamory has its own unique multi-partner terminology and language. One of the most popular styles of Polyamory is Poly-fidelity, sometimes also called closed group marriage. In Poly-fidelity, groups of three or more partners consider themselves essentially married to each other. They usually live together in a single home and share their lives and resources such as married couples do. There may be any combination of males, females and sexual orientations. Polygyny, as it was practiced by the Mormons, is just one example of Poly-fidelity. Classically, Poly-fidelitous groups are sexually

exclusive and do not engage in sexual relations outside the group. However, there are some group marriages which are 'open,' and which do allow for outside romances. In the open marriage style relationships in which the members who consider themselves committed life partners nonetheless permit outside, sexual, romantic and loving relationships outside the marriage in a way that is agreed upon by the marital partners."

These are the basics of that lifestyle, so, what do you think? Sound like something you would love to get into? I certainly disagree with them about the *"modern American nuclear family as an aberration in the course of human history and...that larger, more complex extended families or tribes have been the natural human family structure,"* but maybe I haven't studied the subject as well as they. I must have read different history books, because I still say that one man with one woman is the norm.

When speaking of alternative lifestyles, even homosexuality seems to progress toward monogamy after most seem to have had a great many partners. I remember reading about the man to whom some researcher concluded that the A.I.D.S. epidemic in America could be traced, as this man's having had before he died, up to 700 different partners. That to me was extremely extreme, but not totally unusual within the homosexual community. Promiscuity is rampant, but just as heterosexuality, the tendency to monogamy appears to be very strong.

Homosexuality is wrong! Bottom line! It doesn't matter how you attempt to twist the words of the Bible, it still never changes God's intent. This subject has been hotly debated for at least three decades in the Northern Hemisphere. We know it is not natural due to the fact that it is so rare. The natural way is for males and females to be attracted to each other.

Homosexuality is Wrong

God's creation is supposed to be balanced, i.e. opposites attracting; therefore, males and females get together.

Some of the most dishonest people I have ever observed in my lifetime— besides soccer fans— are some of the ones who are publicly involved with attempting to convince the world that homosexuality is natural. They insist that people are "born that way," and that it is an "acceptable lifestyle," when the facts at least suggest the exact opposite. I say the facts at least suggest the exact opposite because I want to cut the opposing view some slack that maybe their arguments could possibly be somewhat credible. I have just been amazed at how almost no one has picked up on the patterns of the beginnings of this lifestyle for both males and females

From my observation there are three basic ways to enter this homosexual lifestyle. The first and most subtle of the three is a gradual progression into the homosexual lifestyle. I got my first inkling of this tendency when reading about it in a book in the early 1970's. If I remember the story correctly, a woman had written to a minister for counseling because she thought she may be a lesbian, but yet she still had the urge to get married and have children. It seems that she and her female roommate were in a situation where they had to share a bed. This was not totally unusual back before 1970 due to small houses, the amount of money females in the work force could make, and in some areas, the availability of housing. Some nights in bed the two began holding hands for a while to comfort each other, and this touching lead to more touching, which led to lying on top of each other and french kissing. She admitted that she looked forward each day to getting home and in bed with her roommate and she asked if she was a lesbian, because she and her roommate still had the marriage/child rearing urge.

A less subtle way to enter this lifestyle is to make a decision at a point in time to have sexual relations with someone of the same sex. I noticed this while in college with some female athletes who made a conscious decision to have at least occasional lesbian sex. The explanation given for this decision was that they could not get dates with men, so this was their second choice. I honestly think that many of these women were actually heterosexual, but drifted into lesbianism out of what they considered to be a necessity.

The final way that someone enters the homosexual lifestyle will be the heart of this discussion on this lifestyle because I think it is the most prevalent, yet the least understood. I will do this by relating my experience with homosexuality. I have never put this on paper, but I have related it in conversation to several people.

The year was 1975 while I was attending Southwest Missouri State University in Springfield. It was normal to see me hanging out at intramural basketball games. Actually, you could say I was a fixture, since I was well known as a referee and served on intramural committees. This one night as I was sitting along side the court at the Greenwood Gym watching some friends play B-ball, something very strange happened.

All at once, something weighty, like a heavy blanket, came down upon my head and shoulders, and immediately I had an extremely strong attraction for this guy on the court playing in the game.. I am gong to describe this as best as I am able, but unless you have experienced that sensation, it is difficult to understand.

The attraction was specifically for one man and the attraction was within a split second. I went from a hormone-raging heterosexual to a homosexual within a split second. The scarey thing for me, and what I want to get across to the reader, is the fact that at that moment, homosexuality was the most natural feeling in the world. It was as real as the chair upon which I am sitting, and as real as the basketball game I was watching.

But, I wasn't watching for long. No longer than 5 seconds later, I was so scared I practically ran out of the building. I had been sitting alone, and was in the habit of moving quickly at times, because I was involved in so many activities, my actions at that time raised no eyebrows or suspicions. When I was outside and out from under the overhang awning above the sidewalk, this "thing" released from me. I moved so fast out of that chair that I may have left the "thing" there. The only thing I felt after that was fear, as I sure was scared!

In the years since, when relating this incident to others, I may have embellished on the story a little bit by saying that I returned to my dormitory room to check my underwear, but I'm not sure I didn't. I had never been so frightened in my life up to that point. To go from a heterosexual to a homosexual in an instant, is pretty scarey for a normal person, and I don't scare easily.

I cannot stress too much how natural the feeling was during the seconds that I sat there. It was at that instant just as natural to be attracted to that man as it was to be attracted to a pretty woman before that moment And it was that man only to whom I was attracted, another strange part of this episode. The attraction was not to men, but rather to this one man, whom I had known for two years, both he and his girlfriend. To be honest, I never knew if this one man was heterosexual or homosexual. Even though he had been steady with the same co-ed for as long as I had known him, I did not know his status at the time of this incident. [Less than a year later I asked out his ex-girlfriend, so I was certainly attracted to her.]

Why the attraction was to that specific man, I do not know. After having studied the subject for more than 20 years now, I have come up with these two possibilities. The first is that he was homosexual and the attraction was to get me into a relationship with him. The other likely possibility was to seduce me into accepting the homosexual lifestyle, and once I had succumbed to that seduction, I would be hooked and would have to be looking for other partners. I have observed these two patterns over the years since.

At the time of this episode, I had no idea what that "blanket" was that came down onto me. And not having discussed it with anyone else until I got married, it wasn't until after I had been studying the Bible for years that I came to understand that the "blanket" was actually a demonic spirit. Now, I know that some of you are coming unglued at about this point, mainly because you do not want to accept what I am saying and not because you have any information or facts to which you could point to dispute my position on this issue. But, please bear with me.

If my episode was the only time in history that this type of "blanket" experience occurred, then my contention of the demonic spirit could be disputed, but there have been many which I have come across, besides the probable millions of others that I suspect have taken place.

One day after relating this episode to a long-time female friend, she offered that she had experienced the same type of thing, only hers was during her high school years. She told me that she and a friend had been just doing teenage girl things while sitting on her friend's bed one day, as they had done many times before. All at once something came over her and she had this strong attraction for this other girl. As happened to me, she got extremely scared, got off the bed, walked out of the room, out of the house, and never spoke with the girl again. She said the girl never did understand why their friendship ended so abruptly, and she never explained to the friend what happened. I can understand why.

It was this type of encounter which made me suspect that being attracted to a certain person does not necessarily mean that the one experiencing the attraction is a homosexual. The fact is, as the next episode will relate, the recipient of the attraction can be and, from what I have seen, probably is a homosexual, but it is not necessary that they are.

This episode involves a world famous female athlete and a wife of a fairly well-to-do man. This female athlete was a well known lesbian who had become a friend of the family and would stay with them at different times while in that city. One evening, while spending the night, she went into the wife's bedroom to say "Hi" to the wife who was sick in bed. Up to this point, as stated in the wife's book, there had been no attraction to this athlete or to any other woman.

When the athlete sat on the bed to speak with the wife, the story is that the wife instantly had an attraction for this athlete. As soon as I read this, when excerpts of the wife's book were printed in a newspaper, I knew exactly what she had experienced. To my knowledge, the only difference was that in this case the attraction was definitely for a homosexual/lesbian, whereas in the two previously mentioned cases, there was no proof that the attraction was definitely to a homosexual or lesbian. It's for that reason that I gave my two theories for the source of the attraction.

One other episode is familiar to probably millions, as it was in the newspaper. Whether it is true or not, I do not know, but I will relate what the article said. It was relating a statement made by the current lover of a world famous lesbian former TV star. This woman had never before met the star, but as she sat across the room from the lesbian, this woman *"fell immediately in love with her."* [I hope I got that quote right. I know the inference was immediate.] This "falling in love," I am convinced, was the same as the other episodes mentioned above. Love is never immediate, but same sex attraction is almost always, in my opinion, immediate, but very few people have ever attempted to understand this.

I have also seen on TV and read other reports of people who have been prayed for about this same sex attraction. What they related after prayer was that something left them and the attraction left with it. Whether or not this has happened in each case of prayer, I don't know, as I can only relate what I have heard or experienced.

Another aspect to this discussion is the statement I heard on a talk radio show several years ago. The topic was homosexuality, its possible causes, and possible relief. A woman called in to ask the question, *"Can somebody tell me how to not be homosexual?"* Of course by this time my ears were perked up. She went on in this way, *"I don't know anyone who is a homosexual [lesbian] who wants to be one, so just tell us how not to be one."* There are certain times in life where profound statements and events take place, and for me, this woman's call that day was one of them.

This young woman's statement that none of her circle of acquaintances wanted to be the way they were is very interesting. On the show, they did not give her enough time to explain why these people did not like their status, so we don't know why. Was it because of the way society looked at the lifestyle that made them want out of it? Was it the feelings or attraction itself that made them feel dirty inside? Was it the type of people they were originally that made them want to get out? Was it the female desire to have children which prompted them to not be same sex attracted? I do not know for sure, but from what I have heard from others who had been in this lifestyle, I really do not think it had as much to do with societal pressures, as it did with uncleanness inside.

I am by no means an expert on the subject, and there are many out there who have spent more time on it than I. And I cannot be certain that the caller was referring to this, however, according to my studies, these feelings of internal uncleanness are consistent with the above specific incidents when obvious demonic activity is involved. Her response is also consistent with other reports of people who have been involved in demonic controlled lifestyles. Same sex attraction is on the increase today, and it is my opinion that it is due to a seductive spirit which goes from person to person and draws them into the lifestyle.

An obvious example of this demonic activity is the huge prevalence of *"butch"* looking women today [2000] compared to 20-30 years ago. From my observation, when this "seductive" or "same sex attraction" demon comes upon people, their appearance changes over a period of time. I know personally a woman who 10 years ago did not look anything close to "butch." At the time she was divorced, and came somewhat close to seriously dating one of an acquaintance's relatives. She wouldn't move closer to him so it ended. Just a couple of years later she became involved in the lesbian lifestyle. A few years later her looks had changed to where she was obviously *"butch."*

It is the same, yet opposite, with the majority of men involved in a homosexual lifestyle. Even *SEINFELD*, and some other TV shows have figured this one out in their references to the visual characteristics of the male homosexual: Clean-cut, physically fit, trim, aesthetically appealing to females. When you look at a GAY PRIDE parade, what do you see? You see what God specifically did **not** intend! He never intended for women to look like men, nor did He intend for men to be pretty. Any questions on this one?

This is the pattern I have observed for years when it comes to demonic activity. If it is present, you will see a pattern develop, or it will be along a pattern already developed. A few of these obvious patterns which can be traced to demonic activity are conditions such as phobias, anorexia, bulimia, schizophrenia, kleptomania, paranoia, sadomasochism, pedophilia, and similar strange maladies. These are all conditions which begin with demonic possession or oppression and an obvious pattern develops, which allows a person to trace the source of the problem.

Most of the time from what I have been able to surmise, the "same sex attraction demon phenomenon" happens almost at random with no prior inclination toward that type of activity being necessary. Whether that is true in all cases I do not know. As for myself, I had exercised such anti-homosexual activity to the point that I almost pushed off a five story balcony a guy whom I suspected had been following me.

Whether or not you agree with me now, we all need to be aware of what could happen to almost anyone almost anywhere at almost anytime, and that we do not need to accept these demon spirits.

It wasn't until several years after my episode that I understood why the "blanket" left me alone. I was explaining what happened to some relatives and when I got to this part, stating that I had no idea why the demon left me, my oldest brother piped up and said, *"I know why it left! Resist the devil and he will flee from you."* Absolutely correct! My recommendation to everyone who is the victim of strange happenings which are totally out of the ordinary, and do not appear to be a good behavior pattern, then resist immediately.

In this case, do what's natural. Search for someone from the opposite sex with whom to start a family, just the way God designed it.

MAXIMS MAINLY FOR FEMALES

Chapter Twenty-Two

FEMALES, GUARD YOUR HEART!

In the same way that men have to guard their "you know what," females have to guard their hearts. Both genders have a weak point and you will know by the end of this book that I come down pretty hard on the male about keeping his pants on. But, I do not think I have emphasized enough the importance of "guarding the heart" for a female.

Experts say that an average female will fall in love twice during her life. I don't have a problem with that statistic, though I think most females can, and should, fall in love more times than that, as long as they realize that the real love comes when she finds the right one to marry. The other loves are only a partial giving of the heart, or "practice loves." If a female is taught this principle, she will be less likely to give her heart to the wrong man.

You put a normal male in a sexual situation where there is a possibility that he could do something stupid, and there is a high probability that he will do just that. Quite often that stupid thing he does will last someone a lifetime. Obviously, history tells us that for a normal male, sex is his "Achilles heel." History also tells us that the "Achilles heel" for a female is her heart, as she is susceptible to giving it to the wrong man. She is apt to do something stupid that will cause her problems for the rest of her life. Others may also be affected, but seldom as seriously as the female herself.

I am not totally convinced that this maxim/principle should not be somewhere up around Number 2 or 3 in importance, as I have surmised from my research that the normal female is very susceptible to giving away her heart to the most undeserving man on earth, and this is one of the major causes of female problems in the history of the world.

When some people hear the term "female problems" they think of physical problems that need medical attention. When I hear the term, I think of a female that did something stupid with the love section of her heart. The former may have been a high cause of death for more females throughout the ages, but the latter has certainly caused more of them to live in hell on earth.

Many women speak of their first love as being the one which they remember most, and therein lies the problem. The normal female falls too hard the first time. What females have seldom been taught in the past is that this first love is just one of many that they will have until they marry. And when was that marrying age, again? This is what has been missing from the parental equation when teaching growing girls. Parents have failed to communicate to their daughters about when to begin contemplating marriage, and they've neglected to warn them that until that time comes, they need to guard their heart.

For a female, this problem many times begins with the father. Sometimes I wish Dani Lee would be totally sold on her daddy, but she is not, which is the way I honestly know it should be. I want her to look at me objectively, to know that I have deficiencies. One of the main reasons I want that is because I do not ever want her future husband to think that he has to compete with me to please his wife.

During my survey I came across a good number of males who resented or regretted that the wife had thought so much of her father and it caused friction in the marriage. The wife wanted the husband to live up to the standard of her father, and/or the husband always looked upon the father-in-law as a competitor for the loyalty of the wife. This is not good for any party in the transaction.

During the first few years of our marriage, Nancy Lee, kept expecting me to be as handy around the house as her daddy. But, after a few years she came to realize that I could never meet up to her daddy's standard in fixing and building things. After a while it became a joke around the house about my "unhandy-Dan" tendencies. Fortunately, she came to the realization that she could hire out the work or invite daddy for a visit to solve her repair problems. Unfortunately, she is still searching for any qualities in me that would come close to her daddy's, but she likes me anyway.

So, the moral of this story is: Remember females, you save your heart for the man God has chosen for you to marry. Until then, have fun and keep those other males guessing.

Chapter Twenty-Three

FEMALES, DON'T EVER SELL YOURSELVES SHORT!

Go ahead. Call me a sexist. I know good and well that both males and females sell themselves short, but I notice it more with females than with males. Also, I figure that males, being physically stronger, should know better than to settle for less than they should.

We cover the male psyche in the chapter about living your dream, and from what I have gathered, living your dream is more important to males than females. It has been my observation that a female is more likely to be satisfied with the progress of her family than with the progress of herself. That still does not give her an excuse for settling for less than what God wants for her. [A key phrase, but more on that later.]

To me, the most obvious area where females sell themselves short is in their recognition of their looks. Too many females never realize how beautiful they are. Spoken like a man, I know, but I think I am pointing out something important here that too many females fail to take into consideration.

Hey! You all have seen or heard of a beautiful woman who is stuck on a real scuzzbag, lowlife, possible descendant of pond scum, and certainly a poor excuse for a man. Too often she ends up physically beaten on at least one occasion, if not seriously injured or killed, with the bottom line of a miserable life. One big reason this happens is because she sold herself too short. She refused to realize how wonderful or beautiful she really was, that she did not have to settle for the first man to come along.

Females, Don't Ever Sell Yourselves Short!

In another part of this book I mention the good looking Hispanic females who should have been working the runways of New York, whom I found with three kids each in roach infested apartments I was inspecting. By just looking at them I was quite positive they were just two of the millions, if not billions, of females who could have done better. It was obvious to me that they had either gotten married too young or had at least gotten tied down to the same man too early in life.

This is not an unusual situation for a female to get herself into. [Here comes that sexism again.] That's right. It's not an unusual condition for a female since God made the normal female to desire comfort, and security.

This desire to find a comfort zone is not necessarily bad — it is a good balance for the "on the edge" males out there. [Certainly, my wife did not marry one like that.] Females just have to keep this desire for comfort in perspective and use it at the proper times. Unfortunately, too many are not taught how strong this instinct is in them. They don't know when it is to be used and when to shove it to the background and not let it be the controlling instinct. It is a positive aspect that females have this instinct that tells them to seek comfort, but it needs to be trained so that it controls at the right times.

Females, you're too good to settle for less than what God wants for you, especially when it comes to a man to marry.

Chapter Twenty-Four

DO YOU PLAN FOR THE MARRIAGE, OR THE WEDDING?

WOMEN, MAKE PLANS FOR MARRIAGE, NOT FOR THE WEDDING!

This sounds like a solution to a non-problem. Wrong! From what I have put together, this is a major malady among those of the female persuasion. A woman will plan for months or years, day and night, for the wedding, the celebration, the pretty things — but she never spends ten minutes making post wedding plans for the rest of her life as a wife!

A wedding is so incidental to a marriage that the only important part of it is the actual covenant making. Nothing else is important for that whole day, yet females seem to spend all their attention and energy planning the entire 24-hour period. Why? Is it an innate trait that causes them to miss the entire purpose of the day?

There is nothing wrong with planning a celebration day. But, when a little girl is motivated to get married so she will have one day in her life where she is the center of attention, it is absolutely stupid! Always has been stupid! Always will be stupid, and it is a stupidity which has permeated our society. One person I know told me about a friend who has her wedding day all planned out with no potential man in sight. What a waste of mental time! Where are her priorities?!

There is no way that my extremely intelligent daughter, who could be successful at almost anything she sets her mind to do, is going to look upon a wedding day as the only day in her life where she will be the center of attention. If her plans continue in the same direction, being a surgeon will be a whole lot more rewarding than one day dressed up in a white dress. The possibility of saving someone's life dwarfs the importance of a single day in a wedding dress with cameras flashing, don't you think?

There is nothing wrong with the female being the center of attention. But it is very poor leadership by the parents to wrongly train a female child to focus on the day rather than the life after the day. It is a serious error which needs to be rectified — too many young girls' lives have been severely damaged by this problem.

I see several ways to remedy the situation. First off, program girls from the time they are small, just as you have to do with the marrying age, that the wedding is a rather minor incident in their lives. Second, change the ceremony in such a way as to take the limelight off the bride and put it on the union of the couple. I believe God would have it that way. Third, program girls to grow up and have at least one vocation with its accompanying rewards which will dwarf the importance of any wedding day.

It is a fact that the wedding day is only a bump in the road of life when put in its true perspective. That day's only important events are the speaking the vows in front of witnesses, and for the married couple, the wedding night. Then life goes on.

Chapter Twenty-Five

SCHOOLING AND VOCATION BEFORE MARRIAGE

FEMALES MUST HAVE A GOOD EDUCATION AND AT LEAST ONE VOCATION BEFORE MARRIAGE

This principle is proven true by looking at history. How many women throughout history got married before they ever got a high school education, much less a college education? You have heard over and over again how a woman whose husband died, and left her to raise the children without having a vocation to fall back on. In the past 30 years in the U.S. alone, look at the millions of women who got married young, had children, then were abandoned by their husbands, and left with no career to go to make a living.

The idiocy of the leadership of the Church Body to not have adequately addressed this issue in the past has amazed me. Why couldn't they have seen the pattern centuries ago? It doesn't take a genius to figure this stuff out! Unbelievable!

Nancy Lee is one of those who could be considered a victim of this type of stupid thinking on the part of Church leadership. As I stated earlier, she has a higher intellect than I do, but she was never encouraged to go on to higher education to expand on that ability. What ticks me off is that she is smart enough to have been a doctor or dentist, and if she had done that, then I wouldn't have to go out to make a living. I could sit around and write books that few people will ever read. Obviously, I'm the victim here! [Just kidding!]

Well, maybe we can solve the problem after this, if we can get parents to program their young girls to grow up, get an education, learn at least one career [preferably two], then consider marriage, in that order. This, of course, follows the principle which forbids young marriage. How can you get married young if you have to get an education and develop a career before thinking about marriage? You can't, can you?

One extremely important reason for a female to have a good education, which is totally unrelated to making a living, has to do with her future children's education. Parents have to be involved in their children's schooling, which means helping with homework. This, in my opinion, will become much more important in the future as new ways of obtaining an education will replace the old socialist classroom concept.

The change will be brought about by new technology such as satellites, VCRs, computers, Internet, etc., all of these will certainly help socialistic school systems to become obsolete. There will still be some classroom style educational facilities, but not nearly as many as certain parts of the world have seen.

Following the principle that mothers stay home with their children for at least the first 4-6 years— preferably longer— it is only logical that with new technology, home schooling will be much more prevalent, economically feasible, and children will be better educated at a younger age. This advance is inescapable, especially when it is coupled with more adults working from the house. It is a natural progression. Mothers without good educations will be doing their future children a great disservice.

Now the world is changing faster than ever and females can no longer afford the luxury of being lazy when it comes to education. I have noticed for many years how a huge percentage of females would love nothing better than to find, at a young age, a man to take care of them for the rest of their life. Any woman with this mentality in the future, in my opinion, is in for a lot of misery. After all, it is this very attitude which has gotten so many women in the pathetic marriage situations they find themselves in.

Schooling and Vocation Before Marriage

Where did the normal female get the idea that she could find a man to take care of her? I have been astounded at the huge numbers of women who just up and decided that they no longer had to work for a living after they got married. I can almost understand this mentality from my wife's generation since they had not totally been programmed with the women's liberation theology which told them they could be in the work place just like a man. The generations of women previous to Nancy's were certainly programmed with the "stay at home" theology, so it was accepted back then.

What surprises me is the high percentage of females who have grown up in the last 25 years who continue to have this "stay at home" mentality. Here we have young ladies, married in their early 20's [victims of the Married Too Young Syndrome] married just a few years, no children yet, who have decided they don't want to work. They want to stay home.

Is this attitude one of laziness, or inherited, or something else? I do not know, but it is amazingly common among certain ethnic groups especially Hispanics. I am sure some of it is laziness on the part of some women, but I really do not think that has much to do with it overall, as the normal housewife/mother is certainly not lazy. You could not pay me enough to do that job.

My honest opinion is that it has to do with the mental aspect of working outside the home, and how it strains the brains of a huge percentage of females. Call me a sexist if you want, but that is what I have observed. Being a mother/housewife is certainly not easier on the body of a woman, but it is much, much easier on the brain. I believe that is why so many women want to drop out of the workforce.

This certainly does not apply to all women, but absolutely applies to a majority of them. Nancy Lee, for instance at the time of this writing, works 2-3 days per week at a dentist's office. It's her choice, as I would just as soon have her quit the dentist's office, but she enjoys just working part-time. Could she mentally handle a full-time job? Sure. Remember, she is smarter than me, but she chooses not to work full-time.

An interesting conversation I had with a 22 year old jail inmate shed a little bit more light on this phenomenon. He told me that several of his friends who were already married, had wives who quit work soon after the wedding. He knew only a couple of young married wives who worked part-time out of the house. His opinion was that they wanted a "sugar daddy." Someone to take care of them.

Can anyone tell me where this attitude comes from? One theory is that God built into the normal female the knowledge that she is to be the weaker gender, therefore she instinctively needs someone stronger than herself. Perhaps if it were not for this weakness a lot of men would never find someone to put up with them. What do you think?

Another young man I spoke with, soon to be a groom, told me that his wife-to-be was the first woman he had dated who would work. I knew immediately what he was referring to, as he had discovered through dating what I had discovered by survey. He was a good looking young man who probably had no problem getting dates, so I would have to conclude that his statement was well founded. It was further proof for me that this female attitude is symptomatic of a huge percentage of females.

This attitude, in and of itself, isn't necessarily bad, but the females of which I write are not the type to be looking forward to taking care of her family. She just wanted an easier life, which would not qualify her for a job as full-time mom. That takes a better person than your's truly.

Chapter Twenty-Six

NEVER, EVER MARRY A CONTROL FREAK!

Please give me one exception to this absolute. Most people have probably known someone who has been married to a control freak, as it tends to be quite obvious. If you stay away from control freaks you probably cannot be controlled by them [unless they work for the government, of course]. After all the murder/suicides which have taken place in the past few years, maybe I should add to the title of this chapter **NEVER, EVER DATE OR MARRY A CONTROL FREAK!!** I remember an incident in 1999 where a woman had dated a man one time, and she ended up dead by that same man. Think he may have been a control freak?

I have been amazed over the years at how people, mainly women, get attached to control freaks. Many of these women were naive enough to think they were going to change them. [Yeah, right! You are going to change a control freak. How many lifetimes do you think you are going to have to accomplish that?]

The bottom line is that most control freaks were not trained properly by their fathers. They needed to have the slack jerked out of them when they were young, then they would have understood that they had no right to control someone else. Try asking a control freak to tell you where it is written that they have a right to control someone else's life. But when you ask, make sure they don't have a weapon handy, as most control freaks do not have a sense of humor when you question their authority. They usually follow a strict chain of command. First there is God, then them. Well, usually in that order anyway.

Here is a quick example of just how controlling control freaks are. One day I was quizzing a man I know as to why he was such a control freak in regard to his family. He had refused to allow his teenage daughters to wear shorts and pants, as he felt it appropriate for them only to wear long dresses in public. [You've seen these styles on women out in public — they stand out like a wart on the face of a super model.] His reply was, *"I like to be in control of my environment."*

I do not have a problem with him controlling his environment when he is by himself, but when other human beings — who have the blood of God flowing through their veins — come into the picture, his control is then limited.

I would love to have a control freak prove me wrong on this issue. Prove to me that you have ultimate control over another human being's life. Where did you get that authority? The above mentioned man contends that God gave him authority and that He had it written into a book called the Bible. What a bunch of hogwash that is! As I quoted him earlier, he likes *"to be in control"* of his *"environment."* In other words, he controls because he likes it, then he interprets the Bible in such a way as would lend credence to what he "likes" to do. It's amazing what you can learn from someone when you ask the right questions. *"Out of the abundance of the heart, the mouth speaks."*

Many of these "Christian" control freaks claim that their beliefs and actions are based upon Biblical teaching. They base a lot of the argument upon Old Testament or Old Covenant teachings. Under that covenant, which only applied to the Hebrews, God seemed to allow the husbands to have more control over their wives. The one characteristic that all Bible-based control freaks have in common is that they are great expounders of Old Testament theology. [Look at David Koresh, the minister/control freak who was murdered by the United States federal government near Waco, Texas. Did he

even know that the New Covenant existed?] You will seldom
find these people quoting passages from the New Testament
or New Covenant. If they ever did, they may be able to see
the error of their ways.

The principle which overrides a control freak's right to
control someone is found at Genesis 2:18.

"And the Lord God said, 'It is not good that man should be
alone: I will make him a helper comparable to him.'"

In the King James Version the term used is "help meet."
The Hebrew should have been translated "co-equal partner
with." You can prove this by what I mentioned earlier about
God being both male and female. He put the male
characteristics in one body, Adam, and then put the female
traits in another body, Eve; and then they come together to be
one, as God is one. If Adam has half of the traits of the
original and Eve has the other half, then which one has the
most? Duh! When was it that Eve or any other female gave
up a percentage of her half? I missed out on that transaction.
The fact is that this controlling principle from Genesis does
not give control freaks authorization to usurp authority from
their spouses or significant others.

The most prominent verses in the New Testament by
which male control freaks usurp authority is, of course,
Ephesians 5:22. *"Wives submit to your own husbands, as to
the Lord."* Another of "The Control Freaks Club
International" favorites is I Timothy 2:11 & 12:

"Let a woman learn in silence with all submission. And I do
not permit a woman to teach or to have authority over a man, but
to be in silence."

And let all the control freaks of the world say, *"Amen!"*

We now need to see how the above verses line up with
Genesis 2:18 which is the controlling principle. The first fact
holds true unless later negated, but that does not happen in
this case.

Paul's teachings are to remain in the time period in which they were written, as do the Old Covenant teachings on married relationships. As I pointed out earlier from *Dake's*, the Israelite marriage relationships mirrored somewhat the tribes around them. With those tribes being ungodly heathen, to accept some of their traditions is probably not a good idea.

Now, back to our control freaks. How do you recognize a control freak? Let me count the ways. How about if they are bossing you around? Do they always have to know where you are? Do they tell you where to go, what to do, whom you can see or know? These are some of the reasons why a control freak so often marries someone younger. A young, naive girl/woman is about the only one who would put up with his crap; hence, the principle — **never marry a control freak.**.

I don't care if people are control freaks when they are single adults, but when they come into a relationship, even as a significant other, the controller needs to agree to give up the right to always be in control of his environment. Another sovereign human being is now involved. What control freaks have never looked at is whether or not they do this every day, as a matter of course. Do they act like they own the sidewalk, roads, stores, elevators, etc? They share things, events, life, all day every day with others and they survive, so why is it that when they get into the family's own home, they feel like they must take control? Tell me where it is written[!] that life for control freaks would be better for them if they are in control?

When a spouse comes into the picture, a person must give up some sovereign authority over himself. That is the law of covenants. In a marriage covenant you are no longer your own, but your spouse has power over you, if it is demanded within a loving covenant relationship, that is. Remember what we saw earlier in I Corinthians 7:4?

"The wife does not have authority over her own body, but the husband does. And likewise the husband does not

have authority over his own body, but the wife does. "

This is a true picture of a covenant relationship. Each spouse has authority over the other at different times and in different situations. This totally negates the opportunity for a control freak to engage in a marriage covenant relationship. You cannot be in a God-like marriage if you cannot submit to your partner.

Children add another factor to the equation. It requires more surrender of sovereign authority since other human beings have been born with some sovereignty of their own. Admittedly a child's sovereign authority is extremely limited, since the exercising of it is limited. But, when the pregnancy begins, so do the child's rights which are to be guarded by the parents. In that way, with that requirement of protection of the child, the controller has again surrendered some authority. Individuals are no longer their own.

What's the big deal about sharing authority? God has always shared authority since Adam and Eve, when He gave mankind dominion over the earth. He has continued to do so by allowing us to come into a covenant relationship with Him through Jesus. When we come into that covenant relationship we then have authority to go to God to demand of Him. In a covenant relationship one party has a right to demand of the other, If you don't like that arrangement then fuss at God, not me. He is the one who started this, when he kicked Adam and Eve out of the garden.

Did anyone yet come up with a legitimate way that a control freak could be in a Godly marriage relationship? There is no way! So, those of you thinking about associating with a control freak might as well forget it, unless you want disaster. The best thing to do for control freaks is to leave them to themselves and then they can control to their heart's content. Or, maybe sterilization is a possibility?

Chapter Twenty-Seven

NEVER MARRY A VIOLENT PERSON!

ONE STRIKE AND YOU'RE OUT!

We all know that the male is the most common offender of this one, but occasionally the culprit is the female. From my survey this is so seldom that it is not worth discussing. Where the female is usually at fault is: #1 — Falling for such a despicable human being, and # 2 — Failing to have him locked up immediately after the first threat. Don't even wait for the swing!

The basic principle is, *"If he hit you once, he will hit you again."* Why can't women get this through their thick hearts? A man who would hit a woman is absolutely <u>not</u> qualified to lead a family, so he should not even be considered as a marriage partner. I know that some of you would love the opportunity to jump all over me about calling women thick hearted, and not putting the blame on the violent male, but please save that jump until you hear me out. This chapter is to publicly lay out a maxim/principle that Christianity should have laid down many years ago, but failed to do.

A temper out of control is not necessarily evidence of a physically violent person, but you'd better be careful. If you have only seen a few episodes of a bad temper without violence you need to stick around without marriage until you see a few more episodes which may result in physical violence. Wait him out to see if he gets more control over the temper tantrums. You probably also need to check out his background to find out if there were any previous episodes of violence in his past.

Never Marry a Violent Person!

If you find evidence of past violence, and if you do not know for a fact that the person has had a definite change of heart, then the best thing to do is to stay away from that person. Of course, if you think all the spouses who have been beaten several times are lying, then go ahead and marry that low life. To be honest with you, I don't have too much sympathy for abused spouses, since I think they should have known better. Most of them fell in love, tripped that female circuit breaker, and wouldn't listen to anyone or admit what was in front of their eyes. While I'm on the subject, let me specify the women that really disgust me — those who refused to press charges, even after the first time. Pathetic!

Ladies, when you have him arrested, which is exactly what you need to do if he gets violent, never let up on him. File the complaint, make sure the prosecutor does the job properly that would put him in prison for a long time, then don't visit him when he is locked away. The last step is to divorce him. Did I stutter?

I have never come close to hitting Nancy Lee, and not just because she informed me before our wedding that if I ever did hit her she would be gone and I would never get a second swing. She has never provoked me to want to swing at her, but she planted in my mind something I would not want to see, and there is no doubt in my mind that she would go, so you won't catch me in jail for hitting my wife. You may catch me there because I ran afoul of some law-breaking government official, but never for spouse abuse. [Some would say that just subjecting Nancy Lee to life with me could be judged as abuse, but I for one, do not hold to that opinion.]

Let that fiancé know before marriage that one hit and he is history, both out of your life and into the pokey. What is so unreasonable about that? If women would do that, we wouldn't have very many abusing men running around loose out there. They would be locked up where they belong.

Never Marry a Violent Person!

Ladies, just think for a few minutes what it is that men really want in this world. If you have not figured it out yet, it is sexual intercourse with a woman, and if you are the spouse or fiancee, then he probably wants that sex with you. If you let him know early on that one strike and he is out, just as a baseball umpire tells a batter that three strikes he's out, he'll get the message pretty quickly. Just let him know that when it comes to sex, you're boss! I don't think you will have many problems with this advice.

For those of you who are prone to become violent, the rule is that you can't ever hit another person except in defense or liberation. In those situations you need to do what you have to do to inflict damage, but how often do these situations arise? If you feel you are becoming too aggressive toward a spouse, then you have to back off and see where your next actions can land you — without clean, regular sex with your wife, and probably in prison.

And that brings us to a situation which has amazed me for many years. We have all seen on the news how some man has killed his wife or ex-wife and sometimes his kids or himself, usually because she left him and he could not deal with it. This jealous control freak, besides being scum of the earth, is really stupid! If he cannot get along with the spouse, can't he meet up with someone else? All he has to do is to let her go and find another woman who will put up with him. Like there aren't more females than males in the world? Hello?!

Chapter Twenty-Eight

ALWAYS REPORT ABUSE

Abuse of wives and children is a terrible, terrible evil in any population group, but it should have never been tolerated, especially among Christian Believers. Why hasn't the Church been at the forefront of exposing this problem as the evil it really is? Could it be that the historic leadership in the Church were guilty as sin of this family abuse, and therefore unwilling to expose it?

Probably not all of them were guilty, but I know that a decent percentage of them were, just by talking to their children and looking at their wives. I remember one incident back when I was doing telephone counseling in Bible College during the early 1980's. A young lady called in to talk about her dad who had been molesting her for years. She was 22 and lived many miles away from her parents for that very reason. But, whenever her parents would visit, the physical contact would begin again. She told me that while her parents were there she had to sleep on the sofa; her dad would wait until he thought she was asleep to come out of the bedroom and start touching her. Rather than open her eyes to confront her dad about this, she just kept her eyes closed and let him touch her.

That is rather disturbing to me, as I hope it is to you. The molestation is bad enough in itself, but she also related to me that the father worked as an executive in the headquarters of a worldwide Pentecostal denomination. Now, that is really disgusting!

I have heard other similar episodes, but this one seemed to stay in my memory, as it was perpetrated by one of those "holier than thou" Pentecostals. And a leader, at that! But since there has been so much hypocrisy from too many of the leaders within those groups, it is hardly surprising. I would bet that this particular young lady is just one of numerous similar incidents.

It is my opinion that sexual abuse of a child is usually caused by a demonic spirit, similar to the homosexual spirit spoken of earlier. This could explain why so many offenders continue to do it, since sexual contact with a child is totally unnatural behavior. A demonic spirit, as I had experienced with the homosexual demon, could cause a normal heterosexual adult to turn into a sexual abuser of children, and if it came upon a person, this type activity would seem natural.

Another possibility exists which might explain how an adult can become convinced that this type behavior is acceptable. It could occur because you are entertaining thoughts in your mind which suggest that this activity is acceptable.

Here is how this can happen. About 17 years ago while attending Bible College in Dallas, we lived in an apartment complex with two-story buildings which required those living upstairs to walk across a balcony walkway to get to their apartments. One afternoon the four year old girl from next door walked by our picture window and out of nowhere I had a thought of molesting that cute little girl. It astounded me because the thought was so strange and totally alien to all I believed. It was literally unbelievable! By that time I had been studying the Word from Bible College and I knew not to entertain the thought — it came and went in a few seconds because I did not allow it to stay around.

As stated earlier, *"Resist the devil, and he will flee from you."* This thought vanished because I resisted it. I did not allow the idea to fester in my mind. I do not remember using the name of Jesus against the thought, but I may have, as at that time in my spiritual growth I could have spoken to this thought, saying something like *"Leave me in the name of*

Jesus," and I have no doubt that it would have departed.
Everyone needs to understand that they can exercise this same authority when these types of thoughts or feelings come upon them. Simply resist by telling them to go away in the name of Jesus.

For anyone who is confronted by thoughts of sexually abusing a child, or, as discussed in the section on homosexuality, an actual demonic spirit lighting upon you, the first thing to do is resist it with the name of Jesus. If there still does not appear to be any relief, the next step is to talk with one or more spiritually mature Believers in Jesus to pray the prayer of deliverance over you, so that you can gain release from this spirit. Any thoughts along this line which are allowed to fester in the mind will possibly lead to scars for both you and a child, which may never heal.

Sexual contact with a child by an adult, or another child, absolutely is wrong! Sexual activity is for adults with other consenting adults and anything else is sexual immorality and should not be tolerated by any society.

Besides sexual abuse, both physical abuse and emotional abuse also afflict many families. In this context, physical abuse entails the improper striking of a child or other family member. Improper or unacceptable striking is easy to detect. It occurs outside simple to understand limits. We touched on this earlier, but repetition won't hurt us.

The humanist line regarding corporal punishment is that it damages the child, and that some are even scarred for life. What a bunch of B.S.! Humanists are not even smart enough to figure out there is a God who got this entire universe started, so why would we listen to much of anything they say or do? I have spoken with thousands of adults who "suffered" the "torture" of spanking, and you know what I found? Not one of them was scarred in any way! On the other hand, I have talked to many who were beaten or abused and they were scarred by their parent's actions.

Corporal punishment requires limits for parents to follow. First off, you have to determine if you have an active child or a calm child, as children are usually one or the other. If you have not made that determination before your youngster starts crawling, I would say you have a "tweener" or you are not too sharp, so get other opinions. As I mentioned before, the first few weeks after Dani was born I knew we had an *"ants in her pants"* active live wire, and were in for some challenges.

If your children are calm you may never have to lay a hand on them for correction, or possibly just an occasional light rap on a hand that is touching something not to be touched would be sufficient. But if you have an active one, the probability is high that more spanking will be needed. Acceptable correction methods are a light slapping of the fingers and hands, a hand or paddle to the butt, or as Forest Gump would say, *"But-tocks."* Striking the arms, legs, back or head is out.

Physical abuse and correction are two totally separate concepts. Corrective spanking should not be done in public if at all possible, and it should seldom be done by the mother. Early on the child needs to learn that it would have been easier to receive it from the mother, mainly because daddy spanks harder. God made fathers to be the disciplinarians and one of the greatest sins a man could commit would be to shirk his duty as disciplinarian.

And, again, I have to blame the Church Body leadership, because for centuries they never stepped up to address these problems of abuse in our society the way they should have. Shame on them!!

Chapter Twenty-Nine

NEVER MARRY A LIAR!

Obviously this one follows the last few principles, and I don't think I could simplify it any further. A lie is simply a misrepresentation of the facts, and if people have lied once, they will lie again. How often will you let them lie before you draw the line and say, *"This is not the person for me."*?

One of the most subtle lies that we all need to be aware of could be described as an "embellishment" or "exaggeration." A brag or an exaggeration is not necessarily a lie as long as that exaggeration does not continue for a long term. As that great American, Will Sonnet, used to say , *"No brag. Just fact!"* In other words, it is not bragging if you can prove it, and it is not a lie if you can prove you did it or can do it. But, the sign of dishonest people appears when they continue to exaggerate about past feats of their ability.

The slickest perpetrators of this type of offense are the ones who evade the truth, or from whom you can never, or seldom, get a straight answer. Although it was not in a love interest, I fell for one of these slick talkers at least once in my life. I moved to his locale to be associated in an endeavor with him. Before making the move it was obvious that he never answered any direct question that I had for him. Another man who was to join us would not accept his lack of answers, but I did. I do not regret my decision to this day, but when dealing with lifetime decisions such as marriage, you want to make sure that you never settle for a spouse who gives you non-direct answers.

Young people eligible for marriage need to be wary of dishonest suitors. According to my survey, this is one of the most common complaints about a spouse, where a divorce resulted from a too-young marriage. As I stated earlier, 80-

85% of all first divorces were caused because of the parties being too young when they got married. The other 15-20% just married the wrong person. A huge share of this 15-20% married liars. It was usually the man who was the liar, but not always. Most of these victims did not know the liar's background, or ever did a past history check with family or friends.

As soon as you do come close to possible marriage, you need to investigate the background of that person you may marry. If you find one lie, you had better re-evaluate the relationship. If you find a major lie, or a gap in their time line for which they cannot or will not account, then you have a liar. Do not feel guilty about checking into the background of the person with whom you plan to spend the rest of your life. Any intended who balks at such a check should be told to hit the trail.

When I look back on our wedding September 1, 1979, Nancy Lee really should have done a check on what I had been doing the previous seven years, because she really had no idea about me during that period, even though we had known each other for about 13 years.

Let me tell our history as an example of problems which could arise if you do not do a background check. Nancy Lee and I first met, so far as we can remember, when we were both 12 or 13 years old because my oldest brother Dwayne was engaged to a friend of Nancy Lee's family. At the wedding reception Nancy Lee caught the bouquet and I caught the garter. I then was forced to put the garter on her leg, which at 13 was not what I wanted to do. [Today, I touch that leg every chance I get, of course.] Up until we graduated from high school, we saw each other occasionally because her family was like family with my brother's clan. You know how these Italians are about family.

The last I had seen of Nancy, we had spent time together Labor Day weekend after our high school graduation. She took me to the New York State Fair and by the end of the weekend we were with different partners. We just were not attracted to each other at that time. As I lived in Michigan and she in Syracuse, New York area at the time, if I was not visiting my brother I never saw her.

A year and a half after high school I went to Missouri for college and totally forgot all about Nancy. I made my home there and truly planned to live there the rest of my life, until it was turned upside down because of a bureaucratic decision at the Missouri State Athletic level. For the next six months I drove a truck around the country and at our Thanksgiving family reunion I happened to mention to my sister-in-law from Syracuse that I was looking to get married. She suggested I come to New York to see Nancy, to which I replied, *"Nah. I didn't like her several years ago."* But I did ask about her friend, the girl I had ended up with that last time I had seen Nancy. I was informed that this girl was already married with a child.

I figured that was going to be the end of the story until about 2 months later, when I had to deliver a load to Niagara Falls, New York. I was going to have the weekend off so I figured I would go check out why Nancy Lee had not been married yet. I figured that she must have gotten fat and ugly. Wrong! She looked better than I ever remembered, as I was sure she didn't look that good 7 ½ years earlier. To end the story, I proposed that weekend and she accepted 2 months later.

The point I am wanting to make with this story is the contrast in situations between Nancy and me. I had no need to do a background check on her, as she had basically had the exact same lifestyle the past 13 years. Those Italians do not change much.

I, on the other hand, had been on my own, nowhere near family or past friends, so she had no idea what I had been up to. I could have lied about everything for the previous 7 ½ years. She basically knew my family, as she saw my parents and siblings occasionally, and she just presumed that I was like the rest of them. But she could have been mistaken, as neither she, nor my family, really knew what I had been into since I moved to Missouri.

I hope you see the point. Do not assume that man or woman is telling you the truth. Put the pieces together for yourself before deciding on a mate. If you find an unaccounted gap in the time line you may have a problem, so confront that person about it. If you find a lie in the background, then confront that person about it. Make sure the answer is solid. If it's borderline [say the answer is *"I forgot."*], make note of it, but if you find a second unsolid answer, you'd better call it off. The rest of your life is too long to spend in the misery that a liar can cause.

Chapter Thirty

NEVER MARRY AN ADDICT or A BOY STILL STUCK ON HIS TOYS

DON'T EVER MARRY SOMEONE WHO IS ADDICTED TO ANYTHING

How many times have we heard a woman say before the wedding? *"I can change him!"*? Or, *"He will change when he marries me."* Or, *"I'm going to be such a good wife that he will change."* Then how many times have you heard a woman after the divorce say, *"I thought I could change him."*? Hello! Is anybody in there?!

I have found a few cases where the female is the one with the addiction problem, but the percentage is pretty low from what I have seen, and most of these females did not have a good father in the house to raise them properly. It is normally the male who is the addict. That is a big reason why women need to check out a potential husband for an addictive history in the family. The studies I have seen show that addiction can be inherited.

A lot of men are addicted to sports, which is one extremely important idiosyncracy of a normal male that few females have been able to understand. The problem in this area of addiction is that there is a certain percentage of men who are addicted to sports. It is my opinion that this addiction should be pretty obvious around marrying time, when he's in the late 20's to early 30's. Is he too busy with sports to have a relationship?

Gambling can certainly be an addiction. Again, normally a male pattern of stupidity, right? Wrong!! How many females are hooked on Bingo, lottery tickets, or the slots? And this addiction is only getting worse from what I can see, as Bingo becomes bigger as a fund-raising mechanism, and more states/reservations have legal gambling. Unfortunately, instead of looking to the Creator of the universe as their source of income, many people look to games of chance as their source. Not looking to the Creator is a terrible sin, because you then are depending upon yourself or luck. Playing games of chance is not evil in and of itself; it becomes evil only when you violate certain principles.

I have a theory that some extreme cases of gambling are caused by a demonic spirit that latches onto a person and there is no way to get away from it without taking authority over it in the name of Jesus. This situation would certainly not be conducive for marriage.

An example of this type of demonic activity was on the front pages of this country's newspapers back in the 1980's. It involved a famous National Football League quarterback who was plagued with massive gambling debts. To me, this was an obvious case of demonic activity because no matter what he did for rehabilitation, he could not shake it.

Drug addiction in modern America is at an all time high [no pun intended], and it's amazing how many males and females marry someone they know is addicted. Not too long after we moved to Texas, Nancy Lee had a friend who married a man she knew was a drug addict, but she had no doubt that she could change him. Not only did she fail to do so, but the husband died within months, and her baby was born with defects and lived only a few short years. How many millions of times has this happened?

There are some lesser forms of addiction, like being a couch potato, computer geek, audiophile, videophile, etc.. These addicts may stay at home, and their addiction may not kill them as drugs, alcohol, or cigarettes do, but they are addicts nonetheless. Do you think your intended relationship can survive one of these types of addiction?

I am probably addicted to reading. Dani gets onto me often about it, because I do not give her my attention when she thinks I should. Maybe it is just a bad habit, but if you told me I would have to do without reading for the rest of my life, I don't think I could. I'm more than a "reading junkie;" it would be more accurate to classify me as an "infomaniac." If I'm not sleeping, I am probably attempting to soak up information. My "infomaniac" tendencies are so bad that if Nancy Lee were to force me to make a choice between sex with her, or reading for the rest of my life, it would be a tough choice, and she certainly knows how much I like sex.

Sex. Now there's an addiction for you. This one is easy for men to succumb to. Almost every man who has had an orgasm wants to have about as many more orgasms as possible. So, how do you recognize a sex addict? You have to ask? How great a percentage of spare time is spent watching sexually oriented materials, or engaging in, or thinking about sexual activity? That's probably the greatest indicator.

Sexual addiction can really tear families apart, possibly more than any other addiction you could name. I've had the misfortune of speaking with hundreds of ex-wives who had to deal with it. Certainly this type of addiction needs to be recognized before marriage, because from what I have seen, it does not get any better without help.

One of the addictions to which many females succumb is the shopping bug. They can be so addicted to shopping that it can totally bankrupt a home. We all have our weak points and shopping can certainly prove to be one for females. I am not sure that there is such a thing as a demonic spirit that causes some females to go overboard when shopping, but extreme cases may be caused by a spirit of greed or a seductive spirit. Remember the general principle. If it is a rare, extreme situation, there is probably a demonic spirit in control. This principle certainly holds true with addictions.

Some people do not need an absolute to tell them not to marry someone who is an addict, but there are others who need to hear this teaching. If you ever find anyone whose marriage survived one partner's addiction, you can chalk it up as a very rare case. [Maybe that person needs to write a book?]

Alcoholism, of course, is a major addiction. I want to touch on a theory on which I am working, which has to do with men and alcoholism. I do this not to be sexist, but to point out a major problem which mainly women suffer because they are married to alcoholic men. My theory may apply to females, but I do not see it as a factor in very many unhappy marriages. Hear me out and you decide if this would apply as readily to females as it does to males. I have never heard this specifically stated as I am going to do.

As you can probably surmise, if I looked at more than 10,000 divorces, then I would have to come across a huge number of women who had to, or did, put up with alcoholic husbands. Indeed I did, and there is a definite yet rather simple pattern that showed itself.

If you find an alcoholic, you have probably found someone who is very unhappy with his marriage or his life in some major way. With male alcoholics, the major factor is that he did not live his dream [a topic we shall discuss in a later chapter]. When what a man is doing on the outside of himself does not synchronize with the dream that is inside him, then quite often alcoholism is the result, and more times than not, the wife gets blamed for it. But, the reality is that it had nothing to do with the wife. He didn't live his dream for whatever reason, and this usually is his own fault. Some people have this problem before marriage, but quite often it starts after marriage.

Many times when a man becomes an alcoholic after marriage it is because he is unhappy in his marriage. Again, from what I have seen, it has nothing to do with the wife, except for the fact that she was the wrong wife for him to marry. Often, his unhappiness sets in fairly early in the marriage, like when he wakes up after 1 ½ - 3 years of good sex and wonders what he is doing in this marriage. Sometimes even before the wedding he has figured out that he should not marry this woman, but he goes through with the wedding rather than admit to the poor choice. Pity, that more men cannot admit before the wedding that a mistake is about to commence. It would save a lot of misery.

And so we have two main factors in alcoholism which begins after the wedding — the husband is unhappy with the marriage [he knows he married the wrong woman or at the wrong time], or he is not living his dream. But, I have noticed another most common reason for the alcoholic's underlying unhappiness. It is of a spiritual nature, that can only be solved by a religious conversion to follow Jesus. I know this may offend some readers, but I feel that there are too many people in the world who refuse to admit this as a fact. To see the proof just look at those whose lives were really screwed up until they experienced a spiritual conversion, and look at their lives now — the peace that they have.

Another fairly common reason for a man's alcoholism is his inability to live up to the standards of his parents, usually his father. From what I have seen, this unhappiness is obvious way before the wedding, so there is no reason that wedding should have ever taken place. Ladies, if you are not smart enough to figure out this type of unhappiness is caused by an overbearing parent, then I would say that you deserve what you get.

One serious result of an unhappy life for a man can take the form of spouse and/or child abuse. Even though I still think that the overwhelming majority of abuse situations are caused by control freak behavior, I honestly believe that some, if not a lot of abuse is caused because the man is unhappy with either being married to the woman whom he married, or he is not living his dream. He is just not honest enough to admit that he made a mistake in marriage or his career choice, so he takes it out on the wife and children. Ladies, if you are being abused, whether physically or emotionally, then do a happiness check on your husband.

There may be a number of other reasons for a man to become an alcoholic after the wedding, but I think the overwhelming reasons are stated above. If you are involved in such a situation, you may have just read the cause of the problem, but what about the solution? Honesty is the solution in almost all cases, but unfortunately, quite often that honesty leads to divorce, and many experts do not agree that divorce is a viable solution.

Michele Weiner-Davis, in her book, _Divorce Busting_, appears to be convinced because of her meetings and therapy with troubled couples that divorce is not the answer.

> _"People can and should stay together and work out their differences...Over the past several years I have witnessed the suffering and disillusionment that are the predictable by-products of divorce. I have seen people who have been divorced for five years or longer who have wounds that won't heal. These people failed to anticipate the pain and upheaval divorce leaves in its wake. I have heard countless divorced couples battle tenaciously over the very issues they believed they were leaving behind when they walked out the door...I have heard too many disillusioned individuals express regrets about their belief that their ex-spouse was the problem only to discover similar problems in their second marriages, or, even more surprising, in their new single lives...The habits that spouses developed over the years go with them when they end the marriage. This may partly account for the saddening statistic that 60% of second marriages also end in divorce." —_

Michele Weiner-Davis, *Divorce Busting* (New York: Summit Books, 1992).

However, I am not always an advocate of holding the marriage together; in fact, I am seldom in favor of holding on to a marriage that should never have been in the first place. My position is based on the fact that almost every divorce is caused by marrying the wrong person, or marrying at the wrong time. My position is that if God does not want the two of you together, then you should not be together, and divorce is the answer. It may not be a good answer, but neither is staying in misery and keeping your entire family in misery. If divorce is the answer, then your obligation after that is to make sure your children do not make the same mistake that you did.

I do hope I have shed some light on this subject of addiction, as it can be a tormenter of many marriages. If addiction can be "nipped in the bud" for many of you young people reading this, then I will feel that the effort is worth it. A bonus for me will be if adults who have experienced this type of marriage, but never understood the cause of the problem, get a better understanding of what happened to them.

Chapter Thirty-One

PRIDE GOES BEFORE A FAILED MARRIAGE

DON'T EVER MARRY A PERSON WHO HAS NOT BEEN HUMBLED

If you are looking for some latent trouble, then marry a cocky, conceited spouse. You may not notice problems right away with the courtship or in the early part of the marriage, but sooner or later pride is going to raise its ugly head and create havoc within your marriage.

Men, especially, have trouble in this area — they are often too proud of themselves — and if anyone ever figures out why this phenomenon exists with men, please be so kind as to let me know. I have never been able to figure out what men have that we can be so proud about.

What got me thinking about this issue were the observations I had made while surveying the inmates with whom I was incarcerated. Quite a few of them had experienced marital problems in the past. [For Texans, that's no surprise!] It did not take me long to discover why they could have had marital problems if the other causes of divorce did not fit their situation. It was obvious that humility was not in their realm of knowledge.

It really came to my attention when a 21 year-old African-American drug pusher/college basketball player came into the cell-block. I am really not sure if any of the above descriptions are contributing factors to what I observed about his behavior, but it was definitely his attitude that got my attention and caused me to begin looking back on those I had surveyed. I then realized I had been forgetting a major contributing factor to marital strife, that being pride.

Now, everyone with half a brain knows there is nothing wrong with having pride, or self-esteem, but when the self-esteem is too far off balance on the side of self, then you have marital problems, especially with young people. But I have been given plenty of stories about much older men who were still not humbled. Occasionally I come across a female with this "chip on the shoulder" cocky attitude, but it is rare.

The 21 year-old African-American drug pusher/college basketball player was a classic case of pride. He was telling me his disgusting story which began with him not having a father around as he grew up. He started having sexual intercourse at about age 8, but waited until 15 to father his first of three children, whose mothers he says he supports by dealing drugs. To top that off he planned to soon be married to a 31 year-old who was not one of his children's mothers. Since he had done such a great job as father of his first three children he wanted at least 5 more. [Now, that's really smart!]

If all the above was not arrogant enough, we spoke about drinking a few beers, an activity he thought was okay for himself, but not for his wife. This young man was obviously a prideful control freak, but I think it goes much deeper than that. His statements and actions, in fact his entire attitude toward everyone and everything was condescending. He viewed himself better than all except his mother so far as I could tell. And this guy was getting married? Let's put it this way — he was going to be involved in a wedding.

The man had yet to go through a humbling experience wherein he learned how vulnerable and human he really is. Until he gets to that point he will not treat others as equal, especially females. How can you have a marriage without at least some semblance of equality?

This emphasis on a humbling experience hits very close to home with me, because I had to go through it myself.

While growing up with four older brothers I was told often, because of my cocky attitude, that *"Someday someone is going to knock your block off!"* It was their way of saying that I would some day be humbled. They were right in a sense, as I was humbled, but certainly not by violence. I was humbled by a bunch of bureaucrats. The important thing is that I was humbled. Then I was almost ready for marriage.

I have covered my humbling experience [getting suspended from sports officiating] in another part of this book, so there is no need to cover it again. Now that I look back on that time of my life, I see that before this humbling experience I could have really been a major pain in the butt if I could have found a woman to marry me. I was bad enough after the wedding, which post-dated the humbling experience, so it was a good thing Nancy Lee did not know me well before. Also, just two years after our wedding I was humbled again, which led to my enrollment into Bible College. It also led to me being a better husband. [Just think how good a husband I would be if I keep having these humbling experiences.]

From what I have seen, not all men need to be humbled, and some women need to be humbled. Usually "easy going" men have less need to suffer a humiliating experience, but it probably would not hurt them to suffer a set back or two. Set backs are not always bad, except temporarily they may seem that way.

Young people, when they are searching for a mate, need to take humility, or the lack thereof into their consideration. If you do not, you have a very good probability of marital problems such as a controlling and/or violent spouse. Remember, before you marry, give your intended the humility test and see if he passes. If he doesn't pass, then you'd better! Better pass on this guy, that is.

MAXIMS MAINLY FOR MALES

Chapter Thirty-Two

LIVE YOUR DREAM!!

Ladies, if you want trouble from a husband in about 15 to 20 years, then marry a man who is not living the dream God put into him to achieve. It's at that time that he is going to leave you and the young'uns and find a younger woman. And of course he is going to blame it on you. He is going to do everything he can to make you believe it was your fault that he is not living his dream. I wish I had a dollar for each time I came across this scenario during my survey

What I noticed is that this behavior is common with men who got married very young, but it is not restricted to this group. For some of us men it also happens when we get married later in life. If a man does not attempt to live out his dream before he gets old he is probably going to be miserable before too long.

It happened to me when I was about 39 years old. There I was over half way through my life and I felt that I had not accomplished anything. What it really came down to was the realization that if I died at that moment, my life had made little difference in the entire history of the world. Nancy Lee, of course, took the female approach by pointing out that I had a successful, happy family, and for almost 10 years, a rather successful small business. To her way of thinking, that was enough, but not for me. I needed to do more.

At that time of my life I could have gone the negative route and taken the wrong road at that mid-life challenge, which I'm sure would have broken up our home, devastating Dani Lee. Fortunately, I took the positive road, and decided that I would leave something by which some people would hold me in high esteem. I got busy completing a book I had written a few years earlier. The process took almost a year and I even had to pay for the publishing myself, but it saved my life. The book was titled, *ETERNAL DAMNATION on TRIAL* and almost every copy sits in boxes on my garage floor, but I did not write it to sell at that time. I wrote it to save my life. Guess what? I am still alive, my wife still likes me, and if I ever get into a discussion about what the Bible says about eternal damnation, I can honestly say *"I wrote the book on it."*

From my survey I have had to conclude that females are much less likely to need to live their dreams than are males. For a female, a successful family is quite often enough of a dream to be happy with life. It is not wrong at all for a female to want to live the dream that resonates inside her, she just has to make sure nothing gets in the way of that dream.

It appeared to me that females give up on their dreams sooner than males. From my observation, the female is most likely to lose sight of, or give up on her dream when she falls head-over-heels in love in her late teens or early 20's. There's just something about what love does to a woman at that age — as I have written about earlier. Too many women fall too hard in love too young.

The same type of situation can happen to males, but I have seen that fewer of them completely lose sight of their dreams at such an early age. That usually comes later for a man.

When a man falls too hard in love too young, they call him a love-sick puppy, or some other crude, if not derogatory term. And a man who falls in love and changes his life's perspective, most often begins losing his dream. It usually goes steadily down hill as more and more pressures add up, and before he knows it, he wakes up one day with his dream only a faint memory. Then the "*nutzo*" stage sets in with the self-induced "mid-life crisis" during which time he lets his eyes and other body parts begin to wander to other women.

These life changes are self-induced since too many young people take their eyes off the prize. They get caught up in relationships that God never wanted them to get involved in, and then the goals are allowed to lapse. If God has given you the dream originally, then He can certainly help you make it come true so that you actually live it.

Some dreams that God gives you are long-term — it takes a long time for them to be shaped, and you might have to go through "hell on earth" before they happen. But, if God has given you the dream He'll keep it alive in you. We are able to see this at different times in the Bible. God gave Abraham the vision that he would be the father of many nations. Look how Abraham messed up, but God still made good on the vision. He was a very old man, but God made a covenant with him, the blessing of which was that Abraham's seed would bless all nations. Genesis 12: 1-3.Abram was 75 years old when God spoke this to him and he had to bide his time 25 more years before God made good on the promise. That is a short time by Moses' standard, which we find at Exodus 2:11.

The dream is not necessarily something you will see at night, but is rather more like a vision, or ambition, which you see yourself doing or accomplishing as you are growing up or after you have grown up. Probably the best way to identify this God-given dream is mainly by how long or how frequently it remains on your thoughts. At times it will be on your mind so strong and so often that it will seem that you are consumed with it. These periods should not last long; minutes, maybe hours at a time, but these periods will be more frequent than other ambitions.

The easiest way that you will know whether or not it is from God, is by judging it up against the commandment to serve. Jesus' commandment to serve your neighbor as yourself must be applied to all human situations. It is certainly applied to this quest to perceive the dream that God wants you to pursue. If you pursue this dream, you will in some way be serving others and probably getting paid for it.

You will know that an ambition is not from God if it does not follow this serving principle, or if it goes against other Biblical principles/commands. If your dream is pursuing the path of riches just to be greedy, it does not follow the serving principle. If you are seeking riches in order to help make life easier for others, that dream is consistent with the serving principle.

Or, maybe your dream is similar to the "Brain" on the television cartoon, *"Pinky and the Brain,"* of the 1990's. The "Brain" wanted to take over the world. That dream in and of itself is not totally bad, as long as the goal is to serve and not to rule. But the "Brain's" purpose was to rule, not to serve. There is a big difference.

My opinion, as I've previously stated, is that children must be encouraged, cajoled, or somehow made to set personal, attainable goals. When parents make a special effort to instill in their children a pattern of positive goal setting, they are much more likely to be children worthy of parental pride. That is, of course, if those goals line up with the dream that God puts into each person.

Chapter Thirty-Three

WHO'S IN CHARGE?

GOD PUT THE MAN IN CHARGE, BUT HE AIN'T THE BOSS!

This one will have the feminists calling for my excommunication. Many women do not want to hear it, but within a Godly organization there must always be one person who has to take the final responsibility. In a family setting that means the male, since he is normally the physically stronger one. This does not, as many men have historically been taught, mean that he gets to rule. In fact, as explained earlier, the exact opposite is true. The greatest one has the obligation to do the greater serving. Jesus dealt with this issue so we do not need to go over it again.

Without a doubt, historically, men could never be considered the better of the two. The female has obviously earned that award. Anyone who will argue with that is either dishonest, or historically ignorant.

Women have a much better track record of holding it together than do males. Very seldom will you hear of a woman, other than one who got married too young, just picking up and leaving the family, as if she had no more responsibility. But how many times have you heard of the man just up and deciding that he was leaving the family?

Where do these men get the idea that they can come home, pack up and move out? It often goes something like this: *"I'm out of here, because, wife, I am no longer in love with you. I will try to send you some money occasionally, so that my children won't have to go on welfare. But wife, you will need to go out and get a job because now that I have my own place I won't be able to pay your house payment along with my rent. It does not matter that you have been home raising the children for the past 10-12 years. Jobs are plentiful. There are some minimum wagers for which you should qualify. And probably you can start tomorrow.*

"If you have any trouble you can call your parents. They have helped us for years, so I am confident that they will make sure their grandchildren do not starve. Rest assured, I will take the kids for one weekend every other month, as I really still love them. I want them to realize that they are my pride and joy and it just kills me to do this to them. If I had any other option you know I would take it. I have to do this for me, so that I can find myself, and I am sure it will only be a slight inconvenience for you. I am the one who is the victim here. You all have each other and I am all alone, so this is going to be harder on me than it is you.

"I will be around over the next two months to get all my stuff and I'll let the kids know my phone number and e-mail address as soon as I get it. Oh, by the way. I had to cancel the health insurance policy on the children as a cost-cutting move since we now have two households to support. Sorry about that. I'll be in touch."

What kind of scumbucket are we talking about here?!! Any of you women out there ever heard something like this before? You've heard something worse?

How many times have you heard of a woman doing something like this? The only times of which I have heard, she was wed at a very young age, she grew up in a few years, and decided that she wanted out. But this scenario is fairly rare. I only came across it a few times — in only 5-8% of the divorces at which I looked did the woman want out of the marriage.

Since it is so seldom that women do that type of thing, which one is the better gender? The desertion of family is probably the most obvious situation in which the female gender rises above the average male. The innate ability of the female to be a servant to her family is also amazing to men like me who sit around analyzing people and situations. It can be taught to some males, but it comes naturally to females.

Yes, most of us males need to have the serving mentality taught to us, as it certainly does not come as naturally to men. I know in my life I had a good example in watching my dad. Probably his greatest asset was the fact that he was a real servant to almost everyone. He gave much more than he ever received and you can ask anyone who knew him if you don't believe me. When you learn under someone of his serving quality, you'd have to be pretty stupid to not pick up some of it.

I believe it is because of the innate lack of this quality that a lot of men have not done an adequate job of leading their families by serving. Serving is normally heart driven, and men have not historically been driven by their hearts. They have been head driven, which is one of the main reasons that God put the final responsibility on the male for the leadership of the family. The family will not be lead properly if it is lead by the heart. The heart is the balance for the head.

In situations where the male might be mentally incapacitated it is necessary for the female to take the reins of leadership. Also, if the male is not offering a Godly leadership, where he may be acting like an ungodly heathen, the female needs to be the Godly leader. This is one area where I disagree with some Christian teachers who say that a woman must follow her husband's leadership no matter where he is leading. That's a bunch of hogwash!

Keep in mind that leadership of a Godly organization shall seldom make decisions. Leadership's job is to make sure that the correct decisions are made. It never matters who gets the credit for the correct decision, just as long as it is made.

Chapter Thirty-Four

PARTY BEFORE MARRIAGE

GET THE PARTYING OUT OF YOUR SYSTEM BEFORE MARRIAGE

Are you a party animal at age 20? Join the crowd, and party civilly! Are you a party animal at age 30? If so, I sure hope you are not married, because if you are I doubt if you will be for long. An old party animal is almost always a divorced old party animal.

Contrary to most religions, true Christianity never outlaws partying, it just says to do it civilly. You can only do it civilly by respecting yourself, your family and others while you are partying. And that requires partying sensibly.

There are probably some of you leaders who may be thinking, in your "holier than thou" mentality, that this subject has no business being in a book on marriage, but little do you realize the huge segment of the American population that grows up anticipating the young adult years of having fun, which almost always includes partying. A huge number of women spoke to me about the "ex" who wanted to party too much, instead of being home with the family. By the time he was an "ex" she had figured out that she had married a growing boy instead of a grown man.

From the interviews I conducted, it seems most young people are party animals because of rebellion against authority, rebellion against a situation like divorce of parents, or as a way to get away from the problems of home or school. Also, there are those who seek the party scene because of their desire for acceptance — something they may not get at home — and peer pressure. These last two are obviously because of the lack of a proper home life. I cannot ever remember speaking with anyone who told me that they had a great set of parents and siblings, but also felt the need to seek acceptance through friends. Of course, I never talked to everyone in the world, so my generalization would not fit everyone's situation.

The above responses were just some of the usual answers given to me when I asked young people why they had or did spend time as a party animal. But what is the correlation of partying to marriage? I believe it's obvious and it's simple. If we solve the Marrying Too Young Syndrome, we might also solve the "party animal" problem.

For example, dancing is one of the characteristics with which a lot of people are born. They seem to come out of the womb with a spirit of dance in them. It doesn't go away. It lasts through childhood, on into maturity, and beyond. A similar argument can be made for some people who like to party — they are just born with an urge to get together with others on a regular basis. You cannot get it out of them. But by the time they're 30, they should have learned to keep their desire within limits, giving regard to everyone else first and themselves last. Then partying is not sinful, just costly. I don't want to spend my money that way, but many do.

Chapter Thirty-Five

DON'T BE A FREE-LOADER!

You may not always have to pay your own way, but you must be prepared to do so, and you must insist on it. It is the adult, Godly thing to do. Only ungodly heathens are free-loaders or ungrateful takers of welfare. Followers of the God of the Bible are believers in faith and have no reason to be beggars.

Believers in the teachings of Jesus are forbidden from expecting a hand out. Jesus forbade it when he said that we must love one another. As I said earlier, He actually said to serve one another. How can you serve someone else if you are expecting a handout from them? There is nothing wrong with <u>accepting</u> a gift from someone as you are serving them by allowing them to give.

You have to be able to give and receive with a happy heart, but the problem arises when you <u>expect</u> someone to give to you, or <u>expect</u> that someone owes you a living, as the old saying goes. Sounds pretty simple to me.

One of the most obvious, seemingly minor points of contention which arises in people's lives is the giving of gifts for different personal occasions or holidays. I say that this aspect of our lives is minor, but it is astounding how many conflicts arise because of hurt feelings over the giving or non-giving of gifts to friends and relatives. Have you ever been offended by not receiving a gift from someone to whom you gave a gift? Did you ever not receive a thank you for a gift or gifts given? Can you count that high?

Perhaps this is such a contentious aspect of our lives mainly because too many people <u>expect</u> gifts at certain times in their lives. Where did we get this custom with its greedy inclinations? Why don't people have parties or special occasions and instead of receiving gifts, they give gifts to those attending? Now, that would be different.

I make an issue of this for two reasons. Obviously, it causes many petty contentions between people, but more important, it is an attitude which carries over into general life, where people begin to expect a handout. They think someone owes them something without having done anything.

The one that really gets me though, is how Christianity got sucked into believing in, supporting, and receiving benefits from a socialist government that gives a handout. The only way a government can give handouts is by forcibly taking money from one person and giving it to another, so how can that type of philosophy be Biblical?

There are times in almost all of our lives when we need some financial help. That's the purpose of the Church Body, and if they weren't spending it on buildings and salaries and overhead, then they would have a lot of money to loan to members. But, apparently, many Christians would rather participate in a socialistic government that runs an ungodly welfare state. It would seem to me that they have done this because it is much easier to have the money forcibly taken from them in a withholding tax, rather than give it of their own free will. How is that Biblical?

If you ever find yourself sliding toward being a taker instead of a giver, then you need to get yourself turned around. We don't need to be free-loading on each other.

Chapter Thirty-Six

TREAT YOUR FAMILY WELL

TREAT YOUR FAMILY WELL, THEY MAY COME IN HANDY WHEN YOU'RE OLD!

One very disturbing observation I have made is that a huge number of people grow old with nobody around to assist them when they are unable to care for themselves. This is one of the most important reasons to marry right. If you do it God's way He will line things up so that these dependency situations are much less burdensome.

In early 1998 I spoke with my friend, Rhonda Bode, who works as a social worker in Michigan hospitals. She related how prevalent this sad situation is. People are dying without anyone to assist or love them through this time.

I had related to Rhonda how my mom was being so wonderful with my dad while he was going through a lot of physical problems and hospitalization. Mom was assisting him at all times, always available with a smile on her face. Rhonda then told me that was not what she came across in hospitals on a daily basis. Instead, she saw dying people, mainly men, who had neither spouse nor children to help make it easier. It seemed that few of the men had prepared for their old age.

I am a firm believer that God did not intend for us to be alone when we grow old. It is for this reason that men and women need to cultivate long term relationships with people who will be able to assist them if or when they may become disabled. Disability can come at an early age, so cultivating good relationships needs to begin at an early age. Marrying the one God has for you will certainly help in this effort.

I remember thinking about this a few months before our wedding. I asked myself whether or not I would take care of Nancy Lee for the rest of her life if she were to have some type of disability for which she would need my almost constant attention. I pictured her in a wheel chair with me having to push her around wherever she needed to go. After a time of contemplating this scenario I came to the honest conclusion that I would take care of her, despite the ambitions I had for my future. I honestly decided that my marriage vows to her were more important than my personal ambitions or goals. I really do not think my decision was based on a noble concept or chivalry, but rather it was based on my faith in God's ability to make my dreams come true if that was what I was supposed to be doing.

The most common real life scenario is that a man is much more likely to become disabled and need the assistance of his wife. Historically, men have died sooner than females, so the wife is more likely to be the one assisting. Unless a man wants to end up paying strangers to take care of him if he gets disabled, for which he'd better have a lot of money, he needs to be good to his wife and children so they will not cut out on him when the going gets rough.

A large number of contemporary married couples apparently were not aware of the need to have children available during their older years. They were so busy with each other and their own careers that they decided not to have children. Rhonda has observed the outcome of this scenario all too often in hospitals, where there were no children at all, estranged or otherwise, to assist these elderly people.

One reason so many of today's young marrieds are not having children is pure selfishness. On the other hand, many of them saw how messed up their parent's marriage had been and decided they do not want a piece of that type of action. And I suspect that there is another reason to explain their childlessness — they are planning for their marriages to fail.

Sounds crazy doesn't it? People are planning for their divorce by not having children, so that if and when they divorce, there are no hurt children. With today's divorce rate running rampant, I honestly think there are few modern marriages where the parties do not suspect a future divorce. [A survey asking about pre-marriage contingency plans might be an interesting one, but I just do not have time.]

I truly believe that married couples are almost always making a big mistake when they do not have children, whether naturally or adopted. Of course, having children should not be solely based upon the idea that you will be more likely to have some assistance when you get old, but there is nothing wrong with that being at least part of the reason to have children. As for myself, the thought never entered my mind. I wanted a daughter because I figured it would probably be one of the greatest experiences and relationships I could ever have while here on earth. Dani Lee has made it much better than I had imagined it would be.

Of all the reasons I have seen for couples to not have children, the main one is selfishness. They like to share with each other, but they have problems sharing with outsiders. They are so much into themselves, or wrapped up in themselves that they do not want any inconveniences [children] to cramp their style. My honest opinion is that this is an unfortunate position to maintain and that it seldom is God's plan that a couple remain childless. There is much to learn from your own children and we all know that God is into learning.

As I touched on in another part of this book, let God give you the vision of how many children you should desire. If you allow Him to do that, then I believe you will have all the children you need to take care of you in your old age.

Chapter Thirty-Seven

FATHERS ARE RESPONSIBLE UNTIL A CHILD IS TWENTY

I met a man named Rob who related to me the story about the last time he saw his father. Rob's dysfunctional parents had split up and he was left with his abusive dad for a short time. At age 13 Rob's dad told him that he was going to be taken from their home in West Virginia to live at Grandma's house in Cincinnati because the father just couldn't raise him any longer.

A major problem which Rob did not know at the beginning of the journey was that Grandma did not live anywhere near Cincinnati. After they arrived, Rob's dad pulled the car over to the shoulder of the bypass around that city and told Rob to get out with his suitcase. Despite Rob's questions and protests, his last sight of his father was of the back of his head and the taillights of his automobile. So, here is Rob, a dumbfounded 13 year old sitting on his suitcase alongside a Cincinnati interstate. That is not the ideal way to begin the rest of your life.

What happened to Rob reflects a major cause of problems in this country — fathers have neglected to take charge of their children's upbringing. Rob's situation is just one of thousands I have come across during my survey. Countless numbers of children's lives have been ruined because they never received the proper parenting. In fact, if you want to put a percentage with it, I would say that 95% of the messed up people in this world could have been changed by the parents. The problem is massive, but the solution is rather simple — hold fathers responsible for the children they create.

Our society has historically only paid lip service to this concept of holding the fathers responsible. In fact, we have not even taken the steps to have the names of the fathers registered with the names of the children after the child is born.

According to the Bible, God holds the father of a child responsible for the raising of that child. How a child is as an adult is a direct reflection upon how successful the father was at raising that child. As I said before, I have almost driven my wife and daughter nuts for many years acting like a broken record with putting the blame on the father. Every time we would hear about some child in trouble or causing trouble Dani and I would say something about the father.

> Ephesians 6:4 "And you, fathers, do not provoke your children to wrath, but bring them up in the training and admonition of the Lord."
> *Dake's* - *"1. Provoke not your children to wrath (v. 4). Avoid severity, anger harshness cruelty. Cruel parents generally have bad children, correct, do not punish. Punishment is from a principle of revenge; correction is from a principle of affectionate concern.*
> *2. Bring up a child in the nurture and admonition of the Lord (v. 4 KJV) The mind is to be nourished with wholesome discipline and instruction which will bend them toward God and Christian living."*

The word "nurture"(KJV) in v. 4 comes from the Greek word, *paideia*, which means child training; education; discipline; correction.

The word "admonition" comes from the Greek word, *nouthesia,* which means warning; admonition; reproof.

This teaching is backed up by Colossians 3:21, *"Fathers, do not provoke your children, lest they become discouraged."* The term "be discouraged" probably should have been translated as "have their spirit broken." That's *Dake's* suggested translation.

There are some people such as Rob's dad, who would not

have cared about what the Bible said anyway. As I see it, there are two problems with that type of attitude. Maybe you can perceive others, but let me describe these two.

One of the pet doctrines in America has been that *"This is a Christian nation."* There is almost no evidence to back this up. It is my opinion that I have never heard an intelligent person make that remark and I have heard it stated hundreds of times. [That lets you know what I think of people who espouse such stupidity.]

If this country had ever been built according to Biblical teachings we wouldn't have the problems we have. We would never have so much juvenile delinquency, the huge prison population, spouse abuse, child abuse, teenage pregnancy, lying by public officials, etc., that we have in the year 2000 in this country. Personally, I think it would be a good idea if we just admit that this country is not and never has been a Christian country. Remember, *"By their fruits you shall know them."* What we do see are the fruits of ungodly heathens, not the fruits of Christian principles. The majority religion of the U.S. may have been Christianity, but it certainly has never been the dominant religion.

The second of the problems I mentioned above is embodied in so-called spiritual leaders in the Church Body who themselves were offenders of this principle of *"Fathers don't provoke your children."* Too many of these men had no intention to abide by this principle, yet a bunch of them preached to others that they should abide by it. While growing up I saw a lot of this type of hypocrisy in churches.

If we had our laws structured in such a way as to reflect Christian principles, the ungodly heathen would be no problem because they would be punished for misbehavior in the raising of their children, physical or sexual abuse in particular. But we have never had that in this country, other than times when the common law was practiced. Under that system fathers could be held liable for damage their children did to someone's property. But, from my historical study, until the last generation there seldom was any punishment for a father who abused his children.

The common law requirement that parents must take the responsibility for the actions of their children has basically been set aside by present governments. This is due in large part to the humanistic teaching that everyone is a victim, so nobody has to take responsibility for their actions. The problem with that type of philosophy is that there is no accountability, and unfortunately, the Christian Church has allowed itself to get sucked into it.

The true Christian philosophy is based upon the Hebrew heritage which required a father to raise a child properly. Proverbs 22:6 is the most common verse pointed to by Believers as God's instruction for child rearing. *"Train up a child in the way he should go, and when he is old he will not depart from it."* Unfortunately, at some point the Christian Church's teaching varies a bit from the Hebrew teaching because the Bible is silent, so far as I can see, in its specific teachings on parental responsibility for children.

I truly believe that my teachings follow Biblical principle to the letter due to the fact that the spirit of the child is energized by the male — if you create it, you are responsible for it. That is also the common law principle which has come down for centuries and has been practiced by countless numbers of people. The father takes responsibility for his children until they grow into functioning, responsible, effective adults.

To help keep children disciplined during adolescence, the law should be setup to enhance the requirement that a father is responsible for the actions of his child. It starts, as stated earlier, with making parents register any children they have at the registrar's office. This may sound odd except for the fact that we have witnessed how messed up our times have been; maybe desperate times call for more disciplined measures. If parents, from the first week, are required by our society to show that they were the ones who created the child, then we all know whose the child is, as it is on public record.

By the time a child is 10 years old, society should be holding children at least partially responsible for their actions. That entails jailing juvenile offenders for mischievous offenses for short periods like weekends, vacations, nights, etc.. I have spoken with men in jail about this as a viable deterrent and they agreed that if they had been locked up at a very young age by themselves in a tiny room with nothing to do, they would not have come close to jail as an adult.

If a child commits a major crime then both the child and the father need to be punished with restitution and/or jail time. This is certainly not unreasonable, as we are not the ones who created that undisciplined child. Until the child reaches the mental capacity of age 20, the father is responsible. If the father raises his child properly in the first four years and sticks with that disciplined lifestyle, that child will not depart from it.

While I am on the subject, I am astounded by parents who make excuses for their children going astray, claiming that *"They got in with the wrong crowd."* Why can't these parents just admit that they failed to instruct their children on how to choose friends? This is just parents shirking their duty to influence their child's lifestyle.

How a child functions as an adult should be a direct reflection on the parents. If the child is a successful adult, then a lot of the credit should go to the parents, and if the child turns out to be a blight upon society, a lot of the blame goes to the parents. Is there anything difficult about what I have said here?

MAXIMS FOR AFTER THE WEDDING,

or

HOW TO LIVE HAPPILY EVER AFTER!

Chapter Thirty-Eight

THE MARRIAGE COVENANT

The marriage covenant is a sacred, binding, unbreakable agreement between a man and woman to come together as husband and wife to function as one flesh the way God intended. When you have found the spouse God has chosen for you it is time to start planning the marriage, not the wedding. As you already know, the wedding, or covenant making ceremony is only incidental to the marriage, and it is for that reason that the marriage needs to be planned for. It is your life.

The marriage covenant is for the rest of your natural life, or your spouse's natural life, just as blood covenants have been since Adam & Eve. It is a sacred, unbreakable agreement between a man and a woman, exactly as most all peoples have had for marriages and for brotherhood, the type of agreement that the Native Americans [American Indians] used to do to become blood brothers. These relationships were not made on the spur of the moment, but normally after much consideration. The parties entering these unbreakable relationship bonds knew the seriousness by which their union was viewed by everyone. Covenant breaker— either party which broke this bond— was really held in low esteem.

Remember, Judas? Remember Jesus calling him, "friend?" That term, "friend," was a covenant term. Sometimes it referred to a blood covenant partner, but sometimes it referred to a more limited covenant, such as a salt covenant. In my opinion, that is the covenant to which Jesus was referring. He and Judas had partaken together of the salt at the table, just hours before, bringing them into a covenant which was widely recognized among the middle-east population at that time.

If you ever watch the movie, _Dances With Wolves_, with Kevin Costner again, you will see a form of the blood covenant quite prominent in the movie. I recognized it the first time I saw the movie because I spent several years studying everything I could find on covenants. In the movie, a blood covenant was made when Kevin Costner [Dances With Wolves] shot a buffalo just before the animal ran over a teenage Indian boy. Within seconds an Indian brave ran up to the animal, cut out the heart, took a bite [yes, a chew] out of the organ and passed it to Costner for him to take a bite, in hopes of becoming a blood brother, or "friend" with Costner. Costner hesitated slightly [Yeah, like you wouldn't!] then chomped down on that heart and did swallow after chewing. Not exactly what you and I would be interested in doing, but it is a custom which has been practiced in many societies the world over since the beginning of time.

Let me explain what the thought process was behind the custom, as it will also give you a little more insight into the marriage covenant concept, so please bear with me.

Throughout the history of the world almost all peoples have believed that the life of a person is in the blood, and the taking in of other blood would give the good characteristics of the one shedding the blood to the one taking in the blood. The taking in of this blood could be done several different ways, including also substitutes for blood, such as wine or grape juice. In _Dances With Wolves_ the "taking in" was by the almost still beating heart of that huge, courageous beast, and in this instance the event was two fold. Not only did they take in the good qualities of that great animal but also the two men became blood brothers.

This fact of brotherhood is shown in two different ways later in the movie, which is also relevant to our subject of the marriage covenant. Just after the sharing of the blood by the two men, there was the gift-giving as confirmation of the covenant being made. This is also Biblical as found in Galatians 3:15, _"Brethren, I speak in the manner of men, though it is only a man's covenant, yet if it is confirmed, no one annuls or adds to it."_ The gift giving in the movie confirmed or sealed the blood covenant of these two men. You'll see this pattern in our marriage covenant.

This other part of the movie which had its source in the blood covenant was right at the end when Dances With Wolves and his wife were leaving the tribe. His blood brother went up onto a high place on the opposite side of the steep gully the tribe was in and he made this statement, _"Dances With Wolves is my friend! He has always been my friend!"_ It is similar to what Jesus said to Judas. The great thing about this scene in the movie was how this brave shouted it from the hills that he had kept covenant and he wanted everyone to know it. He had a two-fold reason for making this pronouncement; one was to remind his "friend" that he would always be there if he needed him, and he wanted to announce to the tribe and the world that he was not a covenant breaker. In that type of society you could not get any lower than a covenant breaker.

What you just read is an abbreviated version of the history of blood covenants, so if you want a more expanded explanation you can pick up my book, *ETERNAL DAMNATION ON TRIAL*; or for the "P.H.D. version" get a copy of, *THE BLOOD COVENANT* by H. Clay Trumbull (Impact Books, Kirkwood, Missouri USA)

Now, what does all this have to do with the marriage covenant? I would hope that you can see that by now. The marriage covenant is similar, and a parallel covenant to the blood covenants whereby men would become blood brothers. Both covenants are for life, or actually until death; and each party has a claim upon anything the other has. It's slightly different within a marriage covenant, where all things are owned in common, so that there is no need to ask for or demand something from your spouse, as it is yours already. [Hey, men, don't even think this applies to sex. You're dreaming on that one. I tried it already.]

When you come into a covenant marriage everything you had before now belongs to the spouse and vice versa. If you had a lot of money before, it's now shared with the other. If you were broke or less before marriage, the spouse now takes on that deficit. You take the bitter with the sweet, or with some spouses, to quote my brother , Don, *"You've got to take the bitter with the sour."* Can I get an *"Amen!"* from some of you women out there? Not you, Nancy Lee!

The main change the covenant marriage makes is that the two come together to become one flesh. It's as if the two are functioning as one from then on into the future. No matter what happens to the rest of the people in the world, it's just the two of you functioning as one. See why you have to marry the right one in order to do it God's way?

The Marriage Covenant

An honest person would not enter into a covenant marriage, and not desire the best of everything for the other. A person truly in love will be entering the covenant just as much for what one can give to the other as they can get out of the marriage. If you are convinced this is the one God has chosen for you then that is the attitude with which you will enter this covenant marriage. You know the two of you are going to have a whole lot fewer fusses, fights, and disagreements because God put you together, so as a couple you are balanced as if you were one.

I started this chapter by stating that this covenant cannot be broken; well, the real truth is, the covenant can be broken, but at such a high price that few ever leave such a covenant. But, among primitive peoples, it was considered sacred and it was for life with covenant breakers being treated like a non-person — like he was never known.

This non-person status [*"Depart from me I never knew you."*] stems from one of the main features of the covenant making [wedding] ceremony. A feature which has been lacking from almost all modern day marriages, this is where the blessings and cursings are spoken and agreed upon. The above stipulation for the breaking of the covenant was derived from the curses spoken over the two parties which would come upon either party that broke the covenant.

For the best example of the blessings and curses spoken over a covenant, take a look at Deuteronomy Chapters 27 & 28, or any other chapters which deal with the covenant God made with the Israelites. You can't get a much better example than that.

If you keep the covenant the blessings are yours. If you break the covenant the curses come on you. You have a choice, just as the Israelites did, of keeping the covenant or walking away from it. Obviously, it is certainly best to choose the blessings over the cursings. Look at what God told the

Israelites in Deuteronomy 30:19 & 20,

> "I call heaven and earth as witnesses today against you, that I have set before you life and death, blessing and cursing; therefore choose life, that both you and your descendants may live; that you may love the Lord your God, that you may obey His voice, and that you may cling to Him, for He is your life and the length of your days; and that you may dwell in the land which the Lord swore to your fathers, to Abraham, Isaac, and Jacob, to give them."

I wanted to show you verse 20 as an example of what it is like to live within the covenant. If you can transform the words of this verse into words which will fit living within a marriage covenant, then you may get a little bit better perception of that type of covenant.

The blessings of a covenant are fairly easy to understand. But most people do not understand the curses, mainly because there is no such thing connected with our marriages today [2000]. There is almost no punishment if you break your marriage vow today.

During the wedding ceremony, where the covenant is made, each of the two parties, or a representative, shall speak the blessings for the other party if the other party agrees to this covenant. Then this same party will state the curses which he/she hopes will come on them personally, if they should ever break the covenant. This is where this ceremony separates the men from the boys, and the women from the girls. If this part of the historical ceremony had ever been practiced, we never would have had so many young children getting married.

Here's a good curse that would not have been unusual to hear centuries ago. A man wanting a woman to enter into a marriage covenant might say something to the effect that, *"If I should ever commit adultery, I agree to be neutered."* When these primitives spoke a curse, they were pretty serious. [Can you imagine an American male hoping a curse like that comes on him? I don't think so!]

But, why not? Why should it be so unusual to state such a curse if you should break the covenant? If you are really giving your life to this woman, if she is really the one that God has chosen for you, with whom you intend to spend the rest of your life, then why wouldn't you do it? What should we think of a man who would not take such a vow? Should we have any respect for him? Is he really serious about this covenant union?

Do you think more husbands would only take their pants off at home if they knew that they had agreed to such a contract? Do you think that would be an incentive for at least some men? Sure would work for me!

If any of you think I am overboard on this issue, go spend two years studying the history of blood covenants, or just do as I suggested and read about Moses and the Old Covenant curses. Talk about some nasty stuff! If I had the choice between the curses of Deuteronomy Chapter 28, or the above mentioned one, my choice is the latter. Those Old Covenant curses were extremely nasty!

When you read this section of Deuteronomy you will discover that God is very serious about covenants, especially covenants with Him. It is my opinion that He wants us to be just as serious about our marriages, and why shouldn't we be so? Obviously, His way is the best way to do it, so why don't we?

I think it starts here, and it starts now. The marriages of Believers should begin with the marriage covenant ceremony, with blessings and cursings spoken by each party, then the vows, then the gift giving, then the partying starts. The only addition which I can think of is the possible inclusion of the couple sipping a little wine [or a substitute], as a symbol of the covenant being made. This is certainly not necessary, or even recommended, but neither is it outlawed as it is simply a symbol. The only thing outlawed is the shedding of blood. Jesus did that once for all.

Let's take a quick look at the order of the ceremony and I'll give you my recommendations as to how it should be structured to make it consistent with a covenant marriage. The important and required parts of this entire ceremony are: the two parties, male and female; the witnesses, at least two or three; the blessings spoken by each party that will come upon the other party if they accept the offer of this covenant; next comes the curses spoken by each party which they hope will, or which they will allow to, come upon themselves if they should break this covenant; the spoken vow by each party that they agree with and accept this lifetime covenant. Last of all is the gift giving where each party must give a gift to the other as a pledge of their intent. [The accepting of the gift is the confirmation that the conditions of the covenant are agreed to.] Anything else is peripheral and unnecessary.

Taking into consideration the required aspects of the covenant making ceremony, the parties can agree upon other non-required rituals or traditions that they desire. Nothing else is important in the ceremony. You are on your own.

The way I see it, from my research here are some suggestions for the process. Planning would begin with the choice of a place to hold the ceremony. The site should be a place important to both parties which can add great memories. The witnesses can be few or by television, but it's not a marriage covenant without witnesses. You should have a host or hostess to lead the ceremony. The blessings should be personally written from the heart and spoken by each party. The curses also must come from the heart as they will describe the worst thing each party can think of which would help keep them from walking away from the covenant. The bad thing about the curses is that there has to be a way for them to take effect if the covenant is broken. The vows follow which, again, should be personal from each party, as this is why the witnesses are there. For the rest of the couple's lives these witnesses will be making sure that this couple adheres to their covenant vows. After the vows you are on your own, but I say, "Party down!"

Certainly you are allowed to add nuances that are unique to the couple, but one direction I am convinced needs to be turned away from is the traditional "Christian wedding ceremony," especially the giving away of the bride. There is nothing Biblical about it, so chunk it away so far it will never be found except in history books. If you would do the research, you would find that the whole concept of "giving away" the daughter has to do with the legal concept of females being the chattel property of the man of the house. Can someone out there tell me where God, under the New Covenant, ever wanted females to be owned by males?

Everybody doing the same thing for wedding ceremonies, how boring! Let's get our thinking caps on out there! Come up with some new places, new vows, new costumes, new witness participation, whatever! Just make it different, unique, interesting, and most importantly for everyone concerned, memorable! MAKE IT YOURS!!!

One other tradition which should be discontinued is the wedding gifts being given to the couple. How many hard feelings have been made over wedding gifts? If you follow the earlier teachings of this book you will notice that couples will be marrying later in life and should be established with two households, so what could you get them that they don't already have, or have the ability to purchase on their own?

Must I discuss who should pay for the wedding? Are the two getting married adults? Then, duh!

Do you have to get a marriage license? Absolutely not! You wouldn't have asked that question if you had done a little research into government control. Any government that would say you need to have its permission to do what God already said you could do, and wants you to do, is a government which needs to be removed by a peaceful revolution. Any government that gets in God's way *must be overthrown!*

I have heard it for years, that you have to obey the laws of the land, so that when you want to get married you have to go get a marriage license. Nothing could be further from the truth, which certainly doesn't surprise me when it comes to Christian preachers.

The Texas statute on the common law is stated in the following way <u>Texas Family Code Section</u> 1.91(a)(2), and it is in this way only that it was necessary to be considered married in the past. *"...they agreed to be married, and after their agreement they lived together in this state as husband and wife and there represented to others that they were married."* Just that simple. All that is needed is for a man and woman to hold themselves out to the public as husband and wife.

The marriage covenant is more like a common law marriage except for the fact that common law marriages are secret agreements. The major problem with this is that God doesn't like secrets, and especially in covenant marriages He wants everyone to hear it, the vows that is. That way there are more eyes and ears out there watching over the adherence to the covenant by each party.

Witnesses have a responsibility in this thing also, so if you don't want that responsibility, then don't be a witness. A witness's responsibility is to help keep this couple together. If you are at the ceremony, then you agree with the couple. If you don't agree with the couple, then you should have made some effort before the day of the ceremony to attempt to get your point across to the couple. But, if you were unable to convince the parties, and you still disagree with the proceeding, then by all means, do not be a witness. Show the world you have some principles.

Let me touch on some of the possible blessings which could be spoken by either or both parties. At least some of them should be unique to each person, with the objective being to entice that other party to enter into this covenant union with you. You'd better have some reasons why that person should enter a covenant marriage union with you rather than someone else. Admittedly, the other party knows them already, or would not be so close to marrying you, but they need to be spoken publicly in front of witnesses. [Again, that witness thing.]

I know for a fact that a lot of men will say almost anything when a woman has him in a certain position, if you know what I mean, but, they seem to forget what they said after that moment. [I wonder why that is?] But if all parties have to say those things publicly, they are more apt to abide by what they said in front of witnesses. These blessings can be spoken by a representative but only if the party cannot talk. If parties will not say publicly what they feel about each other, then how will they act publicly toward each other? Words are easier to say than actions to be done. If you can't say it, then what makes you think you will do it?

The form of stating the blessings does not really matter. You can begin with something such as this,

"Nancy Lee Dimeis, I have invited you here today because I desire to enter into a marriage covenant with you this day. If you should accept this offer today I want to tell you the blessings which will be yours because of this union.

"You will have a husband who has a great work ethic. When it's time to work, you'll find me at work doing my best to provide a good living for the family. But, I will not be content to just work for someone else, and I want you to know that I have an entrepreneurial spirit where I plan to support us with my own business, which will also give us opportunity to travel. I will do everything I can to see that you, and any children that we may have, will never lack for any necessities

of life. You and the family will be the most important part of my life. I may have other interests or hobbies, but never will they be put before the family.

"I truly believe that I am the best man in the world who can balance out your life. In those few areas where you show a little weakness that's where I am strong. In those areas you can lean on me as your support and I am positive you can never find another man as good in those areas as myself. And those areas of your life where you excel, then I will give you the opportunity to use those skills which, with some other man, may go wasted.

"As I am not a control freak, you will be involved in all important decisions affecting the family, and any of your personal decisions that affect just you will be none of my business, unless you ask my opinion. You are your own person to live your life as you please, and you will be encouraged to remain that within the confines of the family. I will not run your life, as my attitude is whatever is best for the family, that is what we need to do.

"I will be an asset to you in your spiritual relationship with Jesus, as we have both been raised the same and adhere to the same basic beliefs. I am going to stick with you for the rest of my life and I will take care of you if you are under attack by sickness or ill-health, and also, during financial challenges I am not going to cut and run. I will be there for you.

"One of the blessings is that I have a track record of being very healthy; seldom sick or injured and I see no reason for that condition to not continue.

"My education requirements are probably completed so that it is a low probability that you would need to support me while I attend college. But, I am ready and willing to continue my education if we together find that we would be better off financially if I should do so. That's a decision we shall make together.

"Another blessing I believe I can provide for you is good breeding stock for your children, and the number of children is up for discussion. Personally, I would like to have a daughter because I'm sure she would grow up to be as pretty and loveable as you. There is no doubt in my mind that you can produce great children as you have already shown signs of being great with children. I want to have as many children as God has given you a vision to have.

"One of the main blessings of this covenant is that I am crazy about you. You would have to search a long way to find a man with my qualities who holds you in such high esteem. No man could hold you in higher regard than I and no man will desire to please you more sexually than I. You will never have to look any other place for good sex, because I am determined to do whatever it takes for you to be satisfied with the sexual aspect of your life.

"Nancy Lee Dimeis, these and other blessings will be yours if you decide to come into a covenant marriage relationship with me today.

[Now for the cursings.] *"And, Nancy Lee, now that I have told you what blessings will be yours if you enter this covenant, I want to let you know what curses I hope will come on me if I should ever walk away from this covenant marriage. If you should agree to form this covenant today with me, I want to announce to you before God and these witnesses that if I should ever walk away from this covenant I will walk away with nothing but the bills which you and the family need to maintain your lifestyle.*

"If I should ever have sex with another while we are married I agree to be neutered, as I would rather be made to look like a female than to break my sexual commitment to you if you accept this covenant proposal."

Each party can go on like that, or less, but there <u>must</u> be curses spoken over the breaker of the marriage covenant.

The Marriage Covenant

When temptations arise a reminder is made of the curse, which is a strong deterrent to straying body parts.

The vow is the next aspect of the ceremony we need to discuss. The vow is the *"I do"* or *"I will"* of our present day ungodly wedding ceremony. It can be as short as *"I do,"* but it should be a bit longer and spoken loud enough for all the witnesses to hear if possible.

The words could be something along this line, *"I, Daniel Lee, Schinzing, do accept your offer to enter into this covenant and I pledge that the aforementioned blessings of this covenant marriage are yours if you do accept this offer. I shall allow the aforementioned curses to come upon me if I should ever break my covenant with you. And in front of all of these witnesses I today give you my life. I'll be with you until the end."*

Even up until this time the female has the opportunity to back out of the offer as she has not made her vow before the witnesses. Until she accepts, there is no deal. It does not matter that she made an offer, or that the male has accepted her offer. Until she actually says the words of acceptance and the gifts are given, you don't have a deal. The same is true for the male. Once each party has spoken the words of acceptance, the contract is signed. Then the gift giving is what seals or confirms the contract. The delivery is when the covenant is registered at the recorder's office in the county in which the vows were made. A copy of the recording should be filed in each recorder's office of each county in which the couple is domiciled. At that time the contract, or covenant is signed, sealed, and delivered.

And they live happily ever after.

Chapter Thirty-Nine

NEVER USURP AUTHORITY WITHIN THE FAMILY

God has delineated certain boundaries of authority within the family structure by way of Bible teaching, but more overriding than that are the basic human characteristics with which males and females are born. When these guidelines are followed, you have peace and happiness within the family unit.

I know these are statements that will bring down wrath upon me from "Christian" fundamentalists, but how smart is that group of people? No! Don't answer that, as this is a family oriented book. My goodness, those people couldn't think their way out of a wet paper bag if you started the hole for them.

God put certain characteristics in the average male and different characteristics in the average female. That was done a long, long time before a book called THE HOLY BIBLE, or even the Pentateuch was written. So, are we going to believe the characteristics God instilled in humans beginning at creation, or are we going to believe our interpretation of what Paul said to different groups of people about what he observed almost 1950 years ago? Don't you really think that a lot of what Paul said should be kept within its time period? To take his observations out of that period and say that they apply 1900 years later is extremely presumptuous, wouldn't you say?

And this is beside the fact that some of our interpretations of Paul's writings about relationships totally contradict the more important teachings of Jesus. Whoa! There is another one that is going to get me in trouble with a bunch of the theologically disabled. [I would have called them theological dipsticks, but my niece Shannon would not like that.]. But, there are certain Biblical principles which override almost all other Biblical principles or Bible verses. I know this is heretical in most Christian churches, solely because of the false infallibility teaching that came into true Christianity from Catholicism. I am talking about a principle that Jesus taught — how the greatest one in the kingdom of God is the one who is the servant of all. Now, you tell me this principle does not override and take precedence over almost all other Bible verses.

Let me start from the beginning of this subject in one short paragraph. Jesus gave us two commandments under the New Covenant, even though He spoke them under the Abrahamic Covenant. Those commandments you have heard all your life and even several times in this and my other books. *"Love [serve] God and Love [serve] your neighbor."* As I have said before, if this instruction had been translated correctly — using the word "serve" instead of "love" — my statement above would not create confusion. If we accept what Jesus said — *"serve God and serve your neighbor"* — as the number one overriding principle, then our interpretation of all other verses must fall in line with this principle.

The next overriding principle is the other one where Jesus says *"The greater one must* [always] *serve the lesser one."* All of Paul's teachings must be consistent with these two principles. Or, let's put it this way, our interpretation of what Paul wrote must line up with these two principles. Therefore, anything Paul wrote about how "wives submit" must be interpreted consistently with our principles.

And our principles forbid the teachings that the wife must always submit to the husband. The real truth is that sometimes the wife submits to the husband and sometimes the husband submits to the wife. Only control freaks want submission going one way all the time, and usually that is in the direction of the husband.

If you demand submission one way then what you are saying is that you are not very bright. [Whoa! Another inflammatory statement by the writer!] It's true! Follow the logic. Why would you marry someone whom you couldn't trust to run part of your life?

As stated earlier, I married with balance in mind. I needed a wife who was detail oriented, who would take care of our home, our daughter, and other details that I was good at screwing up. Nancy Lee has been very good at that so I do not question her often about those things. I might state my opinion, or more accurately, my view of the issue, and normally she will make the decision. Now, that is not to say that I do not disagree at times with her decision, but that still does not say that if I had made the decision that it would have been any better.

Have you seen yet what I am talking about when I say do not usurp authority within the family? I have no business interfering with decisions my wife makes which are within her realm of comparative expertise, just as she does not with me. Each partner has a <u>definite</u> responsibility to question the more major decisions, but the minor decisions should be made without question.

A couple of major decisions that males and females make together would be in choosing a home and an automobile for her. Since most women do not tend to know much about autos, when she finds the one that's comfortable and in the right color, then the husband usually needs to have the mechanical condition checked out for reliability. Choosing a house should go much the same way. Since the female normally spends more time in the house, she should be mostly responsible for choosing the one that is most comfortable for the family.

It amazes me how many husbands and wives do not stay within their areas of expertise within the family. But, probably the most common offenders of this absolute, other than control freaks, are teenagers. Yes. You read that right, and a large percentage of you parents are familiar with this situation. What it really comes down to when teens rebel, in a large percentage of cases, is they're attempting to usurp authority.

Certainly a large percentage of teenage rebellion is caused by unreasonable parents, but even in many of these cases the child has the responsibility to not rebel because God has given parents the authority over the child until age 20. At that time children should be prepared to take authority over their own lives, unless they are still living with the parents. If this latter situation is the case, then they still do not have total sovereign authority, as it is someone else's roof above their heads. This is similar to when I go visit my mother. I'm an adult, but it is her roof. It's a pretty simple rule — If it's your roof, it's your rules.

Teenagers need to understand this principle when they are very young. They need to know that by age 20 they will be expected to be ready to take control of their lives. If from the time they are young they have this goal, and it is stressed by the parents as being their time, then children will be less rebellious. If all they see is being controlled by parents with no relief in sight, rebellion is just a byproduct.

It is extremely important that children understand that their parents have their best interests in mind when they make decisions. And parents need to be on the cutting edge of offering the child more freedom and responsibility as the child grows older and shows signs of being ready for the changes.

An open mind on the part of the parent is a necessity. Control freaks need not apply, as you are not qualified! In fact the best thing you control freaks can do is just go get yourself sterilized, so you won't ever torture any children with your evil ways! Or, you could change your evil ways. When it comes to raising children you have to look out for their interests, not yours. Don't like it? Then fuss at God, not me! He made parents and children and the principle that says the greater one serves the lesser one.

One other area I want to touch on is the idea of little children running the house. Usually this happens when a child has been spoiled, which as you know is an absolute no-no. Even a young child needs to understand who is in charge in the house so that they grow up respecting authority.

Another important issue in our society is grown children dealing with elderly parents. As people grow old, there comes a time when children begin making decisions for their parents. It is just one of the facts of life. If you live to a ripe old age, there is a high probability that you will need to have someone other than a spouse to help you make, or to make without your approval, decisions that significantly affect your life.

At that time you will find out how well you did as a parent, when you surrender much of your authority to your children. It can be a fine line between a parent surrendering, and a child usurping authority. Then, as the age of a parent increases and the mental faculties diminish, it becomes more important that the parent not usurp the authority that the child has now gained over the parent. It will be a smooth transition if you have properly trained your children.

Follow the principles of serving as God laid down, with *the greater one serving the lesser one*, and fewer problems will arise.

Chapter Forty

PLAN YOUR FAMILY

SAFE AND EFFECTIVE BIRTH CONTROL METHODS SHOULD BE USED TO PLAN CHILDREN,
or
WIVES, WHEN HE HITS THE BIG 4 ZERO, IT'S PAST TIME FOR THE "BIG V"!

This has been one subject which the Church of Believers has failed to address adequately. A lot of the Church's teaching on this subject has come from the Roman Catholic Church. When you look at the historical Catholic teaching on birth control you will find that it consisted of the "rhythm method." This basic concept is that you work your sex life around the female's ovulation and menstruation period, but you could not use any non-natural methods such as prophylactics or birth control pills. This method of course caused a lot of unwanted pregnancies which surprised no one.

Even that method I would consider to be better than the one under which I was raised, which consisted of "the Will of God." It came down to this: *"Whatever happens is God's will."* If you had the choice of the two above methods, which would you choose? At least the first one took a reasonable amount of intelligence to pull it off successfully, but the latter one takes no amount of intelligence whatsoever.

It is my conclusion that the latter method takes no thought process at all. How can I conclude that, you ask? I lived with it. That is the method my parents used and they succeeded at having seven children, but they were unsuccessful at giving the children a really happy home life. They argued a lot and that is an understatement. It affected at least one of my brothers a great deal, as he was quite sensitive, whereas it only affected me to the point that I determined I would never live that way when I got married.

The reason my parents argued so much was because my dad wasn't getting enough sex. Simple as that. One of my brothers figured it out years ago and when he informed me about it, I saw it was clearly the truth.

Now, I don't want you to think I am writing this to run my dad down, as that is not the case. He was one of the most righteous men I have ever known. What I want to do is give you an example of the problems that arise when you use the "Will of God" method of birth control. You see, when my mom had their last child, my dad was 36; she told him that his bed was over there and her bed was this one here. In other words, she cut him off. To my knowledge he never had sex again, and that is what caused the strife between the two of them, which carried over to the rest of the family.

I hope that somebody out there has figured out which one was at fault in the dispute between my parents. My dad wanted sex and my mom didn't want pregnancy, and after seven I certainly can sympathize. How about you? The major cause of this problem was that my dad was raised Catholic, meaning that birth control was out of the question, and because of that, so was sex. So he had to go without for the rest of his life because he refused to look into birth control methods. Not only did he fail to use any method of birth control, but he also never attempted to make sure his wife enjoyed the act also. If he had taken the time to learn what he could do to make sure she enjoyed it, they would not have had such a strained relationship and their children would have had a less stressful childhood.

It would have been a bad enough situation to cut a man off like that, but when it affects the entire family, it becomes a more serious problem. It was a problem my dad brought upon himself because of his own stubbornness, and I wanted to relate this story as an example for others to see, hopefully how not to do it. In my case, when I had sex for the first time, I wanted to do most everything I needed to do, to do it again about as often as I could. To do that I knew I had to make sure my wife had a desire for it also. A woman who has had one orgasm is going to want to have another, so men, give and you shall receive.

It has yet to be pointed out to me the two places in the Bible where it shows that God is against birth control. The problem as I see it is that many segments of religion have consistently, up until a few years ago, taught that sex was something evil and was only for procreation. I believe that this teaching is the exact opposite of what God wants us to teach. I have seen marriages in which there was little sex engaged in, and I have seen, and experienced might I add, marriage in which a lot of sex was engaged in, and it is obvious which one is happiest.

The methods used for birth control can be varied, but they must be safe and effective. When the birth control pill came onto the market, a huge percentage of men loved it, but that was certainly not a cure-all. In fact, it caused problems for some women, proving it not to be a very "safe" way of birth control for some. I wonder how many men are going to enjoy a male birth control pill and its side effects? Then we will see their consistency in their views on birth control.

For some reason, men just do not seem to have a sense of humor about the method called abstinence, which was advocated by so many religions throughout history for their religious leaders and some adherents. That type of teaching is non-Biblical. [I would have called it stupid, but I'm sure my niece Shannon would not have appreciated it.] The only abstinence the Apostle Paul suggested was for a period of time, for fasting and praying, but, then after that time the husband and wife are to come together again for sex. Any suggestion by Paul to remain single was because of the persecution crises to which the Christians were subject at that time. No other abstinence is recommended for adults.

I truly believe that most marriages need good sex and romance to help keep them vibrant and alive, where each one desires the other. The sex drive is there just as is hunger and thirst, and the need for shelter, and that drive should not be allowed to get out of control by abstinence for too long a period. The mind begins to wander, and sometimes that leads to hands and feet beginning to wander. Frequent sex with a spouse is a good cure for this.

I do not see why anything short of abortion should not be used to prevent pregnancy [abortion being defined as any internal removal of tissue past 10 days after having engaged in sexual intercourse]. Prior to that time there is no evidence that pregnancy has occurred. No evidence = no penalty. However, it is important to prevent pregnancy before it could possibly occur, and that means abstinence, withdrawal before ejaculation, [messy, but works] mutual masturbation, condoms, vasectomy, etc. for the man. The woman is under no obligation to use unnatural ways to prevent pregnancy. It's not her job. But she should be involved with the prevention if she wants less upheaval in her life.

It is sexual immorality to not use safe, effective birth control methods until it is time for you to become a parent. When the time is right, then have the number of children God has given you the vision to have. Once you have had that number of children, then it is time for a more permanent form of birth control. Before you have more than 4-5 children you need to check out the medical evidence. According to the Medical Tribune News Service/The New York Times Syndicate, C.1997, becoming *"pregnant six or more times"* can lead to a higher probability of stroke.

If that wasn't enough, the same study also found that *"women with multiple pregnancies were more likely to have diabetes, a history of heart disease and less formal education...* " Can you tell me again the names of those religions that have considered it saintly to have a huge number of children? Was one of them in Utah and another somewhere around Rome?

Regarding permanent birth control, at this time from my understanding, the three choices are a vasectomy for the male, a hysterectomy for the female, or just "having her tubes tied." Of these three it appears to me that the vasectomy for the man is a much cheaper and usually a safer operation. It is for that reason that almost every man who plans to possibly have sex over age 39, is sinning if he has not had a vasectomy. A man who refuses to have a vasectomy is either a weenie, or full of pride. Remember, refusing to do it and unable to do it are two different concepts, but few men should have an excuse. [One of my buddies had the "Big V" in the morning and played a softball game that night. Now, that's a real man!]

Some of us had a vasectomy by the time we were 35; in fact, some of us have had two, so there! If I can do two, you should be able to do one. Children should not be mistakes, they should be planned. Planning is not being controlling, it is being smart. Practice it! Remember, if you are married, when it comes to sex, *"Do it long and do it often."* Just be smart about it — you control the hormones, and don't let the hormones control you.

Chapter Forty-One

RAISE YOUR OWN CHILDREN

Before you have children you need to understand that God is holding you responsible for the raising of your children. Do not depend on parents, friends, grandparents, daycare, or government. You need to thoroughly think it out before you create a child, not so much because of the way it affects you, but rather the way it could affect the child's life.

There are too many children and young adults who have no concern for the child they may be creating. Do you remember that 1960's song, *"LOVE CHILD"*? It spoke of this same issue, stating that a *"love child, (is) different from the rest..."*. If you are in a situation where you risk the possibility of creating a "love child," you need to listen to this song for several weeks to let the words get into your mind so that you may think more about this child and less about your hormones.

There is an amazing phenomenon going on in America today with grandparents raising their grandchildren, or at least taking a huge percentage of the responsibility for taking care of them. That would not be a big deal if the grandchild's parents had died or were disabled in some way where they were unable to care for their own children. But the most common situation today is one in which the children are divorced and/or both are working to support their lifestyle, so the parents of these children are expected to assist in caring for the grandchildren like a day care service. Who raised these children to expect their parents to act as a day care center for grandchildren? Sounds as if the grandparents screwed up!

Children have to be instructed, mainly by example and from a young age, that they will grow up to have children and that they will have to take care of them on their own. If parents are not teaching their children this principle, then who is going to teach this principle of responsibility to their children? I certainly hope you are not going to depend on a humanistic, socialistic, government dominated, school system to teach them, because what you will get is what we have in this country right now in 2000, and that is a mess.

Children, when raised properly, are wonderful. When they are not raised properly, they have a negative impact on everyone around them, and that is a direct reflection upon the parents, that they do not care enough about the child to discipline and teach them properly. Parents should not expect someone else, like grandparents or schools, to raise and discipline their children for them.

When I talk about raising your own children, that does not include placing them in day care five days a week. That means the mother or father, preferably the mother, needs to stay with the children at home at least until they go to school, unless you home school. The first four years of a child's life are the most important, and that is not the time to send that child off to day care while you go make money. If at least one of the parents cannot take a sabbatical for 4-5 years away from a full-time job then it sounds to me as if you failed to plan for the child. There are numerous ways to make money at home part-time so there are few excuses.

As I am writing this, Dani Lee is 13 years old and already I am thinking about the fact that she is only going to be with me about 6-7 more years on a constant basis. I really like having her around as she is funny, smarter than me, pretty, goofy, a lot of help, and makes life much more interesting than if she were not around.

Back to the subject of working at home, one story I heard was about a woman dentist who had a chair in her home and worked one day a week. The patients brought their children while the dentist worked at home with her children. The exception to this may be if there is a sudden injury or death, political arrest, etc., which may force both parents or the other parent to leave the house for work.

If both parents are working and they have not experienced one of the above, then probably they are attempting to maintain too high a lifestyle, and are putting their lifestyle above their children. There are only a few greater sins than this one, so don't do it. Lower your lifestyle to save your children. If you gain the whole world and lose your own children, then you are not a success. If you can't serve your own household, then how can you serve the household of God?

If couples are marrying correctly, they have usually been developing their careers since their early 20's. Then when children come along when they are in their 30's, they should be financially secure enough to meet the challenge of a child or children. Too many young people do not make financial plans for the future when children come along, but by moving that time period back to the 30's a lot of that problem will be alleviated for many couples. A major cause of these problems in the past has been the Married Too Young Syndrome, but now that we have exposed that malady as the evil it is, we should have fewer of these problems.

FATHERHOOD - Men, you cannot mail it in!

Career requirements can be extremely divisive in a home. If one of the parents has to be away for extended periods, this can be a major strain, especially regarding the responsibility for raising of the children. Hopefully, by allowing God the opportunity to chose whom we marry, we will, in the future, have less problem with working for extended periods away from the family. When God does the choosing He knows there are situations which will arise in the future that could challenge a normal marriage. He can put the right man and woman together who will be able to overcome those challenges.

When one parent is away for extended periods the children have to be trained to accept the extended absence, or the parent has to change careers. The latter option is not what a lot of men like to hear, but that is too bad. When you father, or give birth to children, they are your top priority and their well-being, most of the time, is dependent upon the family staying close. So, a career change should not be out of the question. Or, at least line your career up so that you also are at home for extended periods to devote long periods to family activities. Your main responsibility is to your family, not to money.

Then there are *"workaholics."* Yes, you know who you are. If someone has called you one, or someone has suggested you be home more often, or not work so much, then more than likely you are one. We men seem to have something inside us that tells us we need to be working when the sun is shining. It is a fine line we have to walk between advancing our career/business and spending time with the family. It is amazing how many of the adults I surveyed complained about dad working too many hours, and many of those said they were adversely affected by the dad's neglect of the family.

Don't raise your own babysitters.

There are a large number of parents who have several children and for some reason get this crazy notion that the older children must be responsible for the younger children. Will someone please show me where that one is written, as I seem to have missed it.

The bottom line is that you are responsible for the raising of your children — your children are not responsible for the raising of your children. The oldest child seems to get the brunt of the sibling babysitting duty and I have seen plenty of them become bitter because that duty was thrust upon them.

Often this occurs when the parents have a wide gap between the last child and a late in life baby. It seems that the parents have raised theirs, and this last child is left in large part for the other children to raise. Parents should raise their own "late in life baby!"

The object of the parent is to serve the child, not the child to serve the parent. How are you serving the child by provoking them to bitterness? Yes, you are serving children when they help out with their siblings, because they are learning about child raising, but for them to have to miss out on childhood events because of having to babysit your other children will probably be a detriment to their well-being.

Since parenthood is such an extremely important calling and responsibility, each prospective parent, before having children, should be reading books on child rearing from many different sources. Dr. James Dobson out of Colorado Springs, Colorado USA is probably the best child rearing authority I know of. I truly believe that the general principles about children which I have given in this book, gathered from experience and surveying, will go a long way in getting you going in the right direction. It would be a good idea for you to add to these general principles through your own research and study.

One other general principle I want to touch on pertains to grandparents. I know that one of the most difficult things for grandparents is to watch their children, or more especially their grandchildren, go without something. But, challenges usually make them tougher, more knowledgeable and better people. Maybe grandparents need to realize their place in life is not to solve all their children's problems, but to help their children solve their own problems. And do not attempt to make up for the mistakes you made with your child by overcompensating with grandchildren. Grandparents need to back off and let their children raise their own children.

Chapter Forty-Two

DON'T SPOIL A CHILD

DON'T EVER CREATE A MOMMA'S BOY
or a DADDY'S GIRL!

I sure wish I could find an exception for this one. But I just can't do that after seeing thousands of lives ruined because a child was spoiled by parents or grandparents. Spoiling a child is a disservice to the child and to society at large; the usual result is that the child ends up hating those who did the spoiling. Ask any parent who made that mistake and see what their advice is. That is, if they have figured out why their child went astray.

I heard a classic example of this on Rush Limbaugh's radio show in the summer of 1997. A man called to tell Rush about his family problems with a teenage daughter who was causing chaos in the house. I thought the call was rather strange because Rush does not deal with personal problems of people, except maybe evil politicians. The caller went on for about a minute and a half about how chaotic the house was because of the daughter. Then he got to the root cause of the problem when he admitted that the daughter had been spoiled as a little girl. As soon as he said that I knew who was at fault. The girl was just doing what she had been trained to do, her own thing. She was not ultimately at fault, her father was at fault.

The father is at fault, basically because God made males to think with their heads instead of their hearts as females are prone to do. The father has been designated as the disciplinarian of the family. The mother was not, I repeat, was not designated by God as the disciplinarian!

Don't Spoil a Child

While males are normally the control freaks, it is often more likely that females will be spoiled. Of course, this does not always hold true, so a spoiled child could take the shape of a male. Either way, male or female, it is totally wrong, as you are not preparing that child for the rest of life. The Bible teaches parents to *"train up a child in the way they should go."* Spoiling a child is the exact opposite of that.

In June of 1999 I found the following letter to *Dear Abby*. I think it lines up with what I am saying about Momma's boys.

*"**Dear Abby:** The verse you printed honoring mothers-in-law on Mother's Day was bound to touch the hearts of many. I have a suspicion, however, that more than a few women felt the sentiments did not speak for them. In honor of these women, I'd like to provide you with a bit of doggerel I composed in response. Perhaps you'll want to share it with your readers. — Maxine Derringer, Las Vegas, Nevada.*

***Dear Maxine:** Your poem is an absolute hoot! I'm sure it will raise more than a few eyebrows. Read on:*

TO HIS MOTHER

"Mother-in-law," they say, and yet
Somehow I simply can't forget
'Twas you who followed him around
To grab whatever hit the ground.
And in your hand, to make it super,
A real gold-plated pooper scooper!

'Twas you who gave him his way when you
Let him demand a separate menu.
Perhaps if he had been a daughter,
You might have taught him to boil water.
His little socks and underwear
You let him throw just anywhere.

'Twas you who taught him how to say,
"What can the world do for me today?"
And so, today, beside me stands
The man that I took off your hands.
You raised him with such cunning knack,
I think I'll let you have him back."

YOU GO, MAXINE!!

Did Maxine hit it on the head or what, talking about a momma's boy. That's one of the results of spoiling a child — someone else is probably going to suffer right along with the parents. And the someone may be, and usually is, several people. A spoiled child is much more likely to be married several times, and each one of those times whole families are affected. If spoiled children don't get their way, they are usually going to take their ball or dolls and go home. That same attitude carries over into adulthood. If they don't get their way in the marriage, they'll take their toys and go to someone else's house — a new marriage — and the cycle starts all over again. All because of parents creating a momma's boy or a daddy's girl.

Why There Is A Mafia?

To get more specific, one group who consistently spoil their first born sons are those of the Italian persuasion. I know this in large part because I sleep with one Italian on a regular basis and have another Italian as my favorite mother-in-law. I had suspected this pattern for years, but never concluded it to be valid until I picked up on it a while back when I was reading the book, _Touch Me, If You Dare_, written by an Italian preacher, Patrick Donadio [Thomas Nelson Publishers, Nashville]. As a child, he had really been a "hell-raiser" and a large part of his book was dedicated to his ill-spent youth as a thug. While I was reading his book I knew this rebellious youth fit the spoiled child syndrome: a child who is spoiled is probably going to rebel as a teenager. So, I got to asking several people some more questions and each of them admitted that the tendency in Italian homes is to spoil the first son.

I have also observed this pattern in Hispanic, Indian, and Jewish families, and am sure there are other ethnic groups who probably have the same tendencies to spoil a specific child in the family. As I only sleep with an Italian, and don't hang around too many people of other specific ethnic persuasions, I could certainly not claim expertise with these other ethnic groups. It would be interesting to see some studies, if anyone has ever done such a thing, but then again, there's probably nobody else in the world who cares about this subject anyway, huh? [I borrowed that last line from the wife. She uses it often, okay, daily, when I get interested in some obscure subject that a normal person would never care about.]

I do not really mean to pick on Italians, but I know a little bit more about them. I have a theory that you have the mafia because of this child-spoiling practice. And look how screwy the Hispanic countries of the world have been historically. Rebellion sets in at a young age and that leads to petty crime, which leads to more serious criminal activity. This then leads to a society that is never based on laws and trust, but on lies and law breaking.

If those involved in the mafia — if there is such a thing — had not been spoiled children, then maybe there would never have been a suggestion of an Italian mafia. But even if my theory is correct, that wouldn't necessarily explain the "Southern Mafia" which has been described as making the Italian mafia look like fine upstanding citizens. Since I do not know enough about either group it will have to remain a theory for now.

Now, back to the subject at hand. I have seen children raised correctly and children raised incorrectly. Wrong leads to problems for both the child [even into adulthood], and for the parent [even after that child leaves the home]. The pattern seems to be that a spoiled child never seems to leave. They and their problems seem to keep appearing at the door. Most parents enjoy having their grown children over to visit, and if you are Italian like my mother-in-law, you want them to live downstairs or down the street, but you certainly should not want them to bring over their problems.

If the spoiled child never seems to want to leave, the other most common pattern I have observed is that the child will grow up hating the parents and probably have nothing to do with them. As for me, I did not want my child to be around for only a few years. I want to see her grow up and her kids to grow up, so I better do it right.

Ladies, one of the worst potential fathers you could ever marry, is a man who is too easy-going, as this type of man may not be a good disciplinarian for your children. You may love him as a nice, gentle, caring, sensitive man, but be careful as to how this will translate into his being the disciplinarian.

Let me give an example of the chain-reaction of misery which lack of being discriminating with marriage can cause. I know of one family where the spoiling of a child affected four generations. The father did not believe in spanking because he was never spanked. He had been easy going, so he seldom needed it. In the 1950's he attempted to raise a very active child without spanking. That proved to be a major mistake. During the 1960's this boy was a teenager and he did the opposite of what the parents' religious teachings instructed.

This rebellious son got married young, had at least one "unspanked at a young age" child, along with two somewhat well behaved sons. An obvious result of the original "non-spanking" of the father took the form of that rebellious son leaving his wife for another woman, of course blaming the ex-wife. His leaving and shacking up may have contributed to the wayward life of his first son who caused his teenage girlfriend to get pregnant. So, now we're into our 4th generation because of a lack of discipline. I would say that we have a "spoiled child chain-reaction" here, wouldn't you agree?

Another interesting situation was described to me by an associate of mine several years ago. He and his wife were having trouble with their two year old second son. He was becoming a little terror! I asked him how often he spanked that son. The answer was, *"We don't spank him."* I recommended that may be where the problem lay. He then related how he did not believe in spanking, and how his oldest son [at that time age 6] had never been spanked and was well adjusted. Then he further described the oldest son as being calm and easy-going. After he disclosed this information it was easy to see why he never spanked the older one. Some children are just born with a calm, easy-going demeanor; they will probably never require more than one or two spankings in their lifetime.

And then there are babies like his younger son, my daughter, and myself. We were squirming, exploring, restless, and down right rebellious from the get-go. This type of children need to have the parents get their attention when necessary. That attention can be arrived at through the usual non-corporal ways, but sometimes a light slapping of fingers or a swat or two on the butt is an attention getter. This corporal punishment has to be mixed with hugs and love so the children know that your actions are taken because you love them, and they will also know you are not German. [Just kidding!]

Parents who are against the use of corporal punishment are extremely misguided in their belief. Their opposition has contributed to the discipline problems we have in the world today. Even so, they did contribute to society many years ago when they questioned the use of corporal punishment, bringing to the attention of the world that a lot of the spanking of children was actually abuse. Even the Church was derelict in this area, where many of the members of the Body were guilty of abusing their children. However, I have never talked to one person who was spanked as a child along with the parent showing love, who ever resented that they had been spanked.

The next time you hear some "expert on child-rearing" espousing their anti-spanking philosophy, just do a background check on what their religious beliefs are at that time. You will probably find that they are from some humanist based belief system. Make sure you question all advice which comes from someone who cannot even figure out which God to serve. How bright is someone like that? If they can't figure that one out, why do you think they might be right on child discipline?

Raising children in a disciplined home is not difficult as long as you start early. When questionable parents are spoiling their children, good parents are making sure their children know that, *"NO MEANS NO!!"*

Chapter Forty-Three

CHILDREN MUST HAVE STRUCTURE

It is imperative that children be raised in a structured atmosphere if they are to grow up to be well adjusted adults. Most of the screwy adults I have seen were for the most part raised by parents who ran a loose ship at home. Don't you just hate it when you go to the grocery store at about 11 PM, and there are several toddlers in the store with their parents? This is certainly not a rare sight at all, as I see it often. I know that some of it is because mom or dad may be working a different shift, but that is rare. Almost every time I see it, the parents are very young and apparently, very stupid.

Very young children need to go to sleep for a certain length of time, eat and bathe at certain times, nap after certain times of being up, etc.. They need consistency. This is another great reason for child bearing years to occur between 30-39 years old. By that time the parents will have more structure in their own lives. How can you lead if you are still a follower?

It is my opinion that structure is very important at a young age, and that it continues to be important as the child gets older. That is opposite of how I look at discipline, as I believe it extremely important that parents be more strict between 1-½ and 4 years and then loosen it a bit after that.

Let me explain why I say that structure should get more important as the child gets older. A very little child normally is going to hang close to the parents, but after a few years the child is able to get out and about alone and wander off from mom and dad. Most discipline problems should be solved by ages 4-5, but then there are other problems dealing with the children's growing responsibility for themselves which require structure, such as picking up after themselves, asking to go outside, manners, eating properly, sleeping times, pre-school activities, playing well with others, etc..

Then as the child gets into school, structure is very necessary to get school work completed, as well as church, sports and art activities which may entail a lot of practicing. If children at this age are not involved in some activities outside the home, probably the parents are not working to expand the child's interests.

It is really the teenage years that I am most concerned about because I have talked to so many ex-teenage criminals who complained that their parents offered them very little structure, such as a curfew. If parents have done a good job of instilling a structured lifestyle in the child from an early age there should not be much of a problem later on, as teenagers need to have limits to their activities in the same way that younger children have. I spoke with a number of children who regretted that their parents did not make them toe the line. A very high percentage of them were among those I met in jail. Some of them said they had been great during the pre-teen years, but their parents offered few rules when they were teens, and as teens they had become unmanageable.

It is not difficult raising children properly with love throughout their lives. Give them discipline when they are young, and structure throughout their lives until they leave your home.

Chapter Forty-Four

DON'T PLAY FAVORITES WITH YOUR CHILDREN

PARENTS MUST RAISE THEIR CHILDREN THE SAME, BUT DIFFERENTLY

One of the most common disappointments which I heard during my survey was the complaint that a lot of people do not think their parents were fair with them as they were growing up. I was somewhat surprised at the large number who mentioned this to me. Now, whether or not the complaints were well founded, we will never know, but even the perception of unfairness is not a good sign, in my opinion. It seems that too many parents had a favorite(s) among their children and the other child or children picked up on it, and to some children it does psychological damage that will last a lifetime.

One incident I remember very strongly happened back when I was in high school, with a family we knew fairly well. In this family there were two sons and a daughter, all teenagers, and it was obvious that the father showed almost all his praise and attention to the athletic son. The daughter got nothing positive from the father at all and she said she was going to get pregnant so that there would be somebody who would love her, referring to the baby. Unfortunately, that's exactly what she did, but lots of misery accompanied that baby.

This whole problem was caused by a pig-headed jerk of a man who knew nothing about being a parent. Also, the other son was not the most well adjusted boy you would ever know, but what do you expect when you have a father who treats one son better than the other son? This whole chunk of misery could have been avoided if this father had grown up and experienced life to find out what makes people tick before he became a father. But, he was young, horny, had typical ignorant parents, got married before he grew up, and continued a chain of misery.

In my own upbringing it was obvious that my dad had two favorites among the five boys, and one of my sisters will protest that all the boys were treated better than the girls. I really think she was right in some respects because we boys were athletes and she was only a cheerleader.

How can I say that I was not one of his favorites? All you have to do is ask someone who was not a parent's pet to know how you can tell. It's pretty obvious, even if the parent's actions are subtle, as they build up like plaque and after a while they become visible. It just takes a little time.

In our family one of the boys was affected by my dad's actions and it caused him some identity problems when he was a child. It all happened because my dad had not grown up when he got married. As I have mentioned before, the favoritism never really bothered me, mainly because I was so cocky that I just set out to excel, to accomplish something that the favored brothers had not done. That is how I coped, and I would say it worked.

From what I have seen from my survey, my dad was better than most, and that's coming from one of his least favorite sons, so don't go thinking we were a dysfunctional family, as that is not even close. There were seven children and today none has been divorced, none votes democrat, all are saying goodby to the Republican Party and joining forces with the Libertarians, only one of the grandchildren graduated from college as a socialist, and only one spouse is being considered for sainthood. Other than these few blights on our family we are in pretty good shape.

Since Nancy Lee and I will only have one daughter, I will never get the opportunity to see if I would have been a fair parent. I think I would have because I spent so many years as a sports official. I believe if I could ever pass one unjust, control freakish law, it would be that everyone should be required to spend at least 2-5 years working as a sports official where you are required to be fair. I do not think there was ever any experience in my life which changed me more than that. To do that type of work well, you have to be fair minded. If you are fair minded for a long enough period of time, you will never go back to the old way of thinking; hence, one child would not be treated better than another.

It is probably easy to grow to like one child better than another, as each child has characteristics of at least one of the parent's siblings [another subject I find fascinating]. To illustrate my point, in my situation my dad was a first born son and I was a last born son. You cannot get two more opposite types in the same household than that, can you? My dad had two sons who acted like first borns, and you know the attraction first borns have for each other. Then when I acted like a classic last born only a clash between my dad and me could be the result.

These are natural conflicts within a family, which if not understood by the parents, can lead to favoritism. When I was young we never heard any information about the differences in children which are determined by the order in which they are born. But there have been a few studies done which explain the characteristics that develop in children as they grow older. Every parent should read about this subject to better understand their children. It would alleviate a large number of problems and conflicts which arise when a parent attempts to force a child to conform to being something that is not within the child's nature.

To illustrate this, let's again look at my situation. My first born dad was an "early to bed, early to rise" type, where my mom and I were the "late to bed, late to rise" type. My attitude since I was little was that someone should pass a law against mornings, and that it should be done immediately. So, with that kind of attitude you can see how I could clash with my dad who thought it was sinful to not be out of bed at 6 a.m. every morning.

Can you see how these favoritism or bias situations can develop over a short time? A perfectionist parent is going to have problems with a classic last born. Conversely, there is no way to alleviate a favoritism situation if the parent is a first born perfectionist with a classic first born and a classic last born for children. In this scenario it is absolutely natural that a favorite will develop on the side of the first born child.

As I see it, the most important method to alleviate the problems which arise when a parent plays favorites among the children is for the parents to make every attempt to understand why their children are the way they are, why they have the characteristics and idiosyncracies which they have, and why they don't have other characteristics that you the parents desire they have. God never wanted parents to mold children into something they were not, but rather to raise them to be moral, healthy, law abiding, lovers of themselves and others, by utilizing the characteristics they do possess.

Parents have to fight off the urge to favor one child over another. Balance provided by the other parent certainly helps, as it results in less problems if each child is favored a little by each of the parents. However, this is not an ideal situation — resentment can build unnoticed for years and you may never know there is a problem until it is far too late to solve it.

One honest simple solution is for parents to be open and honest with their children. Make sure that if your children ever feel they are being treated unfairly by either parent, they know that they have an appeal process with the other or both parents. A family without a simple, clearly understood appeal process is a poorly lead family. Also, if your children do not know beyond a shadow of a doubt that they can always talk to their parents about anything and everything, then you, the parents have not been proper leaders in the house.

Children should always have an open door with their parents. If they do not feel free to go to their parents, the parents are at fault. At least, parents haven't gotten it across to the children that the door is open; at most, the door isn't open at all and the children know it. For a parent to not allow a child an appeal process is inexcusable. It's bad enough to play favorites with your children, but to not deal with the problem, or to not allow children the opportunity to confront the parent with a perceived problem are signs of poor household leadership.

Remember the story in which the father smothered one child with attention, but obviously slighted his other children? This man also suffered because he had given up on his dream when he was young. He had an athletic son, so he was going to live his dream through that son. Here is that Married Too Young Syndrome again, raising its ugly head and ruining lives, but this time it's joined up with the "playing favorites" game. How many lives over history have been spoiled because of parents treating one child better than another?

Well, how then do you raise children the same, but differently? You do it by discovering what makes each child tick — what type of child is he/she? Historically, too many parents attempted to force their children to fit into some mold which suited the parents. You know the old saying, *"You can fit a square peg into a round hole if you hit it hard enough and long enough."* That, unfortunately, has been the attitude of too many fathers who never grew up before they had children. Some mothers fit this pattern also but not nearly as frequently.

God never intended for square pegs to fit into round holes. God made square holes for square pegs, and round for round, but control freaks hate the idea that there are holes and pegs which they cannot control. [Have you noticed that I really have it in for control freaks? They and the devil are the scourge of the earth.] I believe we need to do it God's way, the way He designed it. A parent's job is to find out which type holes their "pegs" fit into and to help locate those holes.

It seems to me that throughout history parents have for the most part forced children to conform to their way of doing things, rather than the parent being the flexible one to fit the child's type. I'm not talking about coddling here. I'm talking about the parents making an effort to understand what type of child they are raising. Children have different temperaments and parents need to, in the first few years, figure out what type that is for each child.

The fact is that most children will fit into one of two categories or types. The first child of a family will be either an active one or a sensitive one; then the next child will be the other type. It is amazing how often I see the pattern in families.

The differences between children are evident very early in their lives and it is the obligation of the parent to figure out those differences and how to deal with each child's specific needs. A parent is required to do this while maintaining a neutral parental position, never showing preferential treatment to any one child. Parents, if you can do that, you will have earned your money. [Oh, you didn't know you were supposed to get paid for this parenting thing? You must have missed that memo.]

Chapter Forty-Five

DON'T DISCOURAGE YOUR CHILDREN

CHILDHOOD, WHERE SELDOM SHOULD BE HEARD A DISCOURAGING WORD

"Where seldom is heard a discouraging word," should be one of the slogans around every home. It amazes me how many adults have grown up being emotionally scarred because their parents or guardians never said anything good about them. How could so many generations be so stupid about the raising of children?

Only the past generation has placed much emphasis on talking about self-esteem and speaking encouraging things to children. I'm not going to laud too many praises upon the majority of people espousing this "self-esteem gospel" because many of them are public school employees or advocates. Socialist education [public schools] have been an abject failure in America in the 1900's because they have not been very good educators of our nation's children. They failed to teach a huge percentage of the child population how to read, so they stress self-esteem to "psych" children and parents into thinking everyone is okay, even if they cannot read. I call this knowledge vacuum *"the false gospel of self-esteem."* I hope you have not been sucked into it.

What I am preaching is a gospel of Godly self-esteem. This concept is taught throughout the Bible. It did not start with the socialist school administrators of the late 1900's — they just think they originated it. If I showed you all the Bible verses which speak about the power of the tongue you would see that this self-esteem concept has been around for thousands of years. The tongue, or mouth, can wound or it can heal. That is why parents, when dealing with their children, need to use their tongues for healing. As an example of what the Bible says on this subject, I want to show you just a few verses that teach this principle. [Probably the best teacher on this subject whom I have come across is an ex-farmer named Charles Capps of England, Arkansas, USA. Some of his cassette tapes and short books are excellent materials for those who want more information.]

Proverbs 18:21 says,

> "Death and life are in the power of the tongue, and those who love it will eat it's fruit."

Since the Bible was written in the Hebrew language originally, whenever you see the English word "death," it is usually a very poor choice of terms. If it had been translated "separation" instead of "death," readers would have long ago figured out that it was not a good idea to speak discouraging words to each other. Instead, for centuries, people read that verse, still spoke discouraging words, nothing happened immediately, so they thought this principle of words had no effect at all. But it takes time for the words to show their effect, whether good words, or bad words.

Another great verse for parental direction is Psalm 34:13, *"Keep your tongue from evil, and your lips from speaking guile."* If discouraging words are evil and bring separation, then how can you Biblically talk that way to your children? And along with this, look at Psalm 45: 11, which says in part, *"...my tongue is the pen of a ready writer."* I see this verse as saying that a parent's words can write things on the lives of their children. Also, there are other great ones:

> "The lips of the righteous [just] led many..." — Proverbs 10:20

> "He who speaks truth declares righteousness [justice] But a false witness, deceit. There is one who speaks like the piercings of a sword, But the tongue of the wise promotes health. The truthful lip shall be established forever, But a lying

tongue is but for a moment." — Proverbs 12:17-19

"A man shall eat well by the fruit of his mouth, But the soul of the unfaithful feeds on violence. He who guards his mouth preserves his life, but he who opens wide his lips shall have destruction." — Proverbs 13:203

One that I really like is Psalm 34:1, *"I will bless my children at all times. Their praises shall continually be in my mouth."* [Look it up for yourself if you do not believe that I quoted it properly.] If you parent as this verse recommends, then you will not have problems with your children. If they need correction, then do it in love. If they need spanking then spank, but do not berate or verbally put them down.

A major problem that a lot of fathers, and some mothers, have had is that they have set standards so high that their children will never meet them. How many children or adults have you come across who felt that they never met up to their father's or mother's standard, and they just never recovered from it? Help your children by setting attainable goals for them, as stated earlier, but don't verbally abuse them if they don't make it.

Children need to have sweet encouraging things spoken to them. Parent's words should speak life and not separation. Negativism is separation. Many children never recover from parental discouraging words. Then you have some like me, who are only temporarily affected by negativity. We keep plugging along no matter what. It is the more sensitive children that are affected by those discouraging words. Parents, if you had to suffer through this type of emotional abuse as a child, determine that you will avoid their errors.. Speak encouraging, life-giving, esteem-building words to your children and they will probably turn out better than you did.

Chapter Forty-Six

CHECK OUT YOUR CHILD'S FRIENDS

Did you ever talk to someone who was in trouble, or had children in trouble, and the reason they gave was, *"They just got in with the wrong crowd."* How can you do that? How does a child get in with the wrong crowd? How can a parent let that happen?

It amazes me that parents can let their children get involved with the wrong kids. Children should be talking every night about their day, what they did, with whom they did it, where they did it, and why they did it. If you start asking those questions every day when children are young, they will automatically be telling you the answers when they get older.

At the least you should know the parents of your child's friends or how else would you know what type of background the parents have? The behavior of children is easier to understand after getting to know the parent, as so many times children pick up bad habits from the parents.

As I stated previously, the first four years of a child's life are the most important when it comes to child raising. I have never had an intelligent person ever disagree with that statement while we were discussing this subject. That is why I was astounded by the sales of a book by Judith Rich Harris, titled, _The Nurture Assumption_. The last time I checked, that book had sold about 500,000 copies espousing the totally false teaching that: the only influence parents have over their children is providing the genetics, and after that the parents have little influence over the way the children turn out.

Dr. Kevin Leman, of _The Birth-Order Book_ fame, disputes this book vehemently by saying, *"Parents make all the difference.* "As I am writing this Dani Lee is 12 years old and already I am practically in total agreement with the doctor — it is my opinion that parents make at least 90% of the influence on their children.

When I first got a look at the cover of the book, <u>The Nurture Assumption,</u> my thought was that it was evil, just because of the color of the cover. My instinct, since doing extensive Bible study, is that something colored black has a high probability to have evil lurking behind it. Go to amazon.com for a picture of the book and see what you think. I'm telling you, there's something evil behind this woman's book, besides that fact that her conclusions are all wrong.

When you go to amazon.com you can read a review by a Rob Lightner in which he says, *"She [Judith] is upset about the blame laid on parents of troubled children..."* Hello! Is anybody in there? Another review states, *"Through no fault of their own, good parents sometimes have bad kids."* How can you <u>not</u> blame the parents of troubled children? If you follow Judith's teachings, then you can blame the child's peers as being at fault for the troubled child! But, why did any parents ever allow their children to hang out with other children whom they knew would not provide good influence on their children? Plainly put, it is just stupid to not know who it is that your child is hanging with, both inside and outside of day care and schools.

And speaking of day care and schools, another thing some parents do that I have not understood since becoming a parent myself, is to send their children off to boarding school. Why would you have children if you don't want to have them around? What am I missing? Maybe I am the one with the problem?

Chapter Forty-Seven

OTHER OBSERVATIONS AND CONCLUSIONS

If you're still with me, I sincerely hope that I have not offended you in presuming authority to set a few relationship ABSOLUTES. I'm sure that some of you would at least relish an opportunity to give me a piece of your mind, if not an opportunity to tear me apart limb by limb. My suggestion to you is to spend as much time on this subject as I have done, then make your conclusions. After that kind of time investment, I think you will more readily agree with my positions.

Just ask yourself this question. Would the whole world be better off than it is at this point, if everyone agreed with these aforementioned maxims/principles? Go ahead. Tell me it wouldn't. Tell me that, and I'll call you a liar or a Democrat. Tell me what relationship problem would not be improved by following these instructions, then look at the peripheral issues that would also be cleared up. If you haven't figured that out by now after reading about 250 pages, then maybe I should have done a better job of explaining my positions. Either that, or maybe the problem is with you.

In this chapter I want to touch on a few issues that I observed over the years of my survey. The subjects are not in any particular order except in the order in which I thought of them. Debate these subjects with your friends and see their reactions. I hope you find them interesting.

Second Marriages

WATCH OUT FOR SECOND MARRIAGES!! Do second marriages ever result in a happy marriage? No? Yes? Often? Occasionally? Seldom? Which one of these will you choose for your answer? My answer, from what I have seen, is somewhere between Occasionally and Seldom.

It may be that the success rate of second marriages is lower than for first marriages. I personally don't have any statistics on it, but from my vantage point, it doesn't look good. I remember a CBS News report several years ago that explored this issue and concluded that second marriages were not all that successful. To some of us, that would seem to be the exact opposite of the way it should be. You made a mistake the first time, so you should have learned from your mistake and not do it the next time. But, that would be logical, and what does logic have to do with marriage, right?

What seems to be the problem with going into a second marriage? Men thinking with the wrong head, and women looking for security? Maybe. Neither one of these reasons is a good way to enter into another marriage. And that, I conclude, is the reason that so few second marriages actually survive happily. These marriages are entered into for the wrong reasons. Now, that bit of information doesn't take a genius to figure out, but that is what it comes down to. People are marrying the second time for the wrong reasons, and anyone in the position of considering a second marriage needs to be totally sure that their reasons for making such a move are correct.

And how do you do that, you ask? The same way that this book suggested you do it the first time. God will let you know what characteristic(s) you are looking for. Look for those specific characteristic(s) and you will not make the same mistake twice.

Men. Look For A Good Wife

The most important decision a man will ever make is in choosing which God he is going to serve. Choosing the right God makes life much more peaceful and happy, so look around, then make a decision.

The second most important decision a man will ever make is in choosing a wife. Just as choosing the right God makes life happy and full, so it is also when choosing a wife. For that reason, it is more important to plan for finding the right wife than it is to plan for the right career. A career is temporary, but a wife is forever — *"until death do us part."* Quite often a career is not chosen until way into the 30's for many men, and for many others, career changes are often temporary. A wife, on the other hand, is found usually between age 25 and age 32, after which there is never to be a change. I, as did many other men I know, made career changes after finding the right wife, and some of us have had several changes. There is nothing wrong with that in my opinion. Each job, each vocation, means more knowledge upon which to draw and usually makes life more interesting.

Along this line I remember a dentist who worked on me while I was in college. After having gotten to know me better, he told me once that he wanted to do something different. He had done dentistry all his adult life and didn't have other career experiences from which to draw comparisons to know whether or not he was doing the best thing for him. Many other people with whom I have spoken have related similar situations. They were just too young when they got involved in their profession. That is one of the reasons I don't encourage high school graduates to immediately go to college. Most should take time off for a year of two, then go to college. They'll usually do better.

This is very similar to what happens when people choose a spouse at too young an age. After a period of time they want a change — it's a normal response in some people. So look around for a good wife carefully, then make a decision. And keep in mind when it comes to choosing a wife, *a good woman trumps a good-looking woman every time.*

Males, Be Wary Of Infatuations

This one may affect men much more often than the normal woman. Men can fall in love at the first sight of a female. Usually she has to have a certain look, but not always. I have found myself looking at a woman who was nothing to look at so to speak, but she was the only woman around. It sounds stupid to a normal female, but most males I have spoken with about this subject have found themselves in similar situations.

One of the worst infatuations for a male is the stupidity of having a crush on a celebrity. This one is very common, mostly among young men or boys. One young man I knew had a crush on Trish Nixon. I was stupid enough to waste my time having a crush on Debbie Boone not too long before I married Nancy Lee. [Funny thing was that she and her husband got married the same day we did.] Was having a crush on Debbie Boone a waste of my time? Sure was, because I had no opportunity to ever meet her, much less have a relationship with her. The waste of time comes in when we allow the infatuation to keep us from having relationship(s) close to home.

Females can also fall into this trap when they get caught up in their adulation of entertainers. Look at the "groupie" culture if you want evidence of this one. How many women was it that entertained Wilt Chamberlain? Infatuation was their motivation, but I would love to do a study on what these females thought about their experience many years later. Would they say that they are proud of their "groupie" lifestyle?

The same type question could be asked of men who have been carried away with their infatuation(s). Are they proud of being swept away in what could be described as fantasy? I, for one, am not as it was a total waste of mental time. For many years now I have gone out of my way to avoid situations that may cause my mind to wander. For instance, you'll never see me hire a good looking administrative assistant, as I don't want the hassle. I really wonder about these men who do their best to hire beautiful secretaries. How short-sighted is that? They're just asking for trouble. That's why I marvel at surveys which conclude that a good looking woman has a better chance of getting a job that a less attractive woman. It should be the opposite of that in an intelligent world. The fewer possible distractions, the better. If you want to gaze at good looking women, then buy a video. It lasts longer and you can't come close to touching them.

Birth Defects

This is just a theory upon which I have been seeking more information. The theory suggests that a high percentage of birth defects are caused because the father and mother married wrong. They were never supposed to marry and have children with each other. I am convinced that the God of the Bible is not in favor of babies being born less than perfect. Of course you could argue that some with birth defects are really being born more perfect in one characteristic than in others. The movie, _Rain Man_, with Dustin Hoffman and Tom Cruise comes to mind. If you have not seen it, then I recommend that you rent it at your local video rental store. Dustin Hoffman plays the part of a savant [_a person with exceptional learning_] who was a whiz at numbers, but lacked in other mental aspects.

Now, I don't want anyone going off the deep end on this issue and quote me as saying that I said all birth defects are caused by marrying the wrong person. I'm just saying that from what I have observed, many birth defects could have been avoided by waiting to marry the one that God chose for that person to marry.

I also think the same holds true for sterility, even though I believe that God can heal such abnormality and does so on a regular basis. Also, I think some sterility is allowed by God so that these couples are more prepared for adoption. Each couple has to decide for themselves which of these is correct, and hopefully that decision is made before a wedding takes place. If you marry the right spouse, then God will show you what plans He has in regard to children.

Let's Help Hold This Marriage Together

This type of stupidity usually sets in with family and friends, or the spouse. There are too many people in the world who are programmed to do almost anything to hold a marriage together. We have a good friend whose daughter got married at a young age, and this friend has to counsel them by phone on a regular basis in an effort to help them hold the marriage together. I asked our friend the question, *"Are you sure that God wants the two of them to be married?"* Her answer was that it was her understanding that every effort must be made to keep all marriages together.

That type of teaching couldn't be further from the truth. It reminds me of the Apostle Paul before he had his experience on the road to Damascus. He believed he was doing God's will by participating in the killing of Christians. Misguided, but sincere is how [Saul] could have been described, as could many people who fight to save a marriage that should never have been.

When a question comes up about "saving the marriage," the first question that must be answered is, *"Does God want this man and woman to be a married couple?"* Why *"kick against the goads?"* No amount of counseling or prayer is going to keep two people together that God never intended to be together. Now, having said that, let me also say that God can and does heal marriages even if the two were never supposed to be together, but I honestly believe that the cases are rare in which He does that. So, before you work at holding a marriage together, ask the question, *"Are these two supposed to be together as husband and wife?"* Wait for the answer— usually when you first wake up— and confirmation of the answer, and head in that direction.

Living Near In-Laws May Create Out-Laws

This is a common problem experienced by many couples after the wedding. Some people can live near their in-laws, and some people cannot live near in-laws. With the latter group, living near in-laws creates out-laws. Or, maybe it just seems that way. This argument usually needs to be settled before the wedding, or too many problems may come up later which will certainly strain the marriage. You have to decide what type of people you and your spouse are, to know if you like the idea of living near relatives, and also how you are going to divide up the holidays with some consistency. If you think this is a minor point, then why don't you give me a dollar for every marriage that broke up in large part because of arguments over family? I'm quite positive that very few people have that many dollars, because for many this is a sticky issue

Moving Away From Family

This one quite often affects females more than males and many times goes hand in glove with the subject above, living near the in-laws. I spoke with a lot of women who had given up their lifestyle to move to another part of the country to marry a man and ended up getting *"burned"* by him. [I probably shouldn't use the term *"burned,"* as a Pakistani Muslim may read this and take it literally.] In other words, the marriage never survived, and the woman was left in an area of the country with not enough money to move back to her pre-wedding lifestyle. This can be a tough situation, especially for a female, who is usually the one putting more emphasis on her family ties. My recommendation, ladies, is that you be 100% totally convinced that this is the right man for you. If you are not 100% on it, then don't do it. Remember, you don't have to accept every invitation to every party.

One problem associated with moving away which sometimes shows up after the wedding is the possibility of having to move because of career, either the husband's or the wife's. Many years ago there was seldom the question of which career took precedence, but in today's society many times the wife can make a greater salary than the husband. A lot of men can't stand the idea that their wives contribute more to the family financial picture than do they, so this can be a problem. Leadership should never be determined by the finances contributed, but rather by the ability to lead.

One story I came across that illustrates this point is a family where the husband is a public school teacher and the wife makes 4 to 5 times more than he does. If teaching is his dream and he is reaching to be the best in his profession that he could possibly be, then there should not be a problem as he is more of a "Mr. MOM" instead of a "kept man" as was Tom Cruise in the movie, *"COCKTAILS."* When a man is not doing all he can to contribute to the finances of the family the wife will usually resent it, and if a man is not allowed to contribute to the best of his ability, then he will resent it.

Are You Sure You Want A Military Man Or Cop?

I've never seen any statistics on this one, but from the people I have surveyed and reports I have seen in the media, I would seriously question anyone marrying someone in the military or desiring to go into the military. Honestly, I think most of these disastrous marriages with military people were a direct result of getting married too young, but there may be other reasons. I'm going to stick to the "too young" line, because I firmly believe it is true.

It was the Vietnam war which really brought this problem into mainstream societal debate, but I think the problem was obvious during previous wars, it just never got the media attention that the Vietnam veterans received. Maybe that was because everyone was attempting to figure out what went wrong in Vietnam, whereas in previous wars we had won, so nobody cared how it was accomplished.

Now I don't have the slightest idea how military psychologists will view my distrust of "military marriages," but they would probably say that men on the front lines during war need someone specifically to fight for, to survive to get back home to. But, I have seen the disastrous lives for them, their wives, and children, [need I mention grandchildren] after their return home even when they weren't in a war. I feel like people should go into military service because of their belief in the cause and it doesn't matter who or if someone is waiting for them at home. The cause should be enough to keep them going.

How many couples who got married before he/she went to war, or before they went into the military, were really happy in their marriages? I say it was a fairly small percentage. The main reason for that, again, was because of getting married too young. If they had waited until being older, their happiness factor probably would have been much higher.

My admonition again is, be careful when dating someone in the military, or with military or police aspirations. Make sure that military or police man/woman has grown up before you consider marriage. I don't mean to seem as if I am belittling military men or cops, because as long as there are control freaks and criminals in the world we are going to need them, but they are generally of a certain mentality that takes a special type of spouse to put up with. Make sure you are a perfect fit.

Please Desire Children

I want to encourage almost everyone to have a desire to

have and raise children, either your own or adopted. Raising a child is probably the greatest long-term experience a human can ever experience. Of course, I have never been a movie star, President of the United States, a brain surgeon, or held any other so-called important public positions, so maybe I'm misguided or delusional. But, I believe I'll die encouraging people to desire to raise children.

One of the main reasons to do this is because it can help keep you humble. Children have an uncanny way of bringing us back down to earth; they encourage us to stop and smell the roses. [The little ones even think it's important for us to smell other, not so nice things, if you know what I mean.] The overcoming of challenges has to be a person's forte when raising children, but isn't that what life is about, overcoming challenges and relationships? Watching children grow is fascinating. To see them face challenges and develop relationships with others is a joy that can be obtained in no other way. Teaching or coaching may be professions that come close to parenthood, but even those experiences are not the same as when it is your own. It's an overall wonderful experience when you do it right.

It's Only Temporary

Most people do not keep this in mind when going through life. There is almost nothing in life that is not temporary. Can you name one for me? Being ugly? That was one of my major concerns when I was younger, but fortunately Nancy Lee's eyesight was too poor to know, and now she's stuck. How about being poor? Been there, done that. It's only temporary. You never know when God will give you that million dollar idea that everyone talks about; that's why it's only temporary. Having a physical disability? That may just mean that you have other qualities that some of us lack. There just isn't very much that we should get bent out of shape about in life because even life itself is temporary.

The True Definition of Pornography

In simple terms, pornography for adults is defined as written, oral, or visual stimuli of sexually immoral situations or activities. For children, pornography can be defined as almost anything deemed of a sexual nature, whether moral or immoral, as society has at least some responsibility to restrict certain things from children.

This one's going to get me into trouble, if none of the others in this book have done so by now. It seems to me that the two biggest proponents of banning displays of nudity, which in the past has been considered pornographic, are females and religious control freaks. Both of these groups have legitimate positions in some respects, but are wrong in other respects.

Religious control freaks, no matter which religion, can be understood because they are who they are, control freaks. They want to control other people's lives because from their point of view, everyone else needs to be like themselves. An interesting aside which I have seen over the years is that a lot of these control freaks are doing what they are preaching against. Remember a guy by the name of Jimmy Swaggart? Or, the preachers that run off with their secretaries or piano players? Did you ever hear any of those stories? One thing I learned many years ago is that if you hear someone belligerently preaching against something, then there is a very high probability that person is doing what he or she is preaching against.

What most females refuse to understand is that males are sexually stimulated by visual means. When they see a naked female body, normal males are going to get sexually excited. In fact, if the truth be known, if men just think about seeing a naked woman they get excited. The normal female doesn't get excited by seeing a naked man; she is usually stimulated by other things first.

That is where the problem arises. Females don't normally function in a similar way as do males, yet they, with their efforts to destroy visual articles of arousal for men, want to get men to be stimulated in the same way that they are. This reminds me of that idiot named Skinner, who attempted to get the world to believe that almost everything we do as humans, whether male or female, is learned behavior. Anyone who believed that malarkey for longer than 10 seconds has to be declared an idiot right along with him, because all studies and facts say otherwise. If you want to do something really stupid that would prove Skinner and his ilk to be idiots, just take your daughter and raise her to be a boy and see what kind of messed up kid you have when she reaches age 20.

Do you see my point yet with women being against "pornography?" There is a very good probability that a female's definition of pornography and a male's definition are totally different just because of the fact that God programmed males and females differently. Another good one along this line of logic would be a man taking a woman to an X-rated movie and expecting her to get sexually stimulated. Probably not going to work. That man would be better off by cleaning the house, washing the dishes for a week, cooking dinner all week, and "getting in touch with his feelings." She would probably be more sexually stimulated.

Some men need, at times, to look at something to get them sexually stimulated. This is especially true when they get older, because of the need to ejaculate as a preventative for prostate cancer. This is a subject that few others want to touch because of the historical negative connotations of sex, [Thank you, Roman Catholic Church!] but it is an important subject that should be dealt with intelligently. [Also, from the research I have seen, I believe that females need to be having orgasms into a relatively older age than has been previously practiced, also because of the health benefits.]

If all the "pornography" is destroyed, then what are the men going to look at to get excited? Their wives? That's a good one. Not that it would not be exciting, but how many wives want to put on a floor show before love making? Not in my house. But, most men need something like that as they get older, and it is for that reason that I am against banning all nudity. It depends on where it is and for what purpose it is displayed. I've heard stories for years about some older women still desiring to have sex, but the husband "can't get it up," so that both end up being frustrated. But, if he had some sexually arousing stimuli, then both of them would have probably been better off health wise, not to mention that less frustration usually means a better relationship.

You tell me which is worse... a frustrated and less healthy wife and husband because he can't perform [which is only going to contribute to marital strife]... or the man observing pictures of nude men and women in sexual situations or positions? I hope you are not going to tell me that years of sexual frustration for a couple is not as sinful as looking at some pictures of nude women. If you tell me that one, then I say you need prayer, and lots of it.

I am of the opinion that God can move on certain people to desire to help people with their sexual dysfunction, and it's none of my business if someone wants to do so. What is so wrong with watching a video or looking at pictures that teach new positions or techniques to enjoy your spouse more? Sorry, can't see anything wrong with it. Enough said.

How Do You Know For Sure

In very basic terms, if you decide to do something, or are at least confronted with a decision, and you wake up the next or subsequent mornings with peaceful feelings about the decision, then it's a good decision. If, on the other hand and more than likely what will really happen, you wake up in the morning in a cold sweat or at least with negative feelings, then back off that decision. I may be considered the champion of making the wrong decisions, or at least the wife thinks so, as I have probably experienced more cold sweats than anyone else before I learned how to know what God was attempting to tell me.

The opposite is also true about getting a positive, peaceful feeling at different times, not only when you wake up. For me the most recognizable instance of this feeling happened when I left Nancy Lee in New York and moved to Texas. The yelling at each other had been terrible, and in the natural, the marriage was over. But, within a few minutes after leaving I felt a peaceful feeling inside me that everything about our marriage was going to work out. Sure could have fooled me!

It works. You have to be cognizant of what God is attempting to tell you, so pay attention and be wary of negative feelings especially. He will help you make the right decisions. I wrote this book to get you close to your spouse, to help you cut through a lot of the false feeling that we have all experienced in our search for a spouse. I hope you take this information as far as it will take you. Then let God lead you to the one He knows will best balance out your life — that one person for whom God has chosen you to be the balance they need to allow them to live their life to the fullest as God wants them to do. If you do this, then I'm betting that you will have a wonderful life.

Inter-racial Marriage

Under the New Covenant there is nothing wrong with it. If people are marrying the ones God has for them, then skin color doesn't matter. One problem that arises is when inter-racial marriage is a fad, as it is today. Look at it this way: in 100 years Hitler's concept of racial purity will be history. And well it should be. Don't all humans on the earth have the "spirit" of the Creator of the universe flowing through their veins? Then, where's the question?

Other Observations and Conclusions

Be Objective About Your Children

Anyone who has ever been a teacher, a youth leader in some capacity, or involved in youth sports or the like, has had to deal with the "Little League Parent." "Little League Parents" are those who believe that their little Johnny or Susy never does anything wrong. They immediately take the side of their child against an adult when there is a conflict. These are some of the world's most disgusting parents because of the disservice they are doing to their children.

The parent should normally take the side of the adult until all the facts are in, which can only be after all sides in the controversy have had an opportunity to clarify their positions. Only then should parents side with their child, when the proof is obvious that the child is right. But, if the facts are otherwise, and the child is wrong, appropriate discipline should be administered. Admittedly, there are times when the adult has a history of being prejudiced, unreasonable, or maybe even a horse's petootie, and if that is the case, you would definitely side with your child. But, those cases are, from what I have observed, rare.

I only used the term "Little League Parent" because others have used it before me, and it by no means is a reflection on the Little League organization that has done wonderful things for boys and girls for decades. Nonetheless, this phenomenon of dishonest parents, or non-objective parents has historically been common among Little League parents. Unfortunately, it has spread into other aspects of life and has caused many school teachers and youth leaders to change professions or vocations. There was never a need for that if parents had been taught to be objective about their child, and admit when their little Johnny and Susy are wrong. There is nothing tough about this at all. Just be honest. Just as with adults, when your children are wrong, then admit it. And when they are right, stand firm. Don't let your child be a liar.

Temptations

One thing that has surprised me about temptations is that, in my opinion, the Bible is true where it says, *"God will not allow us to suffer any temptations beyond that which we can bear."* This may sound corny, but I honestly believe this to be true if, and only if you marry right. God won't let any temptation come your way that you cannot bear. There will be a way of escape.

What has surprised me in my 20 years of marriage is that I have never had an invitation to stray from Nancy Lee and go to bed with another woman. Now, I'm not suggesting that I was looking for an invitation. I'm just saying that I have never had an invitation. Now, you could surmise that is a reflection on how Nancy Lee wasn't too smart to have married a guy that no other woman would want, but I would rather you take the approach that God will not allow a temptation come our way that is too great to overcome.

I think we need to qualify that statement, as I believe it only applies to those who are doing things His way. However, if we do that, it will reflect upon those who had thought they had been doing things His way, but did succumb to temptation. Maybe they really weren't doing things His way, but were off doing something God never wanted them to do. Do something like that and I am of the opinion that God will let you get your butt kicked all over the place until you get back on track.

The moral of the story then, is that if temptations that seem too hard to bear are coming your way, then you are probably going the wrong way. Spend some time away from the temptations and figure out the right way to go. I'll bet the temptations stop after that.

Husband and Wife Working Together

Don't even think about it!! Not a good idea! Except for a short time, maybe. If spouses attempt to work together full-time, they are flirting with disaster! Can you name for me one couple whose marriage survived after they had worked for years together, all day, every day? Now, can you name for me any couples whose marriage broke up after they had been together 24/7? I can name several in the latter group, but none in the first group.

The fact is, if a husband and wife intend to work together, then they may as well intend to plan for their divorce, because, from what I have observed, there is only a small probability that their marriage will survive to a ripe old age. The pressures are too great for most couples to overcome. It is best for the stability of a marriage if the couple has different information to contribute to each other at the end of the day.

Marriage Building

This is a waste of time. Why attempt to build a marriage that was never supposed to be? And if you marry right, there is no reason to build the marriage. Marriages that are God ordained need no building.

If people follow this advice, there are going to be a lot of marriage seminars that aren't going to be making much money. Sorry about that, all you seminar leaders. But, once a couple decides that God wants them together, then they need to make choices to submit to each other, and forget about spending money to sit and let someone tell them what they should be doing already.

Let me use Nancy Lee and myself as an example. [You have to promise me that you won't tell Nancy Lee about this section, because she will not agree about the details. But, the fact is, sometimes she's wrong! This is one of those times.]

For several years in the mid-1980's to the early 1990's we had what I would call stress on our marriage. Now, keep in mind, there was no doubt in my mind that she and I were supposed to be together, but there was a tension there that caused more friction than should have been. I knew it was caused by her refusal to accept the fact that she was supposed to be in Texas. Remember, she's an Italian, and persons of that persuasion think they need to live close to the original family. And nothing God or anyone else says about it matters. Family is first.

Therein lay the problem with our marriage. She didn't like Texas, nor a bunch of the Texans she had met, so she didn't want to be here. That caused a strain, and I knew that was the problem. Being the first-born controller that she has a tendency to be, every time I broached the problem and the solution to the problem, she didn't want to hear about it. Finally, since her pastor at that time was participating in a Marriage Encounter weekend as a counselor, Nancy Lee suggested that we go to it to see if we could get things straightened out.

Admittedly, that weekend our marriage changed. But, it wasn't the Marriage Encounter weekend that changed the marriage. It was the submission of Nancy Lee to the fact that she wasn't going back to New York, no matter what. Finally, she submitted to the fact that God wanted her in Texas as my wife, and any thoughts or actions to the contrary were just unacceptable. That solved almost every problem through which we had been going. After that submission on her part, we had a different marriage.

Now, understand that she was not submitting to me, her husband. She was submitting to the will of God, plain and simple. Had that submission come before the Marriage Encounter weekend, as it should have, there would not have been a need for the seminar. And that's my point with marriage seminars in general. If people figure out what God wants them to do — be married to this person or not, and its peripheral issues — there is no need for marriage seminars.

It's pretty simple. If you are married to the right person, then submit to that marriage and its goals.

Other Observations and Conclusions

Make Good Choices in Life

This admonition is one of the aspects of the meaning of life. There are messed up lives in this world mainly because someone made poor choices in life. Almost everyone who ends up in trouble either made a poor choice or someone else made a poor choice. People choose to marry the wrong person, which affects the lives of those around them. People choose to create a baby before they are married, and they and the child suffer for the rest of their lives.

People choose to get a good education, despite lacking the mental capacity others may have. People choose to work hard despite not being paid very much. People decide to get out of poverty because they don't like it. People decide to live in a comfortable house, rather than a bigger house that may impress someone in the community. People choose not to go along with the crowd when the crowd is smoking, drinking, doing drugs, being destructive, voting Socialist, etc.. People choose to stand in front of military tanks when everyone else stands back. People decide to do what is right. Some choices affect the rest of your life, and sometimes the lives of others.

It doesn't matter how you enter this life, nor what position in society your family is perched upon at the time you are born, but it matters what choices you make from then on. You can make good choices, or you can make poor choices. These decisions are yours.

My purpose for writing this book was to help people make better choices in relationships. I made a choice to write this book when few people could see a solution to the divorce problems in this world today. I could have chosen to not write it, as I gather many religious leaders would have preferred, but I chose to spend the time away from the family and other activities to deliver to you what I had learned about relationships. I urge you to grow or grow up making good choices in life.

Females, Don't Fall For Their Lines

Dear Abby: I'm 17 and have just ended a relationship that lasted seven months. I was a virgin until this relationship. When we began dating, I told "Todd" I wanted to wait for sex until I trusted him and felt I loved him. The time did come when I trusted him and felt I loved him, so I decided to sleep with him. That's when things started going downhill. A month later, he told me he was sick of me.

Abby, I feel so hurt and used. Now I'm starting to view sex negatively. I know I'm young and have years of relationships ahead of me, but now I wonder if all men are only after sex. If so, it wouldn't be worth — YOUNG, HURT AND CONFUSED [10/6/99]

Obviously, one young female learned the hard way that males and females are different when it comes to sex. Men have historically used every conceivable line in the book to get into a woman's pants. It is just a fact of life, and that is why I feel the need to at least once in this book caution females to watch out for the "lines" males dish out. For a male, until near the marrying age, the quest is for sex, and probably more often than not, there is no love involved in the act. It's just sex.

Just as there is a need for a female to guard her heart, she must also guard other parts of her body. Females will be respected more by guarding those parts, than by being a relief mechanism for some young male. A simple solution for the YOUNG, HURT AND CONFUSED 17 year old female might have been for her to wait for an adult love relationship, but even then she can be treated the same way. Always keep this in mind while dating or even while in a love relationship not leading to marriage there's a high probability that — *It's only a line!* Don't fall for it or more likely than not, you'll regret it.

Females, You Have The Power

Now, don't take this wrong, but you should know by now that I am a bit blunt at times, and this is one of those times. It is so important that I have saved this subject for the back of this book, and I have even considered closing this section off from those not of an appropriate age to see what I am saying, as some people are too young to handle this information properly.

Women, to put it bluntly, the future of the world goes between your legs. God has built into the normal male such a strong desire to get between your legs, that he will do amazing things to get there. Some men will use lies, some will use money, some power, some control, some will use flattery, and others will use almost anything to which they have to resort to end up between your legs.

The attraction of a female crotch for a normal male is almost unbelievable, except to another male. I remember an old line I heard back before I knew much about sex with one woman. It was spoken by a well known former rodeo competitor, and if I mentioned his name, a lot of you women would recognize it. Since he may be embarrassed about having said it in an alcohol influenced stupor, I'll keep his identity to myself, but what he said fairly well explains the true desire of the normal male — *"If reincarnation is possible, I want to come back as a barrel racer's saddle. That way I can be between my two favorite things."*

Is there anyone out there who doesn't understand that one? To the normal women's libber it sounds sexist as all get out, but to the normal male, it sounds very true, though some of us would certainly leave out the horse. [Jesse Ventura, the governor of Minnesota, being one. Remember the trouble he got into with his interview with Playboy Magazine in late 1999? He wanted to come back as a certain size bra.]

And this reminds me of another rude, crude, and socially unacceptable line I heard many years ago while living in Syracuse, N.Y. I was working at a company that had an office staff of a few females who worked in close proximity of us men in the warehouse. They hired a nice looking female to work with one married man in the office among several females. This man used to follow this nice looking woman around like a puppy dog. Everyone there saw it, and got a good laugh out of it. This "bean counter" explained his infatuation this way. *"I would eat her s___ for a mile just to see where it comes from!"*

I know, ladies, I know that's disgusting, but his comment is very, very, very typical of the male psyche. We're just made that way! That's why, females, you have the power! When you have the right man, the one that God wants you to be with, you can control him, or you can serve him.

As spoken of earlier, the male has to relieve his sexual energy because God built into the male a dynamo — a self-reproducing organism — which keeps having that desire to create. It is for this reason that the female must have the power, to keep that male desire in check so that the man's sperm ends up in the right place. The male's ejaculate must be released in the proper way, and sometimes the male urge is too strong for him to be thinking clearly.

That's where the power of the female comes in. When a man is thinking with the wrong head, we all know that someone could get into trouble. Unfortunately, historically it has been the female who has had the screws put to her — in more ways than one, might I add — when a male gets into this condition. It is during this condition that a female needs to recognize her power over the male, and inform him as to whether or not this is the proper time and place to relieve the condition. [I know it's crude, but I am dealing with the facts.]

And the fact is that males are nothing like females when it comes to sex. Males want it on a regular basis, and have to have it on a regular basis. That's the bad news, or the good news for females, depending on your point of view. The bad news is that for the normal female, sex is not a priority for sustaining life. The good news is that with a balanced sex life — balanced meaning on a regular basis — that man will meet the strongest needs of the normal female, that being support, security, and protection. If your man is getting what he needs between your legs, then he's going to hold you in such high esteem that you will be fulfilled as the female God intended.

Power has to be used correctly. If it is not, then balance is lost, and God doesn't like things to be out of balance. Sexual balance in a marriage is sexual satisfaction on a regular basis [regular basis possibly having different definitions for females than for males].

The desire that the male has for a female is the balance God built into the system. The male may be the stronger one, but that strength and power isn't going to do him much good if he has to force someone to have sex with him. Any man will tell you that it is much more enjoyable when sex is offered freely by a woman he adores.

Now, this desire of the man for you, the woman, should not lead you to think that you are a sex object, but rather an object of sex. There's a difference. The former means you are used, but the latter means you are desired. God has never planned for females to be used as sex objects, but He definitely planned for the female to be the object of sex. If He hadn't, then He would not have built into the male such strong desire for the female which a normal male possesses, and which gives the female the power over the male.

I know it sounds crazy, but God works in semi-mysterious ways. He had to put controls on the male, or else men would have gotten control-freak crazy with their own importance. There are certainly un-godly heathen societies where men do not treat females as equals, but you'll never find it in True Christianity. It is in this, the only true religion, that woman is put in her proper place — along side and equal with the male, as balance for him.

This reason convinces me that the female must always, probably until your male spouse dies, remain the huntee. I'm convinced that you females need to relate to your man that you could have done better, and that if he — the spouse— doesn't toe the line, you may just go out and find that better one. That message must be understood by the man, or you may find him gone some day.

I take this stance because the normal male has the need to conquer, or at least make submissive, things that are within his sphere of influence. Now, I am not saying that this position is honorable. All I am saying is that it is a strong normal male tendency. And the normal male is what you, the female, is desiring. [Unfortunately for you, God put that desire for the male into you females. Screwy guys like me are sure glad He did, though.]

One of the keys for a female to almost insure a successful marriage, is by the wife keeping the husband guessing! If you keep that man of yours minding his P's & Q's, then you are more likely to have a lifetime marriage. You do that by controlling the object of his greatest desire. If you are putty in his hands, so to speak, you run the risk of him bolting the marriage.

The Stupidest Female in the World

Despite the opinion of some of you, this category of course does not include the woman who married me. I am referring to the woman who suffers from the delusion that she can change a man. If one person could have a dollar from every woman who suffered from this malady throughout history, that would be one of the richest persons in the history of the world.

This category of females never ceases to amaze me, mainly because the category is so large. Will someone answer this question for me? What is it in the female psyche that possesses so many of them to think they could actually change a man? I know I have asked this type of question earlier in this book, but I have yet to figure out the answer.

The problem as it appears to me, is that many females first take a man into a relationship, then attempt to change him. Wrong! That strategy is backwards. The correct approach is to insist that the man change before he gets the honor of having a relationship with you. Remember what I wrote earlier about a man doing almost anything to get between your legs? Well, just change that last phrase *"...between your legs"* to *"get into a close relationship with you."* So now it reads, *"A man will do almost anything to get into a close relationship with you."* That — almost anything — will include changing his lifestyle to fit into your basic lifestyle. If he won't do that, then he is not *close relationship material!* Stay away from that man!

What you have done — if you won't make him change before the relationship begins — then you have become the *hunter*, rather than the *huntee*. Remember what kind of trouble a female can get into when she becomes the *hunter*? The female's self-preservation instinct dictates that she be the *huntee*, and never be the *hunter*. That is how simple it is.

For example, let's say that you, the female going into a relationship, know that it may grow into something serious, but fairly early on you detect a character flaw in the male. It is in your best interest to cut off the relationship immediately, or deal with the character flaw before marriage. The reason to cut it off immediately is because of the female propensity to think that she can change that character flaw. When you think you can change that flaw, and you attempt to do it, then you have surrendered one of the female's most instinctive defense mechanisms, that of being the hunted one, or *huntee,* Can anything be more clear than that?

It is the responsibility of the *hunter* to conform to the basic habitat of the *huntee*. If you are a deer hunter, are you going to be successful by hanging out in Macy's or Nieman Marcus? I don't think so. A deer hunter has to go out where the deer are, in that type of habitat or lifestyle, if they want to bag a deer. That same principle holds true with men hunting for the right woman. The woman — *the huntee* — does not go into a different habitat, i.e. down to the level of a seriously flawed man, to be hunted. The female is to maintain her principles and basic lifestyle and let the man find her.

Remember that all-encompassing principle that governs the average male? He'll do almost anything to satisfy that burning desire to you-know-what. If he has to meet up to your standard, that means he has to change his flaws into assets, and only then is he suitable for a potential relationship. If a seriously flawed man will not change his ways and come up to your standard, then a short-term relationship, or a platonic relationship with you can be his only hope.

Please do not be counted among the stupidest females in the world. Men with serious flaws — a fairly large category — are going to contribute to wasted years, or worse yet, a wasted life. Don't let that life be yours.

True Happiness Comes From Inside

I would be derelict in my objective if I did not inform you that, even after doing everything I suggested in this book, you will never live happily ever after unless you take two more steps. And, I don't mean to sound too preachy, so I'll give you the shortened version. The long version appears in my next book.

One common problem that all men and women suffer from is that we are all born with an emptiness inside of us. Some of us recognize it rather easily, but others of us go through life without ever knowing that there is something missing on the inside of us. Most of us attempt to fill this emptiness with activities such as alcohol, drugs, sex, work, family, love, sports, etc., but this *"hole"* can only be filled in one way. That is by accepting Jesus to come in and fill that emptiness. This may sound crazy to some people as it did to me while growing up, but in simple terms, if we dedicate our life to Jesus, that *"hole"* is filled. It is then that a peacefulness is felt inside, and that emptiness is gone.

The next step is to accept the gift of the Holy Spirit. I really don't have room here to explain it to you, but please, take my word for it. And, if you must have more information, do some research on the subject from many different sources including my next book.

Conclusion

I can now honestly conclude that the normal female is born more intelligent than the normal male. No doubt in my mind! If a female turns out stupid, then blame it on her father. Or, blame it on her, because she wanted it that way. Or, she allowed males to convince her to be that way. Pity!

Also, I sincerely hope that you have gathered a lot of good information from this book, and that it will help you understand what you have seen in the past, and shed some light on your future.

One last thing that I want to get across is that a happy marriage, and all that goes with it, can be about the greatest lifestyle earthlings can have. It is such a peaceful life, knowing that you have a loving, faithful spouse and well-bred children. Then that peace is passed onto the next generation, then the next generation, then the next, then....Who knows, maybe someday we can have an almost 100% success rate in marriage. I just hope that this book will help us move in that direction. Thanks for staying with me.